WITHDRAWN

It's One O'Clock and Here Is
Mary Margaret McBride

SUSAN WARE

It's One O'Clock and
Here Is Mary Margaret McBride

A Radio Biography

New York University Press • *New York and London*

NEW YORK UNIVERSITY PRESS
New York and London
www.nyupress.org

Library of Congress Cataloging-in-Publication Data
Ware, Susan, 1950–
It's one o'clock and here is Mary Margaret McBride :
a radio biography / Susan Ware.
p. cm.
Includes bibliographical references and index.
ISBN 0–8147–9401–7 (cloth : alk. paper)
1. McBride, Mary Margaret, 1899–
2. Radio broadcasters—United States—Biography.
I. Title: It is one o'clock and here is Mary Margaret McBride.
II. Title.
PN1991.4.M37W37   2004
791.4402′8′092—dc22   2004016005

New York University Press books are printed on acid-free paper,
and their binding materials are chosen for strength and durability.

Manufactured in the United States of America

10 9 8 7 6 5 4 3 2 1

To Elizabeth Parker Ware

Contents

PART III Transitions

Preface and Acknowledgments

ARMED WITH MY KNITTING in my lap, I settle into the listening booth at the Library of Congress and try to imagine that I am one of Mary Margaret McBride's loyal listeners. Her Missouri-accented voice comes out of the speakers. It is a warm, comfortable voice, what she calls a good radio voice, "the kind that pushes up against you."[1] For the next forty-five minutes or an hour (this kind of research unfolds in real time), I sit and listen, alternately knitting and taking notes but mainly letting myself get caught up in the experience of listening to one of the best interview shows that radio has ever produced. A lot of old radio seems dated, but these shows remain remarkably fresh and contemporary decades after they were first broadcast. More than once I am thankful that I chose to become a historian, realizing that this is a pretty fun way to make a living.

Except for loyal fans over a certain age, Mary Margaret McBride is no longer a household word today as she was in the 1940s and 1950s. I certainly had never heard of her before I started this project. I found her in a rather serendipitous way: while reading obituaries in the *New York Times* to begin compiling the database for the biographical dictionary *Notable American Women*, which I was editing at Radcliffe. An ulterior but never hidden motive for accepting the position as the dictionary's editor was mining this vast database of dead women for possible subjects for my next book. In fact, at some point I realized that I was reading the obituaries the way other people read personal ads, except that I was looking for a book topic, not a mate, which I already have. When I first read Mary Margaret McBride's obituary, I did not experience a "eureka" moment, but I was interested and let the idea percolate in my head. Intrigued by the chance to explore a new field—radio—in the time period on which I have focused much of my historical work—the 1930s through the 1950s—with a strong biographical focus, I soon decided the project was indeed a perfect fit.

Unlike novelists, historians need sources, and this book would not have been possible without the archival material that Mary Margaret McBride's estate deposited at the Library of Congress in 1977. In addition to correspondence, newspapers clippings, and selected writings, the collection offers almost 1,200 hours of recordings of Mary Margaret McBride's radio shows. Originally recorded on 78 rpm records at the radio host's expense, they later were transferred to tape. These recordings are a treasure trove of interviews with an incredibly wide range of public figures over three decades, for nearly everybody who was anybody in those years appeared on her show.[2] One of the goals of this book is to alert other scholars to the possibilities for using this resource in their own research, and I hope many other historians, as well as documentary filmmakers and radio producers, will find their way to the McBride collection. I promise you won't be disappointed. In fact, colleagues and friends have challenged me to provide readers of this book with the opportunity to simultaneously listen to the shows that are being described, either on the Internet or through a companion CD. The technology isn't quite there yet but maybe will be soon.

Another source that greatly enriched this book was the letters from former listeners who responded to an author's query I placed in the *New York Times Book Review* at the start of this project. These reminiscences and recollections, mostly from fans but also with some negative comments thrown in (like the girl who hated hearing Mary Margaret McBride on the radio when she came home from school for lunch), allowed me to understand how a radio program could be so important to its listeners and how these memories and loyalties could still be warm and strong five decades after her flagship show went off the air. The book also was enriched by the recollections of family members of Stella Karn and Vincent Connolly, two important members of Mary Margaret McBride's radio family, who saw my request and generously supplied information.

I call this book a "radio biography," a term that is meant to draw attention to its hybrid nature as both a recreation of daytime radio from the 1930s through the 1950s and a biography of one of its most important characters. It does not, however, follow the traditional birth-to-death structure of most biographies. As I have been doing throughout my career as a historian and writer, especially in my earlier book on Amelia Earhart,[3] I find myself stretching the boundaries of biography in ways that I hope that readers find successful and stimulating. The book starts with a description of Mary Margaret McBride's radio show at the height of its influence in the late 1940s and early 1950s. After readers have gotten to know Mary Margaret McBride and learned why her program was so successful, the narrative backtracks to tell the story of her upbringing and early career and how she came to radio. The third part picks up the story after World War II and takes it through her death in 1976. An epilogue discusses the contemporary talk show phenomenon with a look back to Mary Margaret's McBride's earlier role.

Even though the numbers of Mary Margaret McBride's former listeners are dwindling, I hope that this book gives them a chance to revisit a favorite radio show through the lens of history and biography. For those who never heard the show, I hope it offers a window on the vital role that radio played in twentieth-century popular culture.

One of the most enjoyable aspects of writing a book is the chance to thank those who helped make it possible. At the top of the list is Janet Wilson McKee, reference librarian at the Recorded Sound Reference Center of the Library of Congress, who probably knows as much (maybe more) about Mary Margaret McBride's radio career as I do. Over the several years that I researched this book, Jan pointed me to favorite tapes, helped me fill in gaps in the sources, and generally served as a sounding board as I struggled with writing a book about a woman who had been almost lost to history, radio or otherwise. My thanks also go to Bryan Cornell at Recorded Sound for his help and his sometimes bemused reactions as Jan and I discussed subjects such as Dromedary Gingerbread Mix, a favorite McBride product still available today. I would also like to acknowledge other Library of Congress staff members who provided help, support, and friendship along the way, especially Rosemary Hanes, Nancy Seeger, Janice Ruth, Barbara Natanson, Sheridan Harvey, Ralph Eubanks, and Sara Day. Whenever I walk into the Library of Congress, I feel very much at home, and I am delighted to acknowledge that debt.

As its genesis in collecting obituaries suggests, this book progressed simultaneously with the massive undertaking of bringing out the next volume of the biographical dictionary *Notable American Women*, which is now completed as well. The project was lucky to be based at the Schlesinger Library, which is part of the Radcliffe Institute for Advanced Study at Harvard University. My thanks especially to my assistant editor at *Notable*, Stacy Braukman, who kept the office running smoothly during my frequent absences from Cambridge while I worked at "Notable North" in Hopkinton, New Hampshire. Even though the Schlesinger Library is not a major repository of material on radio or McBride, it still is a wonderful place to do research and write women's history, and I cherish my long association.

Over the years Joyce Antler has been one of my most supportive and constructive readers, and her comments on an early draft of the manuscript encouraged me to go forward with the project. Joan Jacobs Brumberg, who shares my goal of bringing history to a wider audience than just the academy, is another of my longtime readers and friends, and she offered especially helpful comments on the topic of Mary Margaret McBride and food. Laurel Ulrich gave me an early opportunity to present my work at a Warren Center conference at Harvard devoted to biography. I also profited from the comments of Barbara Haber and other participants at a Murray Center presentation at Radcliffe on Mary Margaret McBride and culinary history. At New York University Press, Eric Zinner got excited about the project as soon as he heard about it, and he and Emily Park shepherded me through an easy progression from manuscript to publication.

On the home front, Don Ware continued his long-standing encouragement of my career as a historian and a writer, making it possible for me to spend time doing what I love while he pursued his own active legal career. Support for good writing clearly runs in his family, and it is my great privilege to dedicate this book to his mother, Elizabeth Parker Ware, who has always been one of my most loyal and appreciative readers.

It's One O'Clock and Here Is Mary Margaret McBride

Mary Margaret McBride enters Yankee Stadium for the celebration of her fifteenth anniversary on radio, May 31, 1949. *Reprinted by permission of Library of Congress, Prints and Photographs Division.*

Prologue

Voice of America

"I ALWAYS AM HAPPY WHEN A WOMAN SUCCEEDS, but when a woman succeeds superlatively, she's an inspiration to all other women."[1] With those words Eleanor Roosevelt greeted the audience of 18,000 women (and a few men) who jammed Madison Square Garden on May 31, 1944, to celebrate Mary Margaret McBride's tenth anniversary on radio. Millions more listened on a nationwide network broadcast.[2] The next day, the First Lady told the readers of her "My Day" column, "I have seen the Garden filled for important meetings, but never before have I seen it as full as it was yesterday for just one woman and a program of radio interviews."[3]

Mary Margaret hadn't been so sure when she left her apartment that the event would be such a success. (Everyone was on a first-name basis with her, and we generally will be, too, in this book.) Ever the pessimist, she was certain that nobody would come, despite the fact that NBC had received more than 44,000 requests for tickets. A favorite cab driver, more dressed up than usual in honor of the event, was waiting outside her Central Park South apartment to take her downtown, and even his reassurances that his wife and daughter were coming did little to allay her fears. "There's nobody here," she muttered as she entered the Garden through a side door. Only when she walked out on to the stage, dressed in a signature navy blue dress with white collar and cuffs and heard the cheers and applause of the assembled crowd did she finally let herself savor the moment. Her instant reaction was that she wanted to shake the hand of every person who came, just as she did after each of her radio broadcasts. "But they're my friends and they've come to see me," she exclaimed. Her skeptical manager, Stella Karn, who had arranged the extravaganza, barely dissuaded her boss from carrying out her grand gesture.[4]

Originally Karn had a more grandiose idea for Mary Margaret's entrance: she wanted her to enter Madison Square Garden astride an elephant. Stella Karn had always had a thing about elephants, probably dating to her days as a circus press agent. No matter that the sight of the short and rather plump radio personality on top of an elephant might have seemed more than a bit comical—once Stella made up her mind, she did not give up easily. This was one of the few times when McBride prevailed.[5]

It was still wartime when Mary Margaret McBride celebrated her tenth anniversary on the air, and the world situation was too serious to have only a party, so the event was dedicated to recruiting women volunteers for the armed forces. Keynote speaker Eleanor Roosevelt, Mary Margaret's favorite guest and longtime friend, told the audience that the men overseas recognized the important contributions that women were making to the war effort. Actress Billie Burke performed a skit about a WAC being decorated for bravery by the president, and the audience also heard from authors Margaret Culkin Banning and Fannie Hurst, as well as war correspondent Margaret Bourke-White. To reinforce the patriotic theme, members of the Red Cross spelled out the victory signal (three dots and a dash) from the balcony, and the event concluded with a fashion show of military uniforms.

NBC president Niles Trammell was so pleased with the broadcast event that he predicted, "I wouldn't be surprised if we had to take the Yankee Stadium to celebrate your twentieth anniversary on the air."[6] His star radio personality beat his prediction by five years, filling Yankee stadium almost to capacity on May 31, 1949, her fifteenth anniversary on radio. This event replicated many elements of the Madison Square Garden gala, except on a much grander scale, with attendance estimated at around 45,000 people.[7] Once again Stella tried to convince Mary Margaret to make her entrance on an elephant. When that failed, she proposed a helicopter to land the guest of honor on the temporary stage set up over second base. Instead, Mary Margaret strode in accompanied by Scottish bagpipers in honor of her ancestral home. Author Rex Stout remarked, "At the next anniversary, they had better use Grand Canyon."[8]

It was a very hot day on this fifteenth anniversary celebration, unusual for late May, and the predominantly female audience treated the occasion like a Sunday picnic. The city had added extra police, but the crowd was orderly, having arrived by car, bus, and the extra subway cars marked "To Mary Margaret McBride's Yankee Stadium" for the occasion. One local reporter described the scene:

> Solid streams of women were boiling up from the Independent subway station. Every incoming train on the elevated IRT station overhead brought additional hundreds. By 11:30 the two streams of womanhood had merged, and it was plain that very few dishes were being washed in the five boroughs, and precious few babies were being rocked.[9]

Many of the women brought box lunches, often filled with the products that McBride endorsed on her show. Concessionaires noticed a definite trend toward ice cream and soft drinks, rather than the usual beer and hot dogs consumed by Yankee fans. The pigeons also were a bit confused. One man in attendance was overheard to observe, "Those birds. They think the Yankees are gonna play a ball game after we get outta here."[10]

More than two hundred dignitaries filled the podium, including Eleanor Roosevelt, actress Eva Le Gallienne, novelist Fannie Hurst, and NAACP head Walter White. (McBride was later rebuked by conservatives for embracing White in public.) Mary Margaret's friends, longtime sponsors, and the members of her radio family, especially Stella Karn and veteran announcer Vincent Connolly, sat proudly alongside the celebrities. Fred Waring and the Pennsylvanians supplied the music, and Waring served as master of ceremonies. Mary Margaret McBride roses—a salmon pink hybrid recently named in her honor[11]—surrounded the stage. There was time for only brief remarks, and many agreed that commentator H. V. Kaltenborn's tribute to a "miracle woman" captured her best:

> Where else can you find one who pretends to be so ignorant when she is so wise—who is smart enough to be willing to sound foolish—who asks a thousand questions to which she knows the answers—who can talk by the hour without giving away a single secret—who is a supersalesman without trying to sell—who makes everyone feel good by just feeling good herself? . . . She loves all the world and all the world loves her.[12]

McBride's reaction to all the hoopla? "I'm not worth it, but I'll try harder after this."[13]

While much of the afternoon was spent with tributes, gifts, and lighthearted stories, the anniversary event (like its Madison Square Garden predecessor) also had a serious component structured around the theme of justice and human rights. Margaret Bourke-White talked about the last conversation she had with Gandhi before his death, which concerned the threat of atomic warfare. Kenneth Spencer sang the African American spiritual "Nobody Knows the Trouble I've Seen," and Lawrence Tibbett sang the Israeli national anthem. Eleanor Roosevelt discussed the Universal Declaration of Human Rights recently passed by the United Nations, to which she was a delegate. The centerpiece was a dramatic skit narrated by actor Melvyn Douglas called "Unfinished Business, U.S.A.," which presented "Negroes" as America's displaced persons, called for the abolition of the poll tax, denounced anti-Semitism and housing discrimination, and endorsed the civil rights legislation pending in Congress. In 1949, issues of intolerance and civil rights were fairly new to the national agenda, but Mary Margaret made sure they had a nationwide platform through her radio program.[14]

Even though Mary Margaret McBride spent her entire career broadcasting out of a New York City studio, she had a surprisingly national reach. In 1934 she started out locally on station WOR as "Martha Deane," a half-hour afternoon show geared toward housewives that ran until 1940, when she turned over it and its copyrighted name to Bessie Beatty. From 1937 to 1941, McBride broadcast a second fifteen-minute show under her own name, this one nationally syndicated but also airing in New York on CBS. For a year after she gave up Martha Deane, McBride also had a fifteen-minute nationally syndicated show sponsored by the Florida Citrus Commission. In 1941 she dropped that and returned to doing a local show on WEAF, the main NBC station in New York, forty-five minutes at one o'clock, her favorite time slot. In 1949 she went to a full hour.[15] In 1950 when NBC refused her requests to take the show national,[16] she bolted to ABC, where she stayed until she gave up her regular show in 1954. Starting in 1951, the ABC show was widely syndicated in a cooperative arrangement in which the New York show was cut down to thirty minutes and local commercials were added by Mary Margaret, Stella, and Vincent Connolly before the new version was distributed by WGN of Chicago.[17]

The wide if selective reach of her program over the yea
why even though the majority of Mary Margaret's loyal listeners wc..
in the New York metropolitan area, she could still count on a nationwide following. While not every radio owner had the chance to hear
Mary Margaret every day of every year, she was definitely one of
radio's best-known stars in the heyday of radio's pretelevision popularity. In addition, as a result of the extensive national media coverage
she received, Mary Margaret had a presence in popular culture that
transcended the millions who were her regular listeners, allowing the
radio personality to reach into corners of the United States where her
radio broadcast was not carried. Her name was a familiar one to Americans across the country in the 1940s and 1950s and can still elicit a
warm, if somewhat vague, response when the three words "Mary Margaret McBride" are mentioned today.[18]

Daytime radio had not seen anything like her when Mary Margaret
McBride debuted in 1934, but by the height of her program in the late
1940s and early 1950s, dozens of radio shows were imitating the ad-lib
interview style she pioneered. *Current Biography* hailed her as "the first
woman to bring newspaper technique to radio interviewing and to
make daytime broadcasts profitable."[19] When she first went on the air,
most radio shows were developed and written by advertising agencies,
who then sold them to stations. For most of her career McBride and
Stella Karn followed a different course, producing the show themselves
and brokering it to New York stations or the national networks. This
arrangement allowed McBride and Karn to exercise unprecedented
control over the show's format. As long as they had enough sponsors to
keep the show on the air (and they always did), they could shape the
program's content and signature style free from outside interference. In
the process, they pioneered roles as independent producers that later
became the norm for the radio and television industries.[20]

Two things were important to Mary Margaret in regard to her radio
slot, and she wasn't always able to have them at the same time. The first
was to reach as broad an audience as possible, preferably on a nationally syndicated show. It sounds sentimental, but she really wanted the
folks back home in Missouri to be able to listen in, and her mother, too,
once she moved to Florida. The second was to have enough air time—
forty-five minutes was her preferred amount—so that she didn't feel
rushed or hemmed in. Hers was a program that needed time to grow on
its listeners; she had to settle into it just as much as they did.[21]

At the height of her popularity, Mary Margaret McBride attracted between six million and eight million listeners, men as well as women, comprising 20 percent of the available broadcast audience in her time slot. Five times a week, her blend of current affairs, literary trends and tidbits, news from the world of Broadway theater and Hollywood film, and more offered listeners a literate yet accessible radio conversation that both entertained and informed. Each show was different—there were no repeats. It is only because producer Stella Karn paid to make recordings of hundreds of selected shows that we have the opportunity to listen again and recreate the experience of Mary Margaret's listeners each day at one o'clock. Her shows remain remarkably fresh and interesting today, more than five decades after their original broadcast.[22]

Revisiting McBride's broadcasts offers a window on twentieth-century America as the country struggled through years of depression, war, and cold war. These were anxious times, and Mary Margaret helped her listeners get through them. She never aspired to be a political commentator along the lines of Dorothy Thompson or Walter Lippmann, and she never pushed an overtly political agenda. During the 1930s she kept her focus fairly tightly on home and hearth. Especially after the Japanese attack on Pearl Harbor, however, she encouraged listeners to become more involved in their communities and the nation at large. By prominently featuring wartime refugees on her show, for example, she helped counter American isolationism and helped prepare her listeners for the revelations of Hitler's "final solution." She also helped lay the groundwork for the postwar civil rights revolution with her outspoken support for tolerance, racial understanding, and human rights. The widening of her political vision paralleled her own personal evolution as she increasingly found her voice not only as a radio personality but also as a concerned citizen.

Even while her show was outdrawing everybody else, McBride often found herself the target of negative stereotypes linked to her gender, her predominantly female audience, her unmarried status, and her ample physique. Covering all those bases, *Newsweek* ran this description of McBride after the 1949 gala at Yankee Stadium:

> Mary Margaret McBride is a 48-year-old spinster with a talent for back-fence gab and an hour a day . . . in which to display her talents. . . . Her audience is almost wholly feminine—fluttery, middle-aged and purely housewife. Men, as a rule, disdain the show. . . . In good

housewifely tradition, she dotes on and drools over anything that pleases her, particularly food. She is built along the lines of a bulldozer, with a face as unlined and pink-cheeked as an English farm girl.[23]

Such demeaning coverage was nothing new to the radio talk show host. In 1940 *Time* titled an article about her with a single word—"Goo"— and later anointed her "radio's queen of endearing mush."[24] *Newsweek* called her a "radio chatterbox" with a "twangy patter" who "chatters rudderless on the radio just as most people chatter in everyday life."[25] By using such dismissive language, commentators made it sound as though her show amounted to nothing more than whatever came into her head, as opposed to a carefully orchestrated show by a shrewd performer who was perhaps the best interviewer radio has ever had.

Mary Margaret McBride took her listeners seriously, and this book takes Mary Margaret seriously. *Collier's* might dismiss her audience as "McBride's Dustpan Army,"[26] but she never talked down to them, which especially endeared her to female listeners tired of being patronized by radio personalities and advertising executives who assumed that all they were interested in was recipes and curtains. At a time when popular culture rarely judged women's intellectual capabilities on a par with men's, Mary Margaret did not discriminate, treating women and men equally when it came to their desire for interesting conversation and involvement in the world at large. She treated her guests just as respectfully. As an interviewer she always put the guest first, carefully disguising her advance research and preparation by making the interview seem like a chat between friends. She never spoke from notes (she had a phenomenal memory), nor would she let her guests use them. All her day-to-day activities—what plays she saw or books she read, which dinner invitations she accepted, what vacations or weekend jaunts she took—were selected according to whether they might produce a good anecdote or an interesting person to be shared with listeners of the show. The radio show truly was her life.

McBride's radio career was something of a fluke. Born in Paris, Missouri, in 1899, she always wanted to be a writer and set her sights early on New York. By 1920, she finally reached the city, where she excelled not as a fiction writer but as a reporter, and then as one of the highest-paid freelance journalists of the decade. Along the way she teamed up with Stella Karn, a hard-talking, no-nonsense character who became her manager and lifelong companion. When the crash wiped out her

and Stella's savings and the Depression dried up Mary Margaret's lucrative freelance career, she found herself at rock bottom. A chance
radio audition in 1934 opened the door to her new career. Stella Karn
served as her producer, and they worked successfully as a team until
McBride gave up her daily show twenty years later.[27]

For someone as famous and successful as she was, Mary Margaret
McBride never really seemed to derive much pleasure or peace of mind
from what she had accomplished. A true perfectionist, her mood swings
were legendary. "If I have a good show, I'm walking on air. But let me
hear it on record and all the glow is gone," she told an interviewer in
1950. "My reason tells me that I could not have remained on the air for
seventeen years without being good, but I really cannot believe it."[28]
Even when she became a radio legend, she never really got over her failure to become a great writer, pushing herself to produce more than a
dozen books and hundreds of articles, most of them far less original
than her radio broadcasts. As she admitted in the last volume of her autobiography, "I can't explain why I should have been so miserable
much of the time in such a happy job. I suppose it's just that I was never
satisfied."[29]

Mary Margaret McBride was one of those people who always saw
a glass as half-empty—or less. While others were amazed that she drew
a near-capacity crowd to Yankee Stadium in 1949, she fretted about the
empty seats. In a revealing television interview with Mike Wallace on
his *Night Beat* show in 1956, she confessed that she always had the feeling that her listeners would find out she wasn't as good as they thought
"and it'll all end." When Wallace asked her why she felt so unfulfilled
despite her success, she couldn't really answer but did admit, "I suppose psychiatrists would say it's something I've never resolved, something that happened to me when I was young." She continued, "We
were poor, I was worried about my mother, I worried about mortgages.
I worried about everything. I was the oldest child in the family and the
only girl. I think that had a lot to do with it."[30] Mary Margaret McBride
went through life always looking back over her shoulder.

As far as her fans were concerned, she needn't have bothered. Mary
Margaret was blessed with one of the most loyal radio audiences ever.
Many of them listened to her for more than twenty years straight, long
enough so that their daughters who were youngsters in the 1930s when
her show debuted could tune in as housewives with young children of

their own at the height of the program in the early 1950s. These were active, not passive, listeners. They structured their day around the program; they learned from it; and they supported it by buying the products that Mary Margaret promoted on the air. The show was a vital part of their everyday life, not just a diversion or a sop, and the connection was mutual. As the radio host said of her relationship with her listeners in 1939,

> I reach for every scrap of glamour and glitter and I hoard it for the best time of all—the time the control room gives me the signal and I'm on the air. I want them to have as much of this mad, lovely city as I've had. In return they give me all of America.[31]

In an image that seems especially apt here, Mary Margaret's listeners were part of what, in another context, Benedict Anderson called an "imagined community."[32] Even though most listeners rarely met in person, they shared a deep bond through their shared activity of tuning in each day at one o'clock to listen to a radio host they considered a dear friend and practically a member of the family. Or to put it another way, they belonged to the same radio nation. Through the act of broadcasting, Mary Margaret drew American women together and reassured them that their lives were important, too. She never encouraged women to abandon their domestic responsibilities but felt strongly that they should have access to a world of ideas and events as well. Accordingly, the radio program addressed the tensions in modern women's lives between traditional gender roles and the new opportunities opening up beyond the home.

But McBride has been nearly forgotten, in both radio history and the history of twentieth-century popular culture, primarily because she was a woman and because she was on daytime radio, a lethal combination. In the 1930s and 1940s, daytime radio was dismissed as the world of the feminine, dominated by weepy soap operas and the crude commercialization typified by the soap companies that sponsored the serials. By contrast, nighttime radio was seen as more serious, less commercial, in a word, more masculine. No matter that women made up the majority of audiences for both day- and nighttime radio: these gendered perceptions ruled and helped consign Mary Margaret McBride to historical oblivion.[33]

Mary Margaret McBride died in 1976, five years after National Public Radio went on the air. The links between McBride's brand of sophisticated talk and reportage and NPR shows like Terry Gross's *Fresh Air* or *The Diane Rehm Show* are unmistakable, but just as striking are the differences, notably McBride's unapologetic acceptance of commercial sponsorship. "Shock radio"—opinionated ranting, usually by men, on sports, politics, and social issues—is another direction that talk radio has taken since her death. Even though McBride would have deplored its lack of civility, there also are clear parallels between today's call-in shows and her program. When thousands of fans regularly wrote to Mary Margaret to tell her their problems and dreams, and she shared those letters on the air, the talk show host and audience were connecting through the seemingly impersonal medium of radio.

Perhaps the closest contemporary parallel to Mary Margaret McBride is the television talk show host Oprah Winfrey. Like Mary Margaret, Oprah is usually referred to by her first name and has problems with her weight. Opinionated yet sympathetic, she connects with her audience through her own life and the lives of the guests on her show. Books are among her favorite topics, and she runs a successful production company that produces her show and other independent projects. More confessional than Mary Margaret and much more closely linked to the identity politics and self-help movements of the past several decades, Oprah takes her audiences seriously and tries to address their needs. Although the line from an early talk show pioneer like Mary Margaret McBride to Oprah Winfrey is not direct, the parallels are unmistakable. Comparing their careers illuminates two important eras in broadcast history.[34]

Looking back over the course of twentieth-century American history, there are hundreds, perhaps thousands, of individuals who were well known in their time but who have gradually faded from public view, Mary Margaret McBride included. Why, then, is it important to resurrect this lost figure? There are many answers, beginning with the ongoing fascination with biography and life narratives. American history is full of stories of men who made good in fields such as politics, business, or popular entertainment. The stories of comparable women are far less well known but just as compelling, especially when they demonstrate the far-reaching transition from a rural and agrarian way of life to the more urban, consumer-based lifestyle that characterizes the twentieth century. McBride captured especially well the monumental changes that can occur in an individual's life span in her description of spending the night at the White House in 1941: "I, Mary Margaret McBride, brought into the world in a kitchen of a Missouri farmhouse by the ministering hands of a scared neighbor woman, was actually spending the night in the White House at the invitation of the wife of the President of the United States."[35] From those humble beginnings, she became one of the leading women broadcasters in the golden era or radio: "The First Lady of Radio." As a broadcast pioneer, communicator, and writer, she reached millions of Americans with her talk and words. Her life story makes an important contribution to twentieth-century American history.

Mary Margaret McBride's career also reflects broader themes in women's history. Her desire for a life more interesting than that of a Missouri farm wife, her struggle for an education and a career, and her attitudes toward feminism and women's roles all were concerns faced by modern women of her generation, and they still are relevant today. Her decision not to marry because of her career, and the dimensions of her often testy but highly rewarding relationship with Stella Karn, which was the most important emotional commitment of both women's lives, speak to the challenge of forging a satisfying personal life while also pursuing an independent career. Probing the often illusive meaning of this partnership and placing it within the larger history of sexuality and same-sex relationships in modern life confirm the importance of looking at the personal as well as the political when charting women's lives.[36]

Mary Margaret McBride's career also has a broader cultural significance, especially when her program is viewed as representative of mid-twentieth-century Middlebrow culture. The term "Middlebrow" was originally coined by Margaret Widdemer in the *Saturday Review of Literature* in 1933 to refer to "the majority reader," and it came to connote a range of cultural tastes and preferences in the interwar years that were distinct from elite highbrow intellectual tastes but more elevated than the lowbrow tastes of tabloid popular culture. The Book of the Month Club, founded in 1926, is the epitome of Middlebrow culture. Like its panel of experts whose selections guide its members' reading choices, Mary Margaret McBride was a guide and interpreter, too, choosing guests from the world of books, theater, and the arts for her audience's daily consumption. Even though the names of figures such as Dorothy Canfield Fisher, Will Durant, Edna Ferber, and Bennett Cerf are no longer very well known, at the time they were a vital part of American cultural life. Using the medium of radio, Mary Margaret McBride was able to bring their ideas to a wider audience as part of her belief that culture should not be just for the elite but should reach the broad middle ranges of American society, including (or, rather, especially) its female members.[37]

Resurrecting Mary Margaret McBride's career also reinforces the importance of radio to twentieth-century popular culture, recognition that has not always been forthcoming in media studies.[38] When making the case for radio history, however, it is important not to inflate the claims. After all, as Gerald Nachman pointed out, a great deal of old radio was "simply cheap entertainment, much of it silly and trashy."[39] And yet, as the content of Mary Margaret's shows demonstrates, important material did go out over the airwaves, content that needs to be treated with the same respect and authority accorded to film, television, and books, all of which survive in forms that are easier than sound is to study and codify into popular and scholarly history.

Reclaiming a spot for radio in twentieth-century American history is as much about restoring the experience of actively listening to radio to our collective memory as it is about specific shows or personalities. This reclaiming goes far beyond nostalgia, although that is part of its appeal. Radio has been a part of everyday life since the 1920s. So many things that individuals do—jobs, family, schooling, recreation, growing up, and growing old—are accompanied by memories of radio. Radio brought not just background noise but also exciting new historical connections: the first introduction to jazz, swing, or opera; a Fireside chat assuring the country that the Depression will end; wartime news of London under siege; teenagers discovering rock and roll on their transistor radios under the bed covers at night; sports fans following the triumphs or losses of favorite teams; news from faraway places like Korea, Vietnam, or China. In our attention to the historical contours of everyday life in all its diversity, radio needs to be a larger part of the story.

Radio also needs to be part of the story of women's history. Radio is one of those cultural spaces in which women have had unexpected latitude to shape and filter messages coming over the airwaves. In fact, women listeners may have a special relation to the medium, especially during the daytime hours when no one else is presumed to be listening. Radio was a piece of women's lives for most of the twentieth century, and as the experiences of Mary Margaret McBride's listeners suggest, women actively, indeed greedily, listened to the radio, taking from its offerings information and ideas to which they would not otherwise have access. These ideas in turn opened a window to a world wider than the domestic sphere, breaking down the societal forces that have kept women isolated and marginalized in their homes. In the right hands—and few hands were better than Mary Margaret's—radio encouraged women to think of themselves as individuals with a stake in modern life and the public sphere.

Mary Margaret McBride is not just a quaint figure from radio's past. Drawing on her years as a freelance journalist for women's magazines, she pioneered the magazine-style format that still structures many talk shows on the air today. Early on, she realized the freedom and power that she could exercise independently of networks and advertisers by producing her own show, which is now the norm for many successful media personalities. Even though she never married or had children, she reached out to and connected with women who had made those choices, offering them the opportunity to stretch their lives beyond the confines of their homebound existence through her daily radio program. Most important, she realized the cultural and political importance of talk radio, and she was one of the first to exploit its potential. The phenomenal bond that she formed with her listeners is critical to understanding popular culture in twentieth-century American life.

PART I

THE HEIGHT OF THE PROGRAM

A familiar image to Americans in the late 1940s: Mary Margaret McBride in front of a microphone. *Reprinted by permission of Library of Congress, Prints and Photographs Division.*

I

"Here Comes McBride"

The typical McBride day is designed for the single purpose of producing a good broadcast. It entails long hours and endless labor.

MARY MARGARET usually woke up around 8.[1] She was never one to leap out of bed, ready to seize the day and take on the world. In fact, she would often lie cowering under the covers, wondering what awful things the day might bring.[2] But then she would pull herself together and get on with it. She was committed to putting on a good show for her listeners, so the first thing she would do was to turn on the radio to catch the day's news. Her housekeeper brought her breakfast in bed, and she scanned the newspapers. Were there events or developments that her guests or audience might be talking about? Had anything happened overnight that might conflict with her plans for the day's show? Then it was time for her mail, which was delivered to her Central Park South apartment by the bag load. From the beginning of her days on the radio, Mary Margaret and her manager, Stella Karn, had decided that every piece of mail must be answered and promptly. It was the radio host's way of keeping in touch with her fans and making them feel connected to her and the show.

Soon the morning was gone and it was time to dress to go out, which meant wedging her ample figure into the corset she always wore in public. In the last years of her radio career she broadcast out of her apartment (which meant she could forgo the corset), but until then, each day around 12:30 she would go downstairs to catch a cab to the NBC studios. There were always several cabs waiting in front of her apartment. Why did she always have such luck in busy lunchtime

Manhattan? The drivers had been instructed by their wives, faithful Mary Margaret listeners, to be available for the radio star.

When she arrived at the studio, she would be greeted by a studio audience who had written ahead to reserve their tickets and assembled, somewhat nervously, wondering what it would be like to see Mary Margaret in person. Taking off her hat and coat as she entered the studio with just minutes to spare before air time, she might ask them where they were from—Brooklyn or the Bronx, Westchester County or New Jersey, visiting tourists from out of town—but she really didn't have much time to warm up the crowd, not that the faithful needed that much warming up. After quick consultations with Stella and her announcer, Vincent Connolly,[3] she would settle down at a simple table and chair with her guest or guests, who might be old friends but were just as likely to be someone she had met only minutes before. Stella would take her place in the control booth or at the table; a gong would strike one o'clock; and the program would begin.

The next forty-five minutes were a mixture of talk, gossip, and, of course, "doing the products"—her phrase for the commercials that made her show possible. She rarely involved the audience in the actual program, and except for occasional titters or rustling noises, you don't know they are there. Mary Margaret was always so intent and focused on her broadcast that she was almost oblivious to anyone else in the room. At various points Vincent might hurry her along, and then as the end rapidly approached, it was up to him to make sure she got off the air on time. "Good-bye, y'all," she would say reluctantly, as if she could have gone on talking indefinitely. Then she would stand by the studio door to personally shake hands with each member of the audience as they left, just as her Baptist preacher grandfather had done at the end of his sermon each Sunday.

Mary Margaret's day was far from over, however. After rehashing the show over a quick lunch with Stella, it was time to start preparing for the next show. On some days, lunch had to wait because she would tape two shows back to back, with the second held for broadcast at a later time. Then she plunged into the preparation for the next day's show, which might involve reading books (although she usually left that until late at night), visiting an interesting spot in the New York metropolitan area, or going to an exhibition or a show. Dinner was almost always eaten out, either in a restaurant whose charms she could share with listeners the next day or at a dinner party or event whose invitation had been accepted precisely because it promised good chatter or new information to share with her listeners. Then it was back home for several more hours of reading and, often, a midnight raid on the refrigerator. She rarely got to bed before 2 or 3 A.M.

That daily routine was the basis for the McBride phenomenon. Mary Margaret realized that it was probably not wise to let her job rule her life, but she really didn't know how to just hang loose. She claimed matter-of-factly not to have done anything for years that was of purely personal interest to herself: "Everything in my life, down to the people I talk to, the hour I go to bed, and the plays I see—everything is run by my job." She once even stopped and took notes on a conversation she was having with her mother over the telephone from Florida because she knew her listeners would enjoy the exchange, and she didn't want to forget it. And that was in the days when long-distance was an extravagance.[4]

Walter White, the head of the NAACP and a good friend as well as frequent guest on the show, recalled a comfortable, friendly program during which the guests forgot the scary microphone and could "pour out their ideas precisely as they would over a cup of tea on the farm where Mary Margaret was born."[5] In 1949 *Newsweek* pointed to a similar aspect of her appeal: "Miss McBride bridges the gap between the celebrity and the housewife smoothly because she possesses the best characteristics of both."[6] Every day she came into the homes of her loyal listeners, a trusted friend who was their link to the events and people of a wider world. Even if they would never meet a famous guest like Margaret Mead, Fiorello LaGuardia, or General Omar Bradley (who was heard to say, "Maybe my wife will appreciate me at last" when he appeared on her show),[7] her listeners felt as though they had gotten to know the celebrity through her half-hour chat. And they lavished fame and adulation on their beloved host. As a female journalism student from the University of Missouri, where McBride had received her bachelor's degree in 1918, wrote to her idol thirty years later, "As every boy at one time or another thinks—someday I may be President—so every girl in J-school dreams that someday she may hold a comparable position to Mary Margaret McBride."[8]

As stimulating and engaging as the show was, Mary Margaret never could have survived on the air for twenty years if she hadn't been able to win commercial sponsorship for her brand of talk show radio. This is where McBride excelled: nobody could sell products in the way that she could. As Bennett Cerf once said, "For my money, Mary Margaret is the greatest impresario radio ever has developed."[9] National radio networks sang her praises to prospective advertisers: "This 'Mary Margaret approval' has a magnetic cash value. It is the power that herds people into stores to buy."[10] She was so popular that she had a waiting list of sponsors wanting to buy time on her show, even though they had to be personally approved by the radio star herself. How could her listeners trust her, she would say to sponsors, if she wasn't absolutely sure that the product was all that its advertising copy said it was? This combination of sincerity and enthusiasm, plus her loyal and established audience, resulted in terrific paybacks for sponsors. As one advertising executive said, "In my entire twenty years' experience as president of an advertising agency, I know of no sponsored program that can accomplish such phenomenal results."[11]

Listeners didn't always know what drew them to Mary Margaret—they just knew that they kept coming back for more. "I listen to you, but heaven knows why, the way you go on. It isn't your voice—and it certainly isn't what you say. I don't know what it is." Mary Margaret could accept such statements only with exasperation: "Right—it isn't my voice! And it isn't the way I 'go on.' But it isn't anything mysterious either. I think it IS what I say and back of it is good hard work—don't let anybody fool you."[12]

Mary Margaret was aware that her name often was mocked in the popular media: "I knew that as a person I lent myself to kidding and even caricature; overweight, unmarried, with a reputation (really undeserved) of babbling on and on forever like the famous brook."[13] McBride was used to comments about her weight and appearance, but nothing infuriated her more than suggestions that her carefully researched and prepared radio program was nothing more than random thoughts pouring out in an Ozark twang. She knew better, and so did Stella Karn, but it was hard to make the press take her seriously.

Having said that, it also is true that not all the coverage that McBride received in the national and local press was negative. Portraits of her in magazines geared to female readers, such as the *Woman's Home Companion* or *Woman's World*,[14] were generally much more positive and sympathetic to her than were the national news magazines like *Time, Life, Newsweek,* and the *American Mercury.* Partly this is a question of whether the articles were written by women, as they often were at the women's magazines, or men, as they presumably were in the unsigned pieces in *Time* and *Life,* but not entirely. For example, journalist Barbara Heggie wrote two profiles of McBride several years apart, one for the *New Yorker* in 1942 and a second for *Woman's Home Companion* in 1949. The tone of the second was decidedly warmer and more sympathetic than the first, although both took her seriously as an artist and radio personality. Years later McBride reread the *New Yorker* profile and had this reaction: "As I nearly always did when being interviewed I talked too much, but when I reread the story, to my surprise I found I liked it very much. I couldn't even remember what I had been so upset about at the time."[15]

Recognition of her skill and success was often hidden, however, with words and phrases that paint them in a feminine, fluttery way that would never have been used to describe a man's professional achievements. For example, a *Time* article in 1946 asserted that Mary Margaret responded to almost any comment by "clasping her hands, pursing her lips, blinking her eyes and exclaiming: 'Goodness!'" In the very next sentence the magazine called her a "brilliant interviewer" but then undercut that statement by describing the brilliance in a demeaning fashion: "With a well-controlled gush she can 'soften up' almost anyone to just the sticky consistency her listeners love. She does it with an air of dithery, appreciative interest that soon has most guests babbling as if they had known her for years."[16] Far too often the temptation to dismiss her because she was a woman who talked to a primarily female daytime audience won out over a more balanced and objective view.

Mary Margaret was an odd combination of being very shy but also enjoying, indeed craving, the limelight. Preferring to be the star rather than the star maker, she could never understand impresarios like Sol Hurok (or probably Stella Karn): "Perhaps it's because I'm such a ham myself, always hankering for credit-lines, that I can't successfully imagine what goes on inside a person dedicated to thrusting somebody besides himself into the limelight."[17] Yet she admitted to being "one of the most timid souls alive," so shy that she compared going into a roomful of people with taking a plunge "exactly as if I were diving into icy water." When she was a cub reporter on assignment, she used to walk around the block several times before daring to venture inside for her interview, even if she had an appointment. In many ways she felt lucky to have had a career in radio, precisely because it gave her an excuse to meet a range of interesting people in the course of her work.[18]

Mary Margaret McBride channeled all her insecurities and self-doubts into her work. In today's parlance, she was a workaholic. Even taking time off on a fall afternoon to go for a drive with Stella caused her to feel as if she were a small child playing hooky. She greeted with considerable trepidation labor leader Walter Reuther's statement that the thirty-hour workweek was just around the corner. What would she do with the extra time? "I've worked—by choice—18 hours a day most of my life," she told readers of her Associated Press column in 1955. "All I hope is I can finish in the same tempo."[19]

Mary Margaret could never have functioned at this tempo for so long had it not been for Stella Karn, her "chief booster, frequent deflator, and head of my radio family" and "a born impresario."[20] (More pointedly, McBride dedicated one of her books to "Estella H. Karn, Genius and Slave-Driver.")[21] Besides handling all the considerable business arrangements for the show, Stella often filled in as a host, impromptu guest, or announcer. She did not have as effective a radio voice as her partner did, but she could hold her own behind the microphone, even if she was more comfortable puffing away on a cigarette in the control booth with the engineer. Her tart observations and frequent jokes at Mary Margaret's expense, plus her engaging stories of her circus days, endeared her to listeners. So firm was their faith in each other that they never signed a contract to formalize their relationship. "I couldn't have lasted on radio twenty years without her," McBride asserted without equivocation.[22]

Stella's main contribution to the Mary Margaret McBride radio phenomenon was her ability as a business manager and public relations wizard. Many people on radio row regarded Stella as a bitch (their word), but she worked twenty years to win the title, and she was proud of it. She devoted herself 100 percent to her job, which was promoting her boss, not simply because it was her job, but because she truly believed in Mary Margaret's importance. "To me, Mary Margaret is an outstanding person. I admire her judgment, her sincerity, her intelligence. She is a great artist—but doesn't realize it."[23] Stella herself never seemed to want the limelight, being happy to bask in the shadows while her client shone out front. If she allowed herself to be featured in a news article, she made sure that the paper ran Mary Margaret's picture instead of hers. That was the essence of her success and pleasure in her job: "A good manager can't afford to be a ham. There can't be two stars in one show."[24] *Life* magazine called them "the most famous female team" in radio.[25]

What Stella did best, everyone agreed, was say no. Once her mind was made up, she could not be moved, and she did not mince words or suffer fools gladly. She always ascribed her success to the combination of "Mary Margaret's ability and my bad disposition."[26] In return for between one-third and one-half of Mary Margaret's income, she fended off all those who wanted a piece of the radio star, including sponsors which she held in special contempt until they passed muster. Giving up all her other publicity accounts after McBride's radio career took off, she saw her job for Mary Margaret as continuing for twenty-four hours a day, seven days a week.

Nothing interfered with her commitment to her boss. Stella would take on radio executives, newspaper editors, and even the pages at Radio City Music Hall where the show was broadcast. She was the bad cop to Mary Margaret's good cop. Sixty years later one of the pages, then a college student at Columbia and later a broadcasting executive, recalled McBride as pleasant but somewhat aloof, although generous with $2 Christmas tips, a big deal when the salary was $65 a month and pages had to provide their own white shirts. And Stella? She was "all over us and hyper-critical of everything we did (or did not do, in her eyes)." Not surprisingly, when she was out of earshot, Stella was the butt of many choice comments by the pages.[27]

Stella's personality and her single-minded devotion to promoting the career of Mary Margaret McBride more than once caused problems at the National Broadcasting Company, McBride's network at the height of her career. WNBC often organized daylong events that saluted specific communities in the New York metropolitan area and deployed radio personalities to participate as a way of building goodwill with the towns and also getting publicity for the radio network and its stars. In 1947 during a fall salute to Montclair, New Jersey, Stella managed to offend almost everyone with whom she came into contact. Although

WNBC took great pains to assure the local leaders that Karn was not an official representative of the network, the damage had been done. This was not an isolated incident, it turned out, and network officials appealed to Mary Margaret about Stella's "sense of public relations gone awry" and gave Stella an ultimatum: either she would attend these events in a spirit of goodwill toward the station, and not just her client, or she would refrain from participating.[28]

Mary Margaret realized that the people who knew Stella fell into two camps, each with strong feelings: "One group (and it was not small) called her unreasonable, hard-boiled, even cruel; the other hailed her as a great woman, a genius, the most generous, loyal friend anybody ever had."[29] Radio critic Ben Gross captured the two sides of Stella well when he characterized her essentially as

> a kind-hearted person with a broad streak of sentiment and a capacity for life-long friendships. But, when it comes to radio, this cyclonic bundle of managerial prowess has only one objective—the greater glory of Mary Margaret McBride. And, if anyone is so foolish as to stand in the way—well, brother, look out![30]

Stella Karn was the kind of person to attract apocryphal stories, except that in her case they often turned out to be true. One time when Mary Margaret was trying to do a remote broadcast from the Virgin Islands, the first batch of recordings sent back couldn't be played because the wire had broken. Stella cabled this terse response: "Get Boy Scout Manual and learn to tie a square knot."[31] The engineers repaired the wire in time for the prerecorded program to go on the air. Another time when Mary Margaret was interviewing Gary Cooper live from her Central Park South apartment, the broadcast was disturbed by audible banging on the pipes from an apartment nearby. Stella located the source of the noise—two plumbers—who happily agreed to stop working if they could meet Gary Cooper. (They got paid for their time whether or not they were working, which prompted Mary Margaret to exclaim, "Radio time and plumbing time.") For the next ten minutes they took over the radio show, and only with great difficulty was Mary Margaret able to wrest the conversation away from them and back to Gary Cooper.[32]

The main announcing duties on the radio show were handled by Vincent Connolly. More than an announcer but not quite a sidekick or buddy like Stella, he emerged as a trusted on-air personality in his own right. "Thanks again, and please say hello to Vincent," wrote one of her guests. "You know, he begins to seem like a member of your (radio) family."[33] When Connolly first joined the program, he would get so nervous about the totally ad-libbed nature of the show that his hands would shake in anticipation of what might happen next, but he soon settled down. A New Yorker profile in 1942 noted that Vincent was a favorite with listeners "because he treats her with the same amused indulgence they feel for her. 'I don't know, Mary Margaret. Tell us,' he says, with an anticipatory chuckle that is probably echoed by most of the ladies listening in."[34] Sometimes listeners got irritated when Vincent disagreed with her or rushed her off the air when her time was up, but listeners were just as likely to chide Mary Margaret for being too rough on him.

Besides his roles as announcer, timekeeper, and product prompter, Vincent was also something of a fall guy. Once when Mary Margaret was interviewing two of the radio Quiz Kids, Vincent mimicked their traditional opening roll call by saying, "I'm Vincent Connolly, announcer for this program, and I'm thirty-five years old," only to have one of the kids whisper audibly, "He seems like fifty."[35] More often, it would fall to Vincent, who was almost as closely associated with the products as Mary Margaret was, to tell listeners how he wrapped his sandwiches in E-Z Cut-Rite wax paper or enjoyed a can of Habitant soup for lunch. Luckily he felt quite at home in a kitchen and was quite conversant about a range of products (which he had to ensure that she mentioned) that were not typically in a man's vocabulary or province of experience.

All listeners knew that Vincent Connolly was a Princeton graduate and a bachelor. An article in Woman's Home Companion in 1949 described him as "a plumpish blond Princeton graduate, pushing forty, whose voice, warm and cloying as a freshly made batch of chocolate fudge, is almost as well known as hers."[36] Mary Margaret called him "an extremely cultivated, likable, and rather conservative young man" who "does not always approve of my unconventional ways." He had grown up in New Rochelle, New York, in a prosperous family (his father was a banker) and dabbled in theater and music in college, his main loves. Unfortunately he graduated in 1932, the worst year of the Depression, and jobs in the theater were scarce, so he was glad to end up with his job as a radio announcer at WOR, which had its offices in the same building as his father did. Connolly did other radio announcing as well and continued to follow the theater and opera avidly. He spoke flawless French and, except during the war (he was not drafted), traveled almost yearly to Europe. A resident of East Thirty-sixth Street in Manhattan, he also for a time after the war ran the Sutton Manor Bookshop, "a well-known literary oasis on New York's East Side."[37]

Vincent took on a role that many men probably could not have endured. Even though the show featured an eclectic mix of guests from all walks of life, it still was typecast as a woman's daytime show, not much higher in prestige than the soap operas. A columnist from the *New York Sun* named E. L. Bragdon once touched off a small firestorm of controversy by saying that "there was one man on the air who should have a vote of sympathy from all men—Vincent Connolly on Martha Deane's program, who was forced, during his duties as announcer, to listen to talk that was sometimes silly."[38] McBride's listeners rallied to Vincent's defense, and Bragdon backed down, but he had hit a bit of a nerve about issues of gender and authority on the airwaves, specifically why a man (the terrible Depression job market aside) might willingly play a part in a realm so thoroughly identified with the female and the feminine. There was nothing effeminate about Vincent—he was, after all, a cultured person with an extensive knowledge of literature, theater, and the arts, which made him such an indispensable companion on her show. And he was secure enough in his self-image to allow himself to take on duties such as helping Mary Margaret test some of her household products. But there still was something slightly "unmanly" about his on-air persona.[39]

One of the running gags between Mary Margaret and her announcer was why Vincent wasn't married. "I don't know, Mary Margaret," was his usual lackadaisical reply to her ribs and taunts. In fact, Vincent was what in those days was called a "confirmed bachelor," which for many men (probably including him) meant that he was what would now be referred to as gay. Writer Philip Hamburger, in a profile of the talk show host that also mentioned Vincent, stated, "His private life, like Mary Margaret's is an open book to the fans," but a closeted book would have been a more apt metaphor.[40] That a gay man served for many years as her announcer, along with the complicated personal relationship between Mary Margaret and Stella Karn, shows that within the radio family, as in many other families, sexuality and gender relations were not always what they seemed to be on the surface.

Two other members of the radio family were central to the show's smooth functioning. Hilda Deichler, always referred to as "Mrs. D.," was McBride's longtime secretary, dating back to her freelance magazine-writing days. She was in charge of all the correspondence and contact with listeners, with whom she developed strong bonds. Among other things, Mrs. D. kept notes on every broadcast and often was the first person that Mary Margaret consulted for reactions after she got off the air.[41]

Just as important to the success of the show was leg woman Janice Devine, who was in charge of doing the background research and who, like Deichler, stayed in Mary Margaret's employ for decades. Mary Margaret might not meet her guest until five minutes before airtime, but Devine would have already conducted a preparatory interview or telephone conversation to make sure that the person was not likely to clam up with the dreaded "mike fright" when the show began. Devine also followed up on the various ideas that fluttered Mary Margaret's way, such as "Have a note from you that simply says '300 Trees in Hall of Fame.' Want anything done about this?" She also fed possible program ideas to her boss: "How about doing the Hippodrome before it's torn down?" Or "Money left to animals—suggested by the recent story of the trust fund cow that died." Like nearly everybody associated with Mary Margaret, she, too, occasionally took her turn in front of the mike, as did her son Michael, born in 1939, one of the flock of infants and youngsters (nephews and various McBride, Karn, and Connolly cousins, children of staff and friends) who were often called upon to perform informally, such as serenading listeners with "Silent Night" at Christmastime.[42]

A diverse set of characters rounded out the show's radio family. A frequent guest was Juliette Nicole, or Madame Nikki, the French-born creator of Mary Margaret's memorable hats and the designer of much of her wardrobe. "We can't understand Nikki but we love her," wrote one devoted listener.[43] Herman Smith, a writer and food expert who was another "confirmed bachelor," appeared regularly to share stories about the inn he ran in South Salem, New York. Children's authors and illustrators Berta and Elmer Hader, friends from Greenwich Village days and the owners of a scenic New Jersey retreat overlooking the

Hudson where Mary Margaret and Stella spent many wonderful week-ends, often shared their doings. Other regulars included Hattie Silver-man, widow of the founder of *Variety*; Patti Pickens, mother of the singing Pickens sisters (whom Stella had discovered); Enid Haupt, or-chid grower extraordinaire and later editor of *Seventeen*; Helen Josephy, Mary Margaret's travel book collaborator from the 1920s; and Olga Petrova, silent film star. Listeners came to know Mary Margaret's housekeeper and cook, first Frances Gallagher and then Myra Wash-ington, and her three Chinese godchildren, Calvin, Lily, and Bo-Lum Lee, whose parents ran a restaurant in Chinatown. And very much part of the program, as a guest when she visited from Missouri and as the frequent focus of Mary Margaret's reminiscences, was her mother, Eliz-abeth Craig McBride.[44]

This extended radio family was always ready to pinch-hit when a guest was sick or canceled, to fill in when Mary Margaret took one of her infrequent vacations, or to take over in time of emergency or illness. They were the core of the birthday celebrations and anniversaries that marked Mary Margaret's increasing number of years on the radio, and they were there, in tears, for the last broadcast in 1954. The best way to think of them is as a permanent repertory company, a funny, quick-wit-ted, and utterly unpretentious group of souls who were devoted to the radio host and stayed with her through good times and bad. Just the way audiences followed the ongoing exploits of the ensemble cast of the *Jack Benny Show*, Mary Margaret's listeners counted the radio fam-ily as their friends, too.[45]

One person who initially dismissed Mary Margaret and then be-came one of the most stalwart members of the radio family was the New York radio critic Ben Gross. After discovering her in her early days as Martha Deane, Gross wrote a highly negative review of her show. But something (maybe it was Stella Karn's insistence) got him to tune in again the following week, and he had something of an epiphany:

> Her words fascinated me! It became obvious that here was no ordinary female gabber; that she had a rich background of experience; that dur-ing her interviews she revealed hidden facets of her guests; that she had a store of amusing and entertaining anecdotes about the great and the humble and, above all, she loved people. The next day I listened

and by the time another week had passed the Mary Margaret hour had become an addiction.[46]

Ben Gross got hooked on Mary Margaret as far back as 1934, and she only got better.

Here Mary Margaret tries out her radio technique on jazz historian Paul Whiteman. *Reprinted by permission of Library of Congress, Prints and Photographs Division.*

2

Mary Margaret's Radio Technique

When I am on the air, the only thing in the world I want is for the guest to show himself in the best possible light. I'm interested only in the guest. I don't care what happens to me. I don't try to make a fool of myself but I don't care if I do. Later, if we play the program back and I hear myself being a fool, I hate it. But while I'm on the air nothing matters except for a guest to reveal himself. And I think that's the reason why he does.

MARY MARGARET MCBRIDE was one of the best interviewers radio has ever had.[1] With a simple "Tell about it," she put guests at ease and then drew them out, often eliciting memories and confessions that they had not planned to share. "I've never spoken like this before," marveled actress Billie Burke, "and it is an odd experience."[2] There was nothing prurient or sensational about these conversations, just an interesting and sincere chat between host and guest. The audience recognized this, and it made them want more. "You always asked just what I wanted to know," remembered one of her faithful listeners, which Mary Margaret considered a high compliment indeed.[3]

McBride's phenomenal radio technique had many sources, but she always pointed to being born and raised on a farm:

We had good neighbors and the talk I heard as a girl was neighborly talk. I acquired the habit of talking like that myself, and it has always helped me get on with people in an easy, friendly way. On the radio I try to speak as simply as I used to hear my mother and her neighbors speak when I was a girl back on the farm.[4]

That Missouri farm girl innocence confused a lot of casual or first-time listeners, who conjured up a vision of a hesitant, bewildered young woman with pigtails and in a gingham dress behind the mike. Nothing could have been further from the truth. "You have to be a professional to realize the terrific genius behind that careless informality," noted one of her rivals with perhaps a twinge of envy. It was not unusual for McBride to finish a forty-five minute show with the back of her dress bathed in sweat, nearly stuck to her chair. For the rest of her life she could tell time almost to the second without looking at a clock.[5]

The first time that many people—especially critics or freelance writers assigned to do a piece about the radio phenomenon—heard Mary Margaret on the air, they often assumed either that it was all an act or that there was nothing to it (two very different, indeed conflicting, assessments). The more time that critics spent with her, however, the more they realized that what they heard on the air was, for better or worse, real and sincere. "I hate to say it," she once told an interviewer,

> but I'm afraid the truth is that I'm not a good enough actress to fake anything. . . . When I sound dumb, it's because I am dumb. When I get emotional—some have called it corny, others gooey—I honestly feel that way . . . I could not fake dumbness or ignorance any more than I could pretend knowledge I don't have, attitudes I don't feel.[6]

Nor could she fake the enthusiasm that came through so strongly over the air. "Maybe I was often too enthusiastic," she later observed, "but I meant every word. I really *loved* a good guest."[7]

What was at work here was a total absence of ego, at least when she was on the air. (Off the air her ego was quite fragile and susceptible to dramatic mood swings on the flimsiest of provocations.) "The prime requisite of a Good Listener is the ability to forget oneself. I can honestly say I never think of myself when I interview someone. I concentrate on my guest. Nothing else exists for me. . . . All I want is to have them shown off to the best advantage."[8] From the other side of the microphone one of her guests described McBride's gift as her "deep sense of appreciation of *you now*," continuing, "We're all so boxed up and lonesome. When she looks at you with those wonderful brown eyes and that kind beautiful face, you say to yourself, 'Here's somebody who cares about *me*.' So far as I was concerned it was a love scene."[9]

There was more to it than just empathy, however. This was hard work: preparation for her forty-five minutes on the air took nearly every waking moment of Mary Margaret's day, seven days a week, fifty-two weeks a year. What her listeners heard was a totally ad-libbed, unscripted show, but she was as overprepared as any first-time teacher facing a room of eager students. When she told Orson Welles, "I've been thinking of you constantly for forty-eight hours," she was telling the truth.[10]

McBride quickly developed several rules, often out of necessity when faced with the terrible prospect of dead air. The first was never ask a question she couldn't answer herself. A variation on that was never ask a guest to tell a story that she couldn't tell herself, just in case the guest clammed up with mike fright or was otherwise uncooperative. Never ask a question that could be answered yes or no, because then she would have to ask another question right away. Never ask a question that closed the door. The television commentator and writer Heywood Hale Broun learned so much being interviewed by her that he later credited her as his "guru."[11]

Another habit that Mary Margaret adopted early on was the technique of repeating, every couple of minutes, the name of the guest she was interviewing. Until you listen to a lot of her tapes, you don't realize how useful and helpful this is, especially for listeners who might have been out of the room or otherwise occupied when the person was first introduced. She even would spell out the person's name for her listeners if she thought they might have trouble with it: "I think you're a very exciting person. That's I. Rice Pereira. P-E-R-E-I-R-A," she said of the artist, then proceeded without missing a beat to a commercial for Dromedary Cake Mix.[12] When one of her loyal listeners recalled sixty years later what made the show so memorable to listen to, she pointed specifically pointed to this trait of repeating guests' names. In her humble opinion, Mary Margaret ranked as "Best Interviewer Ever!!"[13]

While Mary Margaret is spelling out Rice Pereira's name for her listeners, one can almost see the cub reporter, pencil and notebook in hand, asking a subject to spell her name for the newspaper. As much as it helped to have been raised on a farm, having been a reporter and magazine writer was probably even more relevant to McBride's success on the air. Her journalist's training in tracking down and telling a good story was excellent preparation for deciding how to fill her forty-five minutes each day. Indeed, she herself saw the connection. "It's being a reporter, knowing a story when you see it and keeping at it until you've got that story," she told *Radio Digest* in 1941:

It's not talking all the time about MY friends, MY family, MYSELF as one critic maintained. It's the stories—good, solid feature stories, with as much information, drama and fun as you can get out of them that make women remember, seven years afterward and also word for word, parts of broadcasts that even I have forgotten by now.[14]

When she was a reporter, she did not write stories that were to be read only by women, and she applied that same approach to her radio topics and guests: "I maintain that if a thing is interesting in itself, it is just as interesting to intellectually curious, intelligent women (and my listeners are certainly that) as it is to men."[15] This position represented a not-so-subtle dig at the reigning view of daytime radio as a vast, predominantly female wasteland. Mary Margaret knew that irrespective of gender, audiences were eager for good, serious talk, a fact confirmed by her legions of loyal female and male listeners. But don't call her a commentator. "I don't comment. I interview. And I don't editorialize. I only try to tell about the interesting things people are doing."[16] This position, too, may have had roots in her earlier newspaper career, in which the opinions and the personality of the reporter had no place in the story.

Whatever the sources of McBride's radio magic, when she sat down to broadcast, she was so effective, even seductive, that she called her shows a "conversational love affair."[17] From the start she set out these ground rules: "The only rule is that the speaker have something to say and say it in his natural voice, without notes." The other requirement was that McBride have the first right to a personality, whether it be an author like Mary Roberts Rinehart or James Thurber, an explorer like Admiral Richard Byrd or Thor Heyerdahl, or a Broadway figure such as Tennessee Williams, Mary Martin, or Moss Hart promoting a new play or performance. If she was going to have Eleanor Roosevelt on the show to talk about a new volume of her autobiography, she had to have her first. If the guest dared to break that rule to be interviewed on another show before the scheduled appearance on hers, he or she would be unceremoniously uninvited. So well known was Mary Margaret's ability to launch a new book or personality that public relations people and talent bookers rarely challenged this edict.[18]

Her insistence that guests not come in with prepared remarks also set her off from most other radio shows at the time, which were heavily scripted. Bob Hope was amazed to watch her basically ad-lib a show, or as he said, "Mary Margaret, you just flip it." If someone did dare to arrive with notes, she would simply contrive to sweep them off the table or otherwise make them disappear. She herself relied on only a few small slips of paper, usually reminders about the products or letters from listeners. For the most part, she drew on her phenomenal memory.[19]

Guests were never announced in advance. Sometimes Mary Margaret was well acquainted with her visitor, either professionally or personally, but just as often Janice Devine had done all the legwork, and the host was meeting the subject for the first time just before the broadcast. This called for instant rapport, which Mary Margaret quickly mastered: "Even though I might have walked in three minutes before the broadcast and met the person for the first time, I sometimes felt that by the end of the hour we were best friends."[20] Tongues loosened quickly once Mary Margaret put someone at ease. On one memorable occasion, Appalachian writer Jesse Stuart started spinning some racy stories about his childhood, not realizing they already were on the air. "Hell, ma'am, I never would have talked like that about old Grandpaw. I was so comfortable, I thought we were rehearsin'."[21] As McBride later admitted, "The height of my ambition was to have a guest now and then say on the air something he'd never said before."[22]

These moments of self-revelation and epiphany were even more compelling when they came from famous people. Today we live in a celebrity-saturated, tell-all culture in which every detail (real or not) about the lives of the rich and famous is broadcast in the media and cyberspace, but at the height of Mary Margaret's program, Americans were not yet accustomed to getting to know their celebrities quite so intimately. True, the Hollywood and New York publicity machines cranked out biographical material for mass consumption by hungry fans, but it still was quite unusual to hear personal details, such as stories about their upbringing or their struggle to rise to success, from the mouths of well-known personages themselves. Hearing these stories gave the illusion of breaking down barriers, of making celebrities seem more like ordinary folks: if they got a break and made it big, maybe listeners could, too. In these conversations Mary Margaret kept the focus firmly on human interest rather than celebrity gossip, thereby separating herself from scandal-spreading columnists like Hedda Hopper, Louella Parsons, and Walter Winchell, all then at the top of their fame and influence. Accordingly, when Parsons appeared on McBride's show in 1944 to promote her autobiography, *The Gay Illiterate*, they chatted about her life rather than trading gossip about Hollywood stars.[23]

Guest after guest, the famous and the not famous, commented on Mary Margaret's remarkable ability to make them forget that they were on the air broadcasting to an audience numbering in the millions. "You were the perfect hostess," wrote a first-time author from Mason, Texas, named Fred Gipson, "else I would have been so nervous that I'd have overturned two glasses of water, instead of just one."[24] Bentz Plagemann felt that McBride had almost "willed" him to speak deeply, "and afterward I was as exhausted as if I had run a race."[25] One newspaperwoman was so nervous she feared that the radio audience could hear her teeth chatter, and she was not alone. "I want to tell you how much I enjoyed my interview on Thursday night," wrote Jane Engle in 1949. "I have never held hands with a girl in all my life, but holding your hand certainly restored my confidence."[26]

Mary Margaret could make an interesting show out of almost anybody, nervous or not, but she had her favorites. Authors, adventurers, and explorers who had been to faraway places were at the top of her list, and she confessed to a slight preference for male guests over female, although she never explained why. In her experience, "most novelists (I hate generalizations, but this one is fairly safe) write much better than they talk." Comedians such as Ed Wynn, Danny Kaye, Jimmy Durante, and George Jessel appeared frequently on the show, but she always had a hard time with them because they weren't used to being interviewed—they just wanted to crack jokes and be "on." "Bob Hope, I don't care whether you say one single funny thing today—this is an interview. I want to find out about you." Similarly, stage people often froze up when they had to perform without a script, and "sometimes the broadcast was almost over before I thawed them out." Some of her favorite theater folks were Mary Pickford, Billie Burke, and Dorothy and Lillian Gish. And despite her (and the network's) fears about what kind of salacious stories fan dancer Sally Rand might tell, the program turned into a poignant discussion of Rand's childhood on a farm in Missouri.[27]

Sometimes Mary Margaret reached out to her audiences by inviting a well-known guest to talk about a cause that was dear to his or her heart, which almost always resulted in a good show and good publicity for whatever cause was being promoted. Author Pearl Buck started out as a difficult guest—"reserved and suspicious, I thought, of both me and the microphone"—but she became more human when she ___ ___ talk about her retarded child and her work promoting the adoption of foreign orphans. Listeners never forgot the poignant show in which actress Helen Hayes talked about the death of her daughter from polio. Public awareness of a different kind was raised in the 1940s when refugees from Europe brought the horror of the war to listerners.[28]

Even though Mary Margaret's program was much broader than just books, appearances by authors were such a staple that one publicist from Publishers Row boasted of having a sampler sewn by his wife that read, "God Bless Mary Margaret."

> No one on the air, they will tell you, did so much to sell books as she did, or interviewed authors with such skill and tact, even to the extent of treating them not as curiosities but as people who had written something worth publishing. There was, finally, abundant evidence that she had read what they had written.

McBride deliberately capitalized on the news value of books as part of her strategy of bringing contemporary culture and ideas into the homes and lives of her listening public, presenting books and authors as entertainment in addition to cultural enlightenment. In her mind, this dissemination of ideas removed culture from the realm of the elite and deposited it squarely in the hands of ordinary Americans.[29]

Absent for the most part from these author-based programs were the writers who now make up the modernist literary canon—no Thomas Wolfe, Ernest Hemingway, William Faulkner, or Eugene O'Neill. Instead the radio host welcomed a range of authors whose popularity attested to the vibrancy of "Middlebrow culture" in the 1930s and 1940s, a phenomenon predicated on the existence of a strong, general reading audience for hardcover books (this was before the postwar paperback revolution) on a wide range of fiction and nonfiction topics. Many of the authors associated with Middlebrow Culture—writers like Fannie Hurst, Will Durant, Pearl Buck, C. S. Foster, William Shirer, Lowell Thomas, Erskine Caldwell, Cleveland Amory, Cornelia Otis Skinner, Mary Heaton Vorse, and Marjorie Kinnan Rawlings, among others, all of whom appeared on the program—are no longer very well known, but they were quite familiar at the time. In some ways, these Middlebrow writers were the twentieth-century equivalent of the "damned scribbling women" who so angered Nathaniel Hawthorne in the previous century—best-selling writers who reached popular audiences while other now-celebrated novelists languished in relative obscurity.[30]

In book promotions as well as the general tenor of most of her interviews, Mary Margaret always styled herself more as a popularizer than a critic, which made her show more sales pitch than critical assessment. In part this stance came from her temperament, but it also was dictated by the constructs of radio: why would anyone want to hear about a bad book or a play she hadn't liked? Except for occasional soft digs to authors for neglecting the role of women, Mary Margaret rarely made negative comments about the books at hand, preferring instead to offer plot summaries and interesting anecdotes plucked from the text. While she hoped that her listeners would buy the book, or at least search it out at their local library, in effect these interviews functioned as stand-alone performances, in which the intimacy promoted by radio "encouraged the idea that speaker and audience were meeting as equals." Ironically, listening to authors talk in depth on the air about their work allowed her audience to learn something about literature without actually reading the books. Here we can see the beginnings of the culture of personality and celebrity that has influenced book promotion—indeed, contemporary popular culture—ever since.[31]

Transcriptions of the thousands of interviews Mary Margaret McBride conducted over the course of her career would fill volumes and still would probably not fully recreate the spontaneity and bonhomie of her show.[32] But it is possible to use the content of several programs to stand in for the larger project. Her show on Armistice (now Veterans') Day, November 11, 1947, featured the well-known commentator H. V. Kaltenborn and his wife Olga talking about their 42-day, 22,000-mile trip to Japan and the Pacific. The radio host opened on a light note, mentioning that Kaltenborn had recently been named as a co-respondent in a divorce case based on cruel and inhuman treatment: instead of listening to her, one female listener asserted, her husband listened to Kaltenborn on the radio. The conversation then switched to a lively and frank discussion of the challenges that General Douglas MacArthur faced in postwar occupied Japan, the possibilities for rebuilding Europe through the Marshall Plan, the civil war in Greece, and Gandhi's hopes for a reconciliation between India and Pakistan. Reflecting the deepening cold war, Kaltenborn reported on his impressions of a world at war, not peace, with special attention to fears of a Russian invasion of Japan and the vulnerability of Korea. Kaltenborn's rhetoric is strongly anti-communist, which McBride does not challenge, but she does tell him straight out that he ought to include more about women when he writes about his travels in these countries. Then confirming that listeners never knew what serendipity each show would bring, the remainder of the program was devoted to a fourteen-year-old named Don Hutter who had written a book about an itinerant mouse.[33]

By 1951, quite a few radio shows featured the ad-libbed interview format that Mary Margaret McBride had pioneered, and thinking of the competition, she admitted on air that she didn't want to do interviews unless she could get the "juice." Cartoonist Al Capp was her "guinea pig" in a January 12, 1951, interview. The show opened with McBride telling Capp that she had no preconceived ideas about him, that she merely wanted to find out about the real him and give her listeners an interesting program. His response that he was just a simple guy was not the "juice" that she wanted, and she pressed further. Soon he was talking about how he had the same coloring as his mother, whom he recalled as a remarkable woman, and how upset his family had been when he decided to be an artist. He admitted that he got lectured by his wife when his comic strip got too violent or lusty. After he recounted his Horatio Alger success story, Mary Margaret asked him whether losing his leg as a child had something to do with his drive. He admitted that he was very self-conscious about it, a fairly personal and intimate detail. Having pierced his initial cynicism and lack of cooperation, the interview concluded with Capp and McBride talking about the common humanity of all people.[34]

Mary Margaret obviously won Al Capp's trust, but even her skills could not guarantee results all the time. Over the years the radio host came up against her share of guests who had been glib and eloquent in the preparatory interview but then clammed up on the air. Woody Guthrie, for example, was a very hard interview, although he did feel comfortable singing. Luckily McBride always prepared enough to cover what the two of them would have said in a less lopsided conversation.[35] At the other extreme was the guest who would not shut up, despite gentle prods from the host, Vincent's reminders that the products needed to be promoted, and, finally, exasperation. This didn't happen very often either—it was just as hard to shut Mary Margaret up—but when it did, all she could hope was that her listeners would sympathize with her plight (after all, they all probably knew a neighbor who never stopped talking) and still tune in the next day.

Scheduling snafus also called for fast thinking by the radio host. One time Mary Margaret inadvertently invited two feuding authors to appear and then had to negotiate a temporary truce to get them on the air. On another occasion Mary Margaret was expecting Eleanor Roosevelt for a show promoting the Girl Scouts and was greatly perplexed when she didn't show. She started the program anyway and looked out in her audience to see Mrs. Theodore Roosevelt, whose first name also was Eleanor, sitting in the front row. Having prepared to ask the other Eleanor about her recent travels and her column in *McCall's,* Mary Margaret now had to switch gears entirely without any advance preparation. As she recalled, "I am an ad-libber, but I have to know what I'm going to ad-lib about!"[36]

On the rare occasions when Mary Margaret was slighted by a surly guest, her listeners stood up for their idol like "doting aunts."[37] Once a war correspondent just back from the South Pacific appeared on the show and failed to succumb to either her charm or her interviewing skill. "They sat me down opposite her and she began talking this trivia—where she had been the night before, what she had thought, a recipe she'd heard. After the fighting I'd left, I couldn't take it. I was rude to her." The episode did not end there, for when he tried to leave, the guest was surrounded by members of the audience who berated him for being so nasty to the host. "I guess Mary Margaret won our battle of wills," he later admitted ruefully. "Those women made me feel like a heel—and I've felt like a heel about it ever since."[38]

Since this was live radio, there were bound to be things that were said (and aired) that shouldn't have been. Margaret Bourke-White, just back from riding with bomber pilots over Japan, recounted one of the men as saying "Jee-sus!" when her flashbulb exploded unexpectedly, a radio no-no that slipped past Mel Ferrer, later a well-known actor but at that time McBride's director.[39] Loose-lipped Tallulah Bankhead posed a special challenge, especially since her appearance to promote her recently published autobiography in 1952 coincided with a round of memos from network executives that inadvertent swearing had to stop. After commiserating with Mary Margaret about all the trouble she has been having about swearing on the air, Bankhead promptly told a story about a great-aunt who said "damn" on the air in the early days of

radio. Having, of course, to utter the word to tell the story, she
ceeded to tell another story about being at a party when a stuffy dowa-
ger had said to a fellow guest with a harrumph, "*When* is Miss
Bankhead going to do her stuff?" When informed that Tallulah was be-
having normally, the lady said, "'Well, if that's the case—'I can't say *hell*
on the air, can I, Mary Margaret?'" "No, you can't," she answered for-
lornly. "'Well,' the old lady said, 'if that's the case then the so-and-so
with it. If she's going to behave like everybody else, I'm going home!'"[40]

A far more serious breach involved the actress Laurette Taylor, who
while talking about the southern accent she affected for her role in *The
Glass Menagerie* in 1945, referred to it as "a nigger accent." McBride was
mortified but did not challenge her guest, who finished the program
oblivious to the offense she had caused. So upset that she could barely
sleep that night, Mary Margaret knew that she had to do something to
make it up to her listeners. So on short notice she got NAACP head Walter White to appear on the next show, which she opened by referring to
what had happened the day before. "I'd do anything to keep such a
thing from happening on my program," she told her listeners. "When it
does, it breaks my heart. It was not said deliberately nor with malice,
but thoughtlessly; yet I can't help believing that if people understood—
well, they wouldn't allow themselves ever to be so careless." Then she
invited Walter White to talk about the struggles of minorities to be
treated with dignity around the world and the hurdles they still had to
confront, even as late as 1945. The point was made eloquently, although
McBride remained saddened that the incident had happened in the first
place.[41]

The Laurette Taylor incident was unusual, although Mary Margaret
McBride's support of human and civil rights was not. While not totally
devoid of political or social content, most shows steered clear of large
controversies or raging debates. Most of the guests, as well as the listeners, thoroughly enjoyed themselves, wearing, in the words of one
profile, "the bewildered expressions of persons who have fallen under
her spell." "I would rather be with you on the radio than with Cleopa-
tra on the Nile," said one guest with only a little hyperbole. According
to the *Woman's Home Companion*, it was not unusual for a guest to exclaim in the middle of an interview, "Isn't this a nice lady!"[42] Earl Car-
roll once kissed her on mike, and Robert Sherwood gushed, "I absolutely love her. She makes [the broadcast] a lot of fun. It's almost pain-
less; you forget the microphone and really enjoy yourself."[43] Helen

Hokinson, who reassured Mary Margaret's audience that she really did admire the ladies she drew in her cartoons, had such a good time that she asked whether it would be all right to come back from time to time to sit in the audience.[44]

Part of the experience of being on Mary Margaret's show in its final years was being asked to sign a large screen in her Central Park South apartment that ran almost from the floor to the ceiling, filled with the autographs and best wishes of her favorite guests on the show. (Fred Waring had suggested a screen rather than just having them sign the wall, so she could take it with her later.)[45] Comments ran the gamut from "To Mary Margaret—God Bless Her—Norman Vincent Peale" to "It has been a pleasure to be laid bare by you! William Carlos Williams" to "Richard Rodgers loves Mary Margaret." Gary Cooper doodled a sketch, and James Montgomery Flagg drew a charcoal portrait of fellow Missourian O. O. McIntyre, who then added this inscription: "To Mary Margaret McBride with a low bow from her admiring friend." By the time Eleanor Roosevelt got around to signing the screen, it was so full that she had to lie on her stomach to scribble something near the bottom. Whenever Mary Margaret felt nostalgic about her national radio career after her retirement, all she had to do was look at the screen to be reminded of the array of people that she had been lucky enough to interview at the height of the program.[46]

Actually, Mary Margaret's always needy ego had another way of stacking the deck to ensure that she would get compliments from her guests. Immediately after each show she sent a postcard to her guests with a red-penciled note thanking them for appearing, which, given the efficient postal system of the day, would be waiting for them in their mailbox the next morning. Because she usually was faster than they were, many guests then felt the need to write back to her. "It was I who should have written you," wrote Johnson O'Connor of the Human Engineering Laboratory, "but nevertheless I was delighted to receive your card this morning. What I call 'technique' has always thrilled me and I cannot tell you how much I enjoyed the way you handled the broadcast."[47] "Thank you so much for your card," wrote Buel W. Patch of the Office of Defense Transportation. "I was very glad to have it, but I think the thanking should be the other way around, and I regret that you beat me to it."[48] Or here is a young Harris Wofford, then with a group called the Student Federalists:

It was grand of you to write me the note, but I am the one who should have written to thank you for the honor and opportunity of participating in your broadcast. It was a lot of fun and a fine experience. . . . You are now counted as one of our good friends.[49]

She bonded with her guests just the way she bonded with her listeners. Mary Margaret's ploy of soliciting compliments for her program may not have been completely conscious, but it does speak to the underlying insecurity and shyness that in many ways made her an unlikely success on the air. Probably because she had been riding on top of the world in the 1920s until the stock market crash destroyed her financially and the bottom dropped out of her journalism career, McBride never took her success for granted. She often asked celebrities whether they actually felt famous, something with which she herself grappled. The reply from actress Beatrice Lillie could have been spoken by the radio host herself: "Not at all. I'm always surprised when I pull it off again. I always think they'll rumble me, find me out, you know."[50]

Mary Margaret McBride was not a particularly reflective person, but she did have a basic understanding of some of her own psychological foibles and a desire to understand more about herself and her moods. When her friend Cynthia Lowry interviewed her for a piece in the *Woman's Home Companion* in 1954, she was frank about her needs:

Through my program I feel that I talk to all sorts of people. They're all different ages and different temperaments, with different kinds of humor and different understanding. I try to help them. But the real truth, Cynthia, is that some of the time I'm reaching out for something myself. Something like the way I pick up the telephone when I'm in deep trouble.[51]

Or as she once admitted, "Often on the air I try to find out what makes people tick, hoping, I imagine, to discover things about myself."[52] McBride was not afraid to share her problems with her listeners. Once in the midst of an interview, she asked a guest if she ever got depressed, and the woman replied that she did. Then Mary Margaret admitted, "I do get depressed, often. Over and over I say to myself, 'Well, this is the end,' but I hang on and it passes."[53] In another interview with an expert on sleep, she admitted that she hadn't slept the night before because she was sick with worry over a quarrel she had had with Stella Karn.[54] Such candor was quite unusual over the air, and no doubt it was reassuring to members of her audience who also struggled with their own demons or tempers. Whenever her listeners wrote to her asking for advice, her response was straightforward: "You can never be down unless you let yourself be. No matter how many times you're disappointed, if you can get up that last bit of strength and make the effort, things will work out. They always have for me."[55]

On several occasions, however, Mary Margaret felt the need to seek professional help, although it is unlikely that she shared this fact with her listeners. From the surviving evidence of one such encounter in early 1949, little came of the consultation except a dispute about the bill for the psychiatrist's services. "I visited you twice and got the impression both times that you didn't regard the sessions as regular because you were so tired," she wrote to Dr. Flanders Dunbar, who practiced on New York City's tony Upper East Side. When he confirmed that the charges were indeed correct, she sent off a check for $125 and this retort: "My opinion of your methods would cause this paper to sizzle. As I remember, most of the time we talked about your daughter and if that is psychiatry I suppose I must make the most of it."[56] That probably was the end of Mary Margaret's career in therapy.

Mary Margaret was not one to psychoanalyze herself, and it would be unwise to try to do so from a distance of many decades, but there do seem to be patterns that shaped McBride's daily life and career. She never felt secure in her celebrity. She was a workaholic who let her job take over her entire day and night. She was incredibly thin-skinned about criticism and could not abide negative comments. She could be cruel when angered and was a bad sport about losing. (As she once put it, "Even if I could leap, I'd never be one of those who would bound over a net to cry, 'Good show!'")[57] She lavished gifts on friends and acquaintances, in part so that they would have to write back to tell her what a wonderful and generous person she was. She had a temper and liked to sulk. Often a trip to the refrigerator would be the only thing to snap her out of one of these moods.[58]

Happiness, it seems, often eluded her. Mary Margaret knew what made her unhappy—"my compulsion to expect the worst in any crisis"[59]—and, by extension, what would make her happy: "If I could just learn to take life as it comes, the good and the bad together, I believe I'd be a contented person."[60] But even at the height of her career, such peace of mind and confidence often were lacking. Moreover, she was setting herself up for a crisis once she stepped out of the limelight into retirement.

From the perspective of today's ego-driven, host-centered talk shows, a shy, self-effacing host who really enjoyed doing her show day in and day out does not seem so bad. The reason she had such a fine time on the radio, Mary Margaret admitted, was that "I still was queen of the world—my world, anyway—when I sat before my own microphone."[61] But instead of trying to grab all the mike time and focus attention on herself, Mary Margaret was completely comfortable with letting her guests have center stage. She really did make each guest sparkle. No wonder they lined up to go on her show.

It's wartime, and Mary Margaret and her audience hope that this dove will bring peace to America and the world. *Reprinted by permission of Library of Congress, Prints and Photographs Division.*

3

"Under Cover of Daytime"

ONE DAY early in Mary Margaret's radio career, Stella asked her if she wanted to hear a recording of her voice as it sounded on the air. The prospect filled the recent radio convert with glee, although that did not last long. As they walked into the recording studio, Mary Margaret heard a woman's voice in the background and thought, "Another of those women—*I'm* not like *her*!" When she asked who it was, everyone tittered because of course it was her. For the rest of her life she found listening to her voice a torture.[1]

Mary Margaret's voice definitely takes some getting used to. It is not the kind of well-modulated, accentless, and mellifluous voice that one associates today with radio personalities. First and foremost, it is a southern voice, but it isn't especially slow, and when excited and animated (which is often), it becomes very high-pitched and fast. Her voice's singsong quality definitely sounds girlish, rather than mature, and more than a bit gushy, which is probably why many reviewers dismissed her as an unsophisticated hick. With a voice like that, Mary Margaret McBride probably wouldn't have much of a chance breaking into radio today, but luckily it didn't deter her back then.

Before being hired as Martha Deane, Mary Margaret had had scant contact with radio. In fact, she and Stella probably didn't even own one in the 1920s. For someone who had missed out on the experience of sitting down in front of a box and magically hearing voices, music, and talk come over the airwaves, McBride proved remarkably creative at adapting former journalism skills that had depended on the written word into a radio technique that depended on listening, talking, and hearing. From the very start she managed to intuit what and how listeners wanted to hear and learned to present material and conversation in ways in which they were pleasant and stimulating to listen to.

"Radio is not a single, isolated experience such as seeing a Broadway show, or taking a vacation. It is woven into the daily pattern of our lives year in and year out," noted an influential study in 1946 by Paul Lazarsfeld and Harry Field.[2] In that year, American men listened to the radio for an average of three hours a day and women, an hour longer.[3] After sweeping the nation in the 1920s, radio had become one of the most influential forms of media in the twentieth century, challenged only by films and, later, television. Unlike movies, which encouraged moviegoers to escape into dark public spaces, and before the widespread use of car radios or portable transistors, radio was listened to at home, often in the company of other family members or friends. And unlike movies, where actors appeared irregularly and never as themselves, radio featured (in the words of one radio historian) "charming new friends [who] performed only for *you*. They addressed you, hoped you liked their show, told you what had happened in the week intervening, and begged for some kind of return indication of friendship." No wonder letters poured in to radio stations from listeners who personally heeded that call.[4]

There is something quite remarkable (and hard to recreate) about the process of listening to the radio. Lacking pictures and having only sound to rely on, listeners are forced to use their imaginations, which makes the experience richer and deeper than the later act of simply sitting in front of a television. Fred Allen, one of radio's finest comedians, summed it up well: "In radio even a moron could visualize things his way; an intelligent man his way. It was a custom-made suit. Television is a ready-made suit. Everyone has to wear the same one."[5] Making these imaginative leaps could make radio listening incredibly intimate, almost like a secret or a shared passion. Gerald Nachman, who noted that "radio was interactive half a century before it became a cliché,"[6] joins scholars like Susan Douglas who maintain that you cannot appreciate the importance of radio until you understand the importance of listening: "We can passively hear, but we must actively listen." Through favorite shows and ritualized listening, the audience participates in the creation of its own imagined communities.[7]

As a medium of communication, radio has several other distinctive characteristics. As Hadley Cantril and Gordon Allport pointed out, the popularity of radio "is due above all else to its capacity for providing the listener an opportunity to extend his environment easily and inexpensively, and to participate with a feeling of personal involvement in the events of the outside world from which he would otherwise be excluded."[8] Woven into everyday life, radio allows access to a wider world without interfering with daily routines. Radio also functions as a nationalizing force, spreading music, news, and ideas throughout the country over the airwaves. At the same time, as historian Lizabeth Cohen demonstrated in her study of Chicago in the 1920s and 1930s, radio could also reinforce ethnic identities through special language and cultural programming.[9]

One of radio's most important contributions was breaking down the isolation of rural life.[10] In the 1920s, many state universities began airing extension programs targeted at farmers, providing helpful, practical information on agricultural methods and market trends, in addition to the all-important weather reports. They also sponsored programs offering tips to rural homemakers from home economists at the local university or college. Often these programs were broadcast at midday, when farm families would be at home eating dinner together; additional programs would be aired in the evening hours after chores were done. The evening programs often were more broadly educational and cultural than the daytime programs, and farm women responded especially positively to this kind of programming. Just as Mary Margaret's listeners did in the next several decades, farm women welcomed such cultural uplift to help counter the burdens of geographical isolation and heavy household responsibilities.[11]

Sociologists Robert and Helen Merrell Lynd were among the first to grasp radio's importance as a signifier of modern life. When they did their fieldwork in Muncie, Indiana, for their enormously influential study *Middletown: A Study in Contemporary American Culture* (1929), radio was already well on the way to becoming a necessity for many families' standard of living.[12] When the Lynds returned a decade later to study the impact of the Depression, one of the greatest changes they noticed was the increased popularity of radio listening, an inexpensive form of leisure within the grasp of most families, despite economic reverses. Not only did radio take people's minds off hard times, but it also carried them "away from localism," exposing them to new ideas and a developing national mass culture.[13] In fact, radio was one of the few industries that escaped unscathed the devastation of the Depression, and it even prospered. Similarly, the war years, though tough for many Americans, were good ones for broadcasting.[14]

As a medium, radio had certain characteristics linked to its aurality and its impermanence. If you missed a show, there was no way to listen again, unless it happened to be scheduled for rebroadcast. Because of the rigid schedule ("Radio waits for no one"),[15] you had to listen when the show was on, rather than picking up and putting down a book or choosing whether to go to an evening performance or a matinee. You also had to listen in "real" time—there was no fast forwarding, no skimming. In an increasingly regimented world, one of the most predictable characteristics of radio was its punctuality: "Like train dispatching, it is on time."[16] (Think of the trademark opening, "It's One O'Clock and Here Is Mary Margaret McBride.") Once the show was over and the immediacy of the experience had ended, it was hard to recapture or recreate its spell or aura. Radio was ephemeral, almost effervescent, lacking the permanence of the printed word. But it also was magical, powerful, and life enhancing.

While radio (and later television) history is often presented as the inevitable outcome of a series of technological advances, the fact that the medium's development unfolded quite differently in different national contexts suggests that cultural and commercial forces also were at work. For example, in the British Broadcasting Company model, radio operates as a public service funded by license fees and state support. In most other European countries, indeed throughout most of the world, radio is subsidized or controlled by the government. In the United States, however, radio is based on a commercial model that licenses public airwaves for private profit, only loosely regulated by the federal government through the Federal Communications Commission (FCC). Despite calls for broader public access to the ether, the American system has favored large corporate entities such as the Radio Corporation of American (RCA), formed in 1919, over educational, nonprofit, and public service institutions vying for space on the radio dial. By the late 1920s the result was, in the words of one radio historian, a "restricted-access, vertically integrated oligopoly, dominated by two large corporations and supported by increasingly blunt and intrusive commercial advertising."[17]

In a period of political and economic debate about the future of radio, which began with Commerce Secretary Herbert Hoover's first radio conferences in 1922 and ended with the Communications Act of 1934, the industry's basic organizing principle for the rest of the twentieth century, the network system took shape. In 1926 RCA announced the formation of the National Broadcasting Company, the first attempt to send common programming to a string of affiliated stations across the country. (Previously each station produced all its own programming.) A year later the Columbia Broadcasting System was established, and NBC split into the Blue and Red networks. Those networks, which dominated radio (and later television), were joined in the 1930s by the smaller Mutual Broadcasting Network. In 1943, as a result of an adverse antitrust decision, NBC was forced to sell its Blue Network, which in 1945 became the American Broadcasting Company (ABC). Over the course of her career, Mary Margaret McBride appeared on all four of these networks.[18]

The emerging system had limited room for educational and non-profit programming, and American broadcasting rested primarily on a commercial basis—that is, selling time on the air, for money, to advertisers. Although at first it had not been clear how anyone could profit from airwaves that came into homes for free, commercial advertising provided the answer. Since stations had been granted licenses from the federal government with a mandate to operate in the public interest, it was up to them to justify why such an increasingly profitable undertaking was qualified as operating "in the public interest." Since that latter term was never adequately defined, by the 1930s a crass definition had emerged: the public interest was what the public wanted. Although networks and independent stations still sponsored certain prestige programming on the air, such as the NBC Symphony or the Metropolitan Opera (such shows were called "sustaining programs"), the vast majority of programming was paid for by commercial advertising. Confirming the role of advertising even more, by the mid-1930s the bulk of the programs appearing on the air were created and produced by the advertising companies themselves. The heated debates about alternative models for American system of broadcasting quickly faded from popular memory.[19]

Radio was far from a totally male preserve when Mary Margaret McBride broke into the field in 1934. Women had been part of the broadcasting phenomenon from the beginning, working in all parts of the industry: as ham radio operators in the 1910s and 1920s, as on-air broadcasters and performers, as network staff and executives, and as writers.[20] Women often followed different career paths than men did, however, and they did so with less publicity or national recognition. A 1938 study of the "distaff" side of radio noted, "In no case have feminine radio executives come into prominence with a spectacular flourish. Women have gradually 'faded-in' to their jobs, just as the positions themselves have gradually 'faded-in' to the radio industry." The study noted that in radio, just as elsewhere in the business world, women usually had to work twice as hard as men to get the same results—and a lot less recognition.[21]

In its early days, radio had no prestige and no established chains of command, a perfect opportunity for women to find opportunities and challenges unfettered by ingrained discrimination or prejudice. Similar patterns had prevailed in the early days of Hollywood, when procedures were not well established and jobs were not well defined: everybody basically pitched in, with a script girl holding up a piece of lighting equipment and a technician serving as an occasional stunt man. Even areas of politics and government, such as the social welfare programs established by Franklin Roosevelt's New Deal, offered unprecedented early opportunities for women. Later, in all these fields, as procedures became more bureaucratized, as budgets grew and expanded, and as increased numbers of personnel demanded more carefully laid out chains of command and responsibility, women often found it harder to advance or faced more active discouragement.[22]

This pattern definitely held true in radio, which then developed selective amnesia about how central women had been to its early history. For example, Bertha Brainard joined Newark, New Jersey's WJZ in 1922, serving as announcer, program director, and then station manager; in the 1930s and 1940s she was in charge of NBC's commercial programming.[23] Chicago-based Judith Waller, a leader in public affairs and educational broadcasting, started at WMAQ as a station manager in 1922 and later served as the educational director of NBC's Central Division; she is best known for originating the popular discussion program *University of Chicago Round Table*, which NBC carried for more than twenty years.[24] Nila Mack, who developed the popular program *Let's Pretend* for CBS in 1930, captivated children on Saturday mornings with her imaginative adaptations of fairy tales presented by child actors.[25] But these and many other women are rarely mentioned in standard histories, their significant contributions overlooked, just as Mary Margaret McBride's was.

The general public may have had a somewhat inflated view of the career opportunities available in radio for either women or men. Just as all aspiring aviation buffs wanted to be pilots, even though the great majority of jobs in the industry never involved leaving the ground, most of those aspiring to a career in radio probably saw themselves behind the mike, even though on-air jobs (and this included the many actors who worked in radio dramas) made up probably only a quarter of the radio workforce. According to a 1947 Women's Bureau study, "For one Mary Margaret McBride there are thousands of women unknown to fame and fortune who nevertheless have a niche in radio."[26] In 1938, NBC had approximately two thousand employees, one-quarter of which were women.[27] Very few women were employed in the technical or engineering fields, but they were well represented in most other aspects of the radio industry.

The most galling exception was women's almost total exclusion from announcing, one of the most public and prestigious on-air roles. The issue first surfaced in 1924, when *Radio Broadcast* solicited comments from male station managers about women's voices on the air. "Few women have voices with distinct personality," wrote one, while another concluded that they were either affected or stiff.[28] Two years later a poll of five thousand listeners concluded, by a margin of one hundred to one, that the public would not accept women announcers because of their voices. Station manager Charles Popenoe believed that men were "naturally" better fitted for most assignments, because they didn't have the disadvantage of having "too much personality," as presumably women did:

> A voice that is highly individual and full of character is aggravating to the audience that cannot see the face and expression which go with the voice. We resent a voice that is too intimate on short acquaintance, and the woman announcer has difficulty in repressing her enthusiasm and in maintaining the necessary reserve and objectivity.[29]

In their 1935 study on the psychology of radio, Hadley Cantril and Gordon Allport reported the results of a more recent survey showing that 95 percent of a sample of eighty listeners preferred male announcers. Men and women were equally unreceptive to women announcers. Listeners preferred male voices for political reporting, news, and sports; only when "subtle or reflective" material was presented did women seem unobjectionable. Cantril and Allport concluded: "The listeners' chief reason for preferring male announcers is that women seem to them affected and unnatural when they broadcast." How could this be, when listeners were more than willing to accept women as singers and actresses? The only answer seemed to be prejudice. From the late 1920s on, radio managers helped turn the unscientific bias against women announcers into a self-fulfilling prophecy, soon brushing aside women's exclusion by saying there was simply no demand for their services.[30]

Once women were deemed unsuited for announcing, it was very difficult to break into the field. Even though women announcers were as popular as men in Europe, the aversion continued in the United States, although certain areas of the South had "announcerettes."[31] One of the few exceptions to the public's unwillingness to accept women broadcasting hard news was Dorothy Thompson, who crafted a successful radio career in the late 1930s and 1940s built on her popular "On the Record" syndicated newspaper column.[32] Another was Kathryn Cravens, whose News through a Woman's Eyes debuted on the CBS network in 1936. Cravens focused on the human interest aspects of the news: "How does it feel . . . to be mayor of a great city, a congressional lobbyist, a war-torn cripple, a flophouse bum?" Both Thompson and Cravens were among the few women credentialed as radio correspondents during World War II.[33]

By the early 1930s, an informal and formal division had emerged: women's voices almost totally disappeared from nighttime programming but were acceptable during the daytime when "women's" concerns predominated. Historian Michele Hilmes correctly pointed to what was at stake here:

> If the proper business of radio is to broadcast "men's" concerns—such as news, sports, and politics—to a male audience, then the exclusion of women is only "natural." If, however, the main business of radio is to cater to the predominantly female audience—as, indeed, the daytime hours did quite effectively by the late 1920s, populated predominantly by female announcers and talents—then a different order of priorities might prevail.[34]

This nighttime/masculine, daytime/feminine dichotomy is crucial to understanding the history of radio in general and Mary Margaret McBride's place in it.

When people think about the golden age of radio in the 1930s, their memories usually center on prime-time shows. Amos 'n' Andy, the program that first demonstrated the mass appeal of radio, first appeared on network radio in 1929. So popular was the show that restaurants and movie houses were deserted when it aired at 7 P.M. Another popular show that began that year was *The Goldbergs*, featuring a Jewi in New York City whose lives revolved around the wit and wiɔuᴄ its matriarch, Molly Goldberg, played by Gertrude Berg who was also the show's creator.[35] The next new thing to sweep the networks was the rise of comedy and variety shows. In the year 1932 alone, Jack Benny, Fred Allen, Ed Wynn, and George Burns and Gracie Allen all started prime-time programs, soon to be joined by Edgar Bergen and his dummy Charlie McCarthy, Eddie Cantor, and Bob Hope. Comedy shows competed after 1936 with prestige drama productions like the *Lux Radio Theatre* and the *Mercury Theater of the Air*, best known for Orson Welles's 1938 "War of the Worlds" broadcast which was so realistic that panicked listeners were convinced that Martians had landed in New Jersey.[36]

Reinforcing the commercial aspects of radio by the 1930s, all these programs, whether serious drama or light comedy, were sponsored and produced by advertising companies like J. Walter Thompson, which were responsible for hiring the talent, writing the scripts, and overseeing production. The link between products and programs was never very far removed in radio's heyday, as evidenced by these names: the *Chase and Sanborn Hour* featuring Charlie Bergen and Charlie McCarthy; the *Kraft Music Hall* with Al Jolson and, later, Bing Crosby; and the *Jack Benny Program* sponsored by Jell-O ("Jell-O everybody" was Benny's trademark opening). These shows were the top of the line—respectable, sophisticated, serious, and capable of drawing national audiences composed of men and women, young and old, from all sections of the country in the desirable evening hours.[37]

What went on in the daytime hours was less prestigious, in large part because of the assumption that the audience was almost entirely composed of women. Women also made up the majority of the evening audience, but that "fact" was conveniently overlooked in the gendered world of radio broadcasting, as was the "fact" that almost 30 percent of the daytime audience was made up of men. Pioneering soap opera writer Irna Phillips pointed out this disconnect when she asked why advertisers pitched their ads one way during the day and another at night, even though they were reaching the same audience: "Does the I.Q. of a housewife change after six o'clock, or doesn't she listen? Or does the advertiser, who knows that approximately 98% of all products used in the home is purchased by the homemaker, ignore the daytime serial listener after six o'clock?"[38] By stigmatizing the daytime audience as less desirable than the nighttime audience, the implication was that women lived in their own ghettoized existence, barely considered part of the general public who ruled at night.[39]

At first, sponsors were not even so sure that there were enough listeners tuned in during the daytime hours to warrant sponsoring programs, but they quickly figured out that they did not necessarily need huge ratings because the production costs were lower, thereby making the return on the advertising dollar much higher. Since women were presumed to make most of a family's decisions about which products to buy—with the exception of expensive items like automobiles or refrigerators—it did not take long for sponsors to realize the enormous potential audience of daytime consumers just waiting to be tapped. This discovery partially confirmed a vision articulated by Bertha Brainard back in the 1920s:

> I am looking forward to the day when you and the sponsors realize that the daytime hours are our most important selling times and the rates for the daytime hours will be double those of evening, in view of the fact that all our real selling will be done to the women in the daytime, and the institutional good will programs will be directed to mixed audiences after 6:00 P.M.

Brainard concluded, "I am such a confirmed feminist that I thoroughly believe this is going to take place, and in the not too distant future." She was only partially right. Advertisers did discover the daytime market, but the money to be made there was never enough to support the sustaining programs in the evening hours. These, too, remained beholden to advertising.[40]

Like the prejudice that kept women from being announcers, daytime radio can be seen as a series of self-fulfilling prophecies. Since the audience was presumed to be primarily female, programs had to be geared toward them, with the homemaker or "women's hour" shows being the most popular and easiest to produce at first. The prevailing wisdom was that women were supposed to do women's shows, and only women's shows. This, of course, created opportunities for women on the air at the same time that it restricted them to certain formats and certain time slots. In actuality, as Mary Margaret McBride's Martha Deane program demonstrated, many programs geared toward women quickly moved far beyond just recipes and household chat to include interviews, book reviews, and general public-interest information. By the 1940s these formats often featured male hosts or a husband-and-wife team: the morning variety-talk show typified by Don McNeil's *Breakfast Club*, *Arthur Godfrey Time*, Tex McCrary and Jinx Falkenburg, and Ed and Pegeen Fitzgerald. Rather than make the case that Mary Margaret was unusual, it is better to think of her as part of a wide range of talented talk show hosts (including, by the 1940s, some men) who offered a variety of interesting programming in the daytime hours.[41]

The problem is that when people, then and now, think of daytime radio, they think of soap operas, or "serials," as they were called then. While soap operas were the largest category of daytime radio, they did not own a monopoly of the airtime. In fact, there was quite a diversity of programming available at various times, and listeners had a large selection of options with which to fill their radio hours each day. Some figures from 1948 suggest what the daytime lineup looked like. Serials accounted for 51.6 percent of the shows, followed by audience participation (25.4%), news and commentary (4.9%), popular music (3.7%), and miscellaneous (14.4%). Unfortunately, the creativity and interest of many of these programs, including Mary Margaret McBride's, was lost in the stereotyped and limited view that daytime equaled soaps, and soaps equaled drivel. Since women made up the majority of listeners to the soaps, this made it even easier to dismiss them as inconsequential.[42]

No other form of media has been vilified or subjected to such contempt as the soap opera. Irna Phillips produced the first serial, *Painted Dreams*, in 1930, and between 1933 and 1937, the year in which Phillips's most successful show, *Guiding Light*, premiered, serials became a staple of daytime radio. From 1937 to 1942, an additional seventy-four shows were introduced. Sponsored by companies such as Procter and Gamble, Pillsbury, American Home Products, or General Foods, the shows filled the daytime hours with revenue-producing programming at a comparatively low cost. Those characteristics still apply to television soap operas today.[43]

One of the most interesting things about the serials, and what is lost in the general dismissal of them as "serialized drool,"[44] is how much they were marked by their debut during the Great Depression. Anne Hummert, who along with her husband Frank helped popularize the serial format, explained:

Nobody can understand the phenomenal success of the soaps without knowing when they were born. It was during the Depression. The housewife was at home worrying about everything. Would her husband lose his job? Where was the family's next meal coming from? They found escape in the lives of the people on the soaps.

With their open-ended stories and lack of closure, which had roots in the serialized fiction commonly carried in popular women's magazines like the *Ladies' Home Journal* or *Woman's Home Companion*, the "stories" (as they were often called by listeners) foregrounded women's concerns in a way that was rare on the airwaves, or indeed anywhere else in popular culture. The narratives acknowledged the potential for conflict between the sexes, showed that men could often be ill tempered and even wrong, and provided strategies for women to cope with the uncertainties of everyday life, an especially important skill during the Depression and the war years.[45]

Advertisers and radio executives quickly sensed that the soaps drew an incredibly loyal audience, but they were hampered by the absence of reliable ratings to back up their claims. In the primitive field of audience research and reception, one of the areas that received the most attention was daytime serials. Critics regarded soap operas as formulaic and unworthy of attention or scrutiny, but social scientists found them intriguing: radio serials "are particularly suited to show the mutual dependence of community and individual from the point of view of the home situation," one study found. While investigating who the audience was and why they listened, the surveys also offered a window on the world of the woman at home during the day.[46]

Herta Herzog, who took her Ph.D. at the University of Vienna before emigrating to the United States and becoming the second wife of radio researcher Paul Lazarsfeld, did some of the most interesting studies. She began with a list of probable characteristics of the estimated twenty million daytime serial listeners during the early 1940s: women who followed the serials would be more isolated from their communities; they would be less intellectual than nonlisteners; they would be especially interested in personal problems, perhaps because they themselves were "beset with anxieties and frustrations"; and they might be distinguished simply by how much they enjoyed listening to the radio in general. Of those factors, the only ones that held up were that serial

listeners were somewhat less educated and generally fe
tively about radio than nonlisteners did. In many ways, althoug..
search did not explicitly say this, the study found hardly any psychu
logical differences at all. In other words, the psychological makeup of
women who listened to soap operas every day was remarkably similar
to that of those who did not.[47]

Some of Herzog's most evocative material came from one hundred
personal interviews concerning what the serial programs meant to listeners. She identified three major types of gratification. First, listeners
enjoyed the serials as a

> means of emotional release. They like "the chance to cry" which the se-
> rials provide; they enjoy "the surprises, happy or sad." The opportu-
> nity for expressing aggressiveness is also a source of satisfaction. Bur-
> dened with their own problems, listeners claim that it "made them feel
> better to know that other people have troubles, too."

Second, listening offered opportunities for wishful thinking, "to fill in
gaps of their own life, or to compensate for their own failures through
the success pattern of the serials." The third type surprised the researchers: listeners enjoyed the serials because they learned things from
them, using them for advice and guidance for their own lives. "If you
listen to these programs and something turns up in your own life, you
would know what to do about it" was a typical comment.[48] Note that
every one of those characteristics would apply to Mary Margaret
McBride's listeners as well, perhaps even more so than to listeners of
the soap operas.

Another study, by Rudolph Arnheim, looked at the content of the
serials by surveying forty-three shows for three weeks in the spring of
1941. Most of the shows were set in medium-size or small towns rather
than large cities, and most of the characters were solidly middle class,
with professional men and housewives the most typical and nary a
working-class character in sight. Arnheim compared the plots less "to a
stream hampered by a dam" than "a stagnant lake which is troubled by
a stone thrown into it." Major catastrophes and problems were a con-
tinuous threat to individual and communal well-being, especially problems linked to personal relations. As the characters struggled to deal
with these problems, fictional female radio characters took on major

roles, larger roles probably in fact than they were granted in everyday life, thus offering the women in the audience a chance to identify with them.[49]

Obviously the soap operas must have been reaching out to listeners in important and significant ways if so many women listened to them regularly. The messages and lessons that listeners absorbed from these programs were far more nuanced and multifaceted than the stereotyped view of women's weepies assumed. Radio historian Michele Hilmes used the phrase "under cover of daytime" to convey the ways in which daytime radio could serve as an open-ended challenge to the restricted domestic roles offered to American women through the media, mainly by daytime's willingness to place women's concerns at the very center of the broadcast experience and by its recognition of the tensions inherent in modern women's lives. Instead of dismissing women as passive consumers of the radio experience, this view foregrounds women's agency. Women actively participated in a daytime milieu that took their concerns seriously and allowed them to connect with other women facing similar concerns and challenges. To be sure, this cultural space was circumscribed by such factors as commercial interests and a narrow definition of what constituted the home, but it still offered open-ended possibilities for the creation of new social identities that moved beyond traditional gender roles.[50]

The success of Mary Margaret McBride's show makes more sense when placed against this backdrop. In a way similar to soap operas, the program answered the needs of many women (and more than a few men) who listened to the radio during the day for interesting conversation, useful information, including descriptions of new consumer products, and a small dash of current events. The radio host insinuated herself into their lives, becoming as much a part of their routine as doing the shopping, making the beds, or cleaning the kitchen. But she gave them more than mere household hints—she stretched their minds and offered them a respite from those very domestic chores that filled their days.

Mary Margaret was hardly trying to get the nation's housewives to collectively drop their mops and leave their families for exciting lives of their own. She knew that by choice or necessity (or both) the lives of most women in her audience—indeed, most American women in general in these years—were defined primarily by matters of home and family. But that domestic sphere did not have to be as narrow as it was often portrayed. Listening to radio programs like Mary Margaret McBride's made the home less isolated, and women, more connected. McBride offered access to a vision of lives for women that, housebound or not, was infused with engagement with powerful ideas, charismatic people, and new ways of doing things. In her commitment to interesting and stimulating programming, Mary Margaret McBride demonstrated her belief that the daytime audience was a significant force and should be taken seriously. Her claim to radio history lies less in being the "first" to do ad-libbed interviews or host a talk show than in her unerring ability to speak to the nation's women in a way that reinforced but ultimately challenged traditional gender roles.

Mary Margaret greets a flock of loyal fans, predominantly female (and all with hats), along with at least three brave men. *Reprinted by permission of Library of Congress, Prints and Photographs Division.*

4

Mary Margaret's Bond with Listeners

EACH DAY when she sat down in front of her microphone to broadcast her radio show, Mary Margaret McBride kept a clear picture in her mind of her typical listener: "When I am on the air, I imagine that I am talking to a young married woman with a couple of children. A woman who at one time had a job and is still interested in the jobs of other people, the business world. So I talk about people who do things, the world at large. I try to give her the vicarious thrill of going places and meeting people. When I describe a restaurant where I had dinner . . . I try to look at it as she might . . . and share her enthusiasm."[1] As the host herself put it, "It's our program, you see—not mine."[2]

The medium for this dialogue was, of course, radio, and Mary Margaret knew well "the strange intimacies that can grow up through air contact."[3] Her program lacked the call-in features of modern talk radio and did not depend on audience participation from the small number of people who watched the taping of each show. Yet she managed to establish a deep bond with listeners who made the program part of their daily routine. Once Vincent Connolly opened the show with his familiar refrain, Mary Margaret's listeners would enter into an intimate, one-to-one conversation with her and her guests that took them away from their ordinary lives for the next forty-five minutes. "At the appropriate time, my Mother would curl up in her chaise lounge, turn on the ole portable beside her and all was well!" remembered the daughter of a loyal listener. "A day for my Mom was not complete without listening to Mary Margaret. Nothing but nothing interfered."[4]

Mary Margaret McBride had the ability to reach across a broad demographic range, once even getting a good review in the *Daily Worker*, the Communist Party's newspaper.[5] One perceptive magazine writer described how the radio host seemed to fit the needs of multiple age groups:

The younger woman sees her as the warm mother—confident, tolerant, understanding, and brimming with life; to her contemporaries she is an extension of themselves, the woman who gets around and relates to them the things that chance confines their doing; to the older woman she is the good daughter, the one who has gone far in the world but who has never forgotten her own mother and the training she received at home.[6]

Another magazine article from the 1940s pointed out that the radio host did this all with a "complete lack of snobbishness," that the individual listener felt "that were it not for some trick of fate, she too could be meeting all of these interesting people and having such experiences." The article concluded, "And they respond by believing every word she says. This belief in a single person's integrity is the most astounding phenomenon in radio."[7]

Listeners recognized that Mary Margaret sincerely cared about them, wanted to be part of their lives, and always took them seriously. "You really are different from some of those women on the air who patronize and talk down. You never talk down," wrote one fan. "You bring the whole world into my home," wrote another.[8] Said a third, "I go with you to the White House and Florida and Williamsburg—visit Eleanor Roosevelt and Esquimeaux [Eskimos]."[9] Like the soap opera serials that shared the daytime hours, McBride's program focused primarily on women's lives, foregrounding and validating women's daily concerns and values in a way that was rare in popular culture at the time. Even if society dismissed or rendered invisible women's contributions to their homes and families, Mary Margaret recognized and validated their hard work and commitment. Her basic respect for the complexities of modern women's domestic lives and their simultaneous yearnings for connections with the broader public sphere was the core principle of her radio philosophy.

Mary Margaret's listeners showed their loyalty in many ways. Buying the products advertised on the show was one of the most concrete (to say nothing of delicious) ways of supporting the program, but listeners kept the lines of communication open in other ways as well. If a woman relocated to a new community, one of the first things she might do was seek out other Mary Margaret fans as an introduction to her new neighbors. They named pets and animals after her (she was especially partial to a pair of goldfish named Martha and Vincent) and sent snap-

shots, recipes, and special presents, often her favorite foods. No visi.
left her apartment without a care package of some sort. When she was
sick, they suggested remedies. When she lost her temper, they chided
her, not because she wasn't occasionally allowed to be cross, but because listeners feared that "somebody strange" might be listening in
that day and think she was like that all the time. One devoted fan from
Staten Island sent her yellow roses (her mother's favorite) every year on
her mother's birthday and the anniversary of her death.[10] Just thinking
about these acts of kindness could move Mary Margaret to tears: "I
know it's sentimental and I don't care. They are so unbelievably sweet
and it's such a thrilling feeling to have them worry about me."[11]

Some of the contacts with listeners were more bittersweet. An old
woman came to one of Martha Deane's early studio parties, and after
the show she stood in line to shake hands with the host, who noticed
that she had been crying. It was still the Depression, and times were
hard. Mary Margaret mumbled some endearment or encouraging
words, and the woman thrust a small wrapped package into her hands,
which contained a cut-glass bowl and this note:

> Tomorrow they are coming to take me away to the poorhouse. This is
> the only thing in the world I have left that I value. It's been handed
> down in my family for generations. I won't let the sheriff get it when
> he comes for my bed and chair. You mean more to me now than any-
> body so I'm giving it to you as a keepsake.

There was no name or address on the package, and neither Mary Margaret or Stella were ever able to trace its owner.[12]

Mainly listeners sent letters. "People don't write letters like those
anymore," exclaimed Mary Margaret,[13] who realized that she heard
more regularly and fully from many of her listeners than she did from
her closest friends, from whom she was lucky to get a scribbled card at
Christmas. "I don't believe anybody could stay completely smug, self-
centered and narrow after people have written such letters to her," she
said of herself.[14] As she confessed in 1960 in her autobiography, "I felt I
knew my correspondents better than many members of my own family.
I loved them, too. After all, they were making possible for me a life I
love, and I wanted to embrace them all, I was so grateful."[15]

Many radio shows received large amounts of mail, testimony to
the urge that many listeners felt to continue the conversation with their

favorite radio personalities after the show was over,[16] but the amount of mail that Mary Margaret received was phenomenal. "Write me lots of letters," she repeatedly told listeners, and they did. When she first started on the radio as Martha Deane, "the most thrilling event" of her day was stopping in front of the window marked "artists' mail." She lugged that mail around in grocery sacks waiting to be read until her agent said that that looked undignified and had the mail delivered directly to her apartment. In 1936 she claimed that she still answered almost all the mail herself: "I know if I'd poured out my heart to somebody whom I considered a friend and maybe felt a little foolish afterward, I'd hate to think a secretary was reading and answering the letter."[17] But as McBride's fame spread and the number of letters mounted, they often were turned over to a secretary, despite her good intentions. What a window on the worlds of ordinary women in the 1930s and 1940s those letters would have been if they had not been donated to various paper scrap drives during World War II: 3.5 million pieces of mail![18]

One of the characteristics of McBride's radio career was how she made these letters from her listeners into a regular part of her show. For example, in her early days on the air, she usually devoted the *Martha Deane Show* on Saturday entirely to letters from listeners. Later, as part of promoting the products, she often shared anecdotes from the listeners about the program's sponsors. The advantages of this strategy are clear, starting with its being an easy and fun way to fill the time. More broadly, sharing these letters on the air was yet another way of building connections with the radio audience and reinforcing the perception that the show was just a chat between friends. Imagine the pride and delight when a listener heard her letter mentioned on the air, but also note the performative feedback loop at work, especially in regard to the products: listeners endorsed her endorsements through their letters, and then she in turn reendorsed them by reading the letters on the air.[19]

Obviously Mary Margaret did not share private confidences over the airwaves, but these personal letters were what made broadcasting so meaningful to her. She learned to glance through the piles for her regular correspondents who wrote to her as often as several times a week. "There are thousands of women (and some men) whose handwriting is as familiar to me as that of my oldest friends, and just as dear."[20] So devoted were some of her correspondents that "I honestly believe I'd recognize their houses and their children and their gardens if I saw them.

I know what their husband likes for dinner, how the new d
curtains hang in the breakfast room and just how the garden _
when the poppies are in bloom."[21]

In pondering why her listeners wrote to her so often about their
hobbies, gardens, pets, memories, and dreams for their children, Mary
Margaret thought it had to do with her role as a friendly outsider in
their lives. "Partly because they felt sympathy in me, I suppose, but
mostly because I was not bound up in their families, communities,
friendships, and feuds, so they were unself-conscious about telling me
ideas and emotions they felt they couldn't confide to anybody closer to
them."[22] In this way she functioned as something of a sounding board,
or even a therapist, for women and men who were perhaps lonely or
who had nowhere else to turn. She also was there for those who just felt
the need to reach out to their favorite radio friend as they would to any
other acquaintance. (Evelyn Birkby called this a "neighboring style" in
her memoir about Iowa radio homemakers.)[23] Rather than seeming like
a distant celebrity, listeners believed that Mary Margaret was accessible
and always willing to listen. Furthermore, these connections kept intimacy at a comfortable distance. Listeners rarely turned up on her Manhattan doorstep, so the radio host never had to interact with them in
person about their hopes, fears, and problems.

Since it was not feasible for her to write a personal letter in response
to every piece of correspondence, Mary Margaret early on hit on the
idea of sending to every correspondent an autographed card or a postcard with a brief message in her distinctive red pencil. Those postcards
(she might write four hundred a night) and other communications relating to the radio show were often kept as treasured mementos by fans
long after Mary Margaret went off the air. "I could hardly believe my
eyes when the postman handed me your card. I never dreamed you
could find time to answer letters from your radio listeners," wrote a
grateful recipient. "Yet *you* wonder why some women claim you helped
them rebuild their lives."[24]

The more routine correspondence was handled by sometimes as
many as fifteen secretaries, whose salaries were paid by the radio host
and who worked out of her apartment. One of their tasks was to forward any mention of a product to the appropriate sponsor, which could
be quite a task, since some correspondents might mention ten or twelve
products in a single communication. One recent Vassar graduate who
worked on Mary Margaret's mail right after the war found the work

boring and didn't last long on the job. Noting that Mary Margaret "did not communicate with a lowly worker!" her main memory of the experience was the waft of pine bubble bath that would overwhelm the apartment in the morning while the talk show host got dressed for work. "I became an aficionado of pine bubble bath too, and until now never equated it with Miss McBride."[25]

Mary Margaret McBride's audience was as diverse as the letters sent to by her listeners, but common themes and connections linked her entire listening public. As would be expected with any daytime radio show, some of her most loyal listeners were shut-ins, confined to their homes by temporary or incapacitating illnesses. One of Mary Margaret's favorites was "a blind woman sitting all day in a wheelchair, who writes to cheer *me* up."[26] Another woman, who had initially dismissed her mother's infatuation with the show as "a forgivable, whimsical quality of a gentle old lady who brightened her life by an over indulgence in radio," changed her mind when a chronic illness forced her to return home to live with her mother for a while.[27] In the 1930s a recuperating pneumonia patient bonded with Mary Margaret and her guests, who became "daily visitors" in his reclusive life. He developed this odd sense that he was one of very few listeners, even to the point he felt sorry for Mary Margaret "because I thought she must be as lonely as I was as a bedridden pneumonia victim." It was almost as if she were broadcasting the show only to him.[28]

Not quite in the category of shut-ins but homebound nonetheless were the women with small children who were a large part of her audience. For them, the show was a lifeline to a world beyond their domestic experience. "I was an at-home Mom in the fifties," remembered one listener almost fifty years later, "and all those programs were a Godsend to us."[29] A woman from suburban New Jersey who listened to the show regularly from 1946 to 1952 recalled recently, "I learned much as a young housewife—some of which still is sticking today."[30] Another listener from Saddle Brook, New Jersey, noted that she listened to Mary Margaret McBride every day, used and recommended her products religiously, and bought any publication or book that she wrote, concluding, only half in jest, that she "more or less had you dominating my life where there could be a connection." This listener was sure that she was not alone.[31]

Like many of Mary Margaret's fans, another woman had started listening with her mother and then kept up the habit when she went to college. "I don't believe I have ever been as up on Broadway and the current novels as I was in those years."[32] Another daughter remembered her mother, a loyal listener, as a "typical, intelligent housewife with no opportunity for higher education who faithfully listened to Mary Margaret McBride. The program stimulated her interest in a wide variety of subjects and provided many of the elements of a liberal arts course of study." As a young adult, the daughter became an avid listener, too, and even started using the products sponsoring McBride's show, including Sell's liver paté, which she recalled as "a rather exotic purchase in our family!"[33]

Children often had strong memories of hearing Mary Margaret McBride on the radio when they came home from school for lunch or when they were home sick. "As a grammar school child, I came home for lunch every day," remembered one boy, "arriving, just in time to share my sandwich and my glass of milk with my mother, Miss McBride, and her guests."[34] Sally Sacks's father was a dentist whose office was in their apartment building, so he came home for lunch every day, just as she did from elementary school. Her father adored Mary Margaret's show, which always accompanied the meal, but she "couldn't stand her voice and was utterly bored by the program. . . . It was a relief when I entered high school and no longer came home at midday!" Yet she remembered how avidly her father listened each day, often passing along to her mother recipes and other tips that he learned on the show.[35] Other husbands took the time to thank Mary Margaret for giving their wives something interesting to talk about at dinner.[36]

A young Bert Greene was such an avid listener to Mary Margaret's show that his mother would invariably begin the family dinner table conversation each night with this question: "Well, what did Mary Margaret have to say for herself today?" Greene, who later became a well-known cookbook writer, credited the show with providing him with "a ticket to the future—awakening (across the air waves) my burgeoning senses to a world of books, theatre, and art." His mother, who could not listen regularly because she worked outside the home, had this to say after listening in one weekday holiday: "I don't trust people who won't listen to Mary Margaret. I don't know why, exactly—but if people can't recognize an *honest* human being when they hear one, that's a good reason to be leery of them!" When Greene fulfilled a lifelong ambition to write a book and be a guest on her show thirty years later, he recounted that story to the radio host. She sighed, "Oh me. I'm sorry I never met your mother. True fans are hard to find."[37]

Some of the most compelling memories of listening to Mary Margaret came from recent immigrants who used her radio show to improve their language skills and learn about American culture in general. A sixteen-year-old girl who arrived in New York in 1937 as a German Jewish refugee remembered Mary Margaret as "one of my first and best teachers": "Listening to her helped me to learn English and taught me a great deal about the United States."[38] Another girl, the only daughter of immigrant parents, also learned English by listening to the radio, where she was enchanted by McBride's "mellifluous" voice: "her interesting questions, her worldliness, her sweetness captivated me, and whenever I cut school or spent the sultry summer vacation days alone in a tenement apartment I listened to her." When Mary Margaret held her tenth anniversary celebration at Madison Square Garden, this young girl tried to convince her classmates to skip school to attend, but none of them knew who the radio star was. She didn't go to the celebration and took her schoolmates' ignorance of her idol as a sign that she should pursue her own interests and passions: "Her subjects, guests, reviews of books and events fed my curiosity about the world beyond my door, and I am forever grateful to her."[39]

This adulation and loyalty that listeners showered on McBride was very much a two-way street: she needed to hear from them just as much as they needed to reach out to her. Her dependence on her listeners for validation, which was similar to her feelings of despair when she had a bad program and felt she had let down her listeners, explains why she was often so devastated by the few negative letters she received. A dashed-off note stating, "I can't stand a woman's voice on the air. Why don't you stay at home and take care of your family,"[40] could literally ruin her day. True, Mary Margaret was always incredibly thin-skinned, but it was almost as if she experienced these letters as personal wounds. "I've learned through headaches and silly tears that there will always be a few 'poison pens,' usually unsigned, and that it's no good worrying over them. Then I read one nasty, carping letter and I'm in the dumps again." Luckily the friendly letters were the majority, or "I'd be a case for a psychiatrist, I guess."[41]

There are no accurate statistics on the size or composition of Mary Margaret's listening audience, because the ability to measure audience share on the radio was still in its infancy during the years she was on the air. The A. C. Nielsen Company did take a special survey in 1954 of the age of housewives who listened regularly to the show and reported these findings:

Age	% of audience
18–34	20.0
35–54	57.6
55+	19.4
not a housewife	3.0

This market research suggests that most of McBride's listeners were older women, probably married or widowed, whose children had left home or were already in school.[42] Reflecting this demographic, a promotional flyer from radio station WEAF proclaimed in 1944, "Her fans are probably the grandmothers of Frank Sinatra's fans."[43]

If all the letters consigned to the wartime paper drive miraculously resurfaced, it might be possible to calculate a more precise breakdown of the gender, age, region, and class of McBride's audience. Even without this, though, there are plenty of clues to the show's composition and how fans listened to her show each day. First, they generally listened in their homes. Although by 1945, 40 percent of American cars had radios,[44] that is not where Mary Margaret's listeners heard the show. Many women did not drive or have access to the family car, which would have been seen as part of their husband's domain. Instead, they spent their days at home, doing heavy cleaning, child care, and all the other chores that more than filled their day. While the more affluent members of the audience might have new labor-saving appliances like vacuum cleaners or washing machines, housework was still time-consuming, hard—and dull. Mary Margaret provided a midday break in the monotony.[45]

Because most of McBride's radio career came before the massive suburbanization that reshaped the American economy and countryside after World War II, Mary Margaret's listeners were much more likely to live in Middletown (as described by the Lynds in their classic 1929 sociological study) than in Levittown, the pioneering postwar suburban development. Many listeners probably lived in small towns or urban neighborhoods filled with families with the same racial, ethnic, and class backgrounds who had lived there all their lives. Like most Americans at the time, probably only a minority owned their own homes; they were far more likely to rent or live with relatives. These families were not destitute (after all, they owned radios) but were likely to be a mixture of lower-middle-class families who hoped to better themselves and middle-class families who had recently established themselves. Perhaps the best way to think of Mary Margaret's core listeners (and to distinguish them from their postwar suburban counterparts) is as members of the preaffluent society, battered by depression and war and still struggling to get by, with little margin for error or misfortune.[46]

These listeners also would have been in the large majority of American women, especially married women, who did not work outside the home. In the 1930s and 1940s, the lady of the house was almost always in. Even though between one-quarter and one-third of women were gainfully employed in these years, with many new workers responding to patriotic appeals to get a war job in the 1940s, between two-thirds and three-quarters of women still were not working. Even though women's roles were certainly changing, especially during the war, gender definitions had a solidity and permanence that ruled most women's lives. Men's and women's worlds remained quite separate, with women in charge of the domestic sphere and men responsible for dealing with the outside world. Obviously those rigid gender distinctions were more fluid in practice, but nonetheless women were still defined primarily in terms of home and family. Not until 1963, almost a decade after McBride had gone off the air, did Betty Friedan publish *The Feminine Mystique*, her best-selling critique of postwar domesticity and gender roles.[47]

Most likely the great majority of Mary Margaret's listeners would have been white, although precise figures on racial listening patterns are nearly impossible to find. It is certainly reasonable that she had a core of dedicated African American listeners, especially in cities like New York, Philadelphia, and Chicago where her program was regularly broadcast. Her support for civil rights in general and for individual black performers, writers, and artists was well established long before the emergence of an organized civil rights movement and no doubt attracted minority listeners.[48] But like almost every segment of American popular culture in the middle years of the twentieth century, the world of radio revolved around white folks, with people of color welcome to participate and partake but without being seen as its central consumers.[49]

The lives of women in her audience would likely also have been limited in their access to education and other opportunities. Many of

McBride's listeners probably had not even finished high school, taking jobs to fill the time before marrying and having children. College would have been a dream for most, as would travel to many of the places described by guests on the show.[50] But just because they had been thwarted by circumstances from taking advantage of opportunities available to later generations of women does not mean that they were not just as eager and hungry for news and connections to the world beyond their homes. "They may do their work at home," the radio host observed, "but they listen to me—their letters prove it—not so much for household advice as for stories about the world." Mary Margaret recognized that hunger and fed it for forty-five minutes every day.[51]

Edward R. Murrow once said of radio, "You are supposed to describe things in terms that make sense to the truck driver without insulting the intelligence of the professor."[52] Mary Margaret was more likely to be talking to the wives of truck drivers and the wives of professors, but she did have Murrow's knack of reaching an audience that stretched from the working poor to college-educated listeners and sophisticated New York urbanites. She also managed to attract a sizable minority of men.[53] The challenge was the same: to stimulate interest and expose an audience to new and exciting material. One of Eleanor Roosevelt's favorite sayings was that if you have to compromise, you should always compromise up. When choosing her material and setting the tone of her program, Mary Margaret always talked up, not down, to her audience.[54]

Perhaps every radio talk show host forms a symbiotic relationship with his or her listeners, but there does seem to be something especially tight about the bond that developed between Mary Margaret McBride and her millions of devoted fans. She gave her listeners a daily link to a world of books, Broadway shows, broader social issues, celebrities and ordinary folks, and, yes, the products, all done with gusto and sincerity. She was there for them during the hard times of the Depression, the patriotic sacrifices of wartime, and the uncertainties of the cold war that followed. Even though she was herself a celebrity, listeners felt that she was a dear personal friend to whom they could turn in good times and bad. She was someone they could see dropping by their home and sharing a cup of tea and a piece (or two) of cake. Her radio popularity demonstrated the level of intimacy and personal connection possible between listeners and a radio personality and fundamentally challenged any notion that radio listening was a passive activity. Her loyal and engaged audience was just as much a factor in the show's success as were Mary Margaret's guests or radio technique.

Mary Margaret McBride was well aware of the "terrific responsibility" that she had taken on for the well-being of her listening audience (until the late 1940s, her phone number was listed in the Manhattan directory in case fans wanted to contact her directly), but she wanted to remind them that they had an important responsibility, too:

> They have to substitute for a family, for that rambling farmhouse with its white garden and for the host of old friends I haven't even time to telephone. They take up all my days; I eat queer foreign food so that I can tell them about it. I don't go to a play or drive off for the week-end unless it'll make a story. They practically run my life.

Just in case there was even the slightest doubt about how she felt about this turn of events, she added, "and I *love* it!!"[55]

5

"The Appetite as Voice"

If I were doomed to eat the same meal every day for the rest of my life and could have my pick of all the food the world offers, this is what I'd choose and be tickled to death at the chance, *only*, of course, it would every bit have to be fixed the way my mother did it: delicate butter-milk biscuits so hot you can't pick them up and have to slather butter on their delicate insides by the catch-as-catch-can method, mashed po-tatoes that have been hand-beaten with cream and butter until they are fluffy as a cloud, baby chicken fried to crisp brownness, and cream gravy made in the skillet with all the little brown crumbs to give color and flavor, tender young mustard greens boiled with side meat and, to finish off, hot apple dumplings rich with cinnamon, butter and brown sugar and thick yellow country cream to pour over!

MARY MARGARET and food—the bond between them was as strong as the one she shared with her listeners.[1] Food also was a critical com-ponent of her radio success. On the face of it, radio would not seem like a good place to cultivate a love affair with listeners over food, but food was so central to Mary Margaret's life, and Mary Margaret was so im-portant to her listeners, that it is impossible to disconnect the two. On almost every radio show, food was practically a guest itself, providing a common language, a voyage of discovery, a way of making connec-tions. Food truly was, as she titled a chapter in one of her books, "my favorite subject."[2]

"Mary Margaret's preoccupation with her stomach is celebrated in radio," *Collier's* noted in 1948. "It takes only the slightest jab to turn Mary Margaret's thoughts toward food."[3] When she remembered major world events like the outbreak of World War II, the memories were often linked to the food she was eating when she heard the news. In fact, almost every significant stage or moment in her life was associated

So many choices, so little room on her plate . . . *Reprinted by permission of Library of Congress, Prints and Photographs Division.*

with food: her childhood, her early days in Greenwich Village Stella taught her "to eat in twenty-eight languages"),[4] her travels abroad (Paris was her first onion soup, Rome was ham cooked with fresh figs), her culinary adventures throughout the United States, and even her recurring periods of depression, when Stella learned that the best way to snap her friend out of the blues was to arrive with a quart of ice cream or a box of chocolates.[5] Food was an integral part of her workday, too: after each radio broadcast Stella and Mary Margaret would rehash the day's program and plan the next by adjourning to a nearby Schrafft's for a meal that nearly always ended with a dessert topped with two scoops of ice cream.[6]

In her radio work, unlike journalism, Mary Margaret gave herself her own assignments, and many of them, not surprisingly, were related to food. She interviewed chefs at work at their restaurants, sharing her descriptions of her culinary adventures (including multiple tastings, of course) with her audience. Showing how far she had strayed from the journalistic ethics of the 1920s, she was quite happy to accept complimentary meals in return for her plugs. She also shared details with her hungry fans of her encounters with a variety of American and ethnic cuisines (including, but not limited to, Hungarian, Scottish, Italian, Swedish, Austrian, French, Japanese, and Chinese, as well as southern-style barbecue and New Orleans Creole), which invariably produced "an avalanche of requests and demands that I eat more good dinners and report back."[7] In turn, listeners sent in favorite recipes for her to try, and packages of delicacies arrived regularly at her apartment or the studio, as did freebies from her multiple sponsors. Even if this woman had wanted to go on a diet, she would have been unable to, because she would have lost her favorite topic and, by extension, her voice.[8]

Mary Margaret's love affair with food dated from childhood. "Boys never did interest me *nearly* as much as food," she often said, without the least bit of exaggeration or embarrassment.[9] There was always plenty of good, hearty food on the Missouri farm where she grew up. Even when the family was struggling to make ends meet, friends who dropped by or out-of-town relatives who came for an extended visit were welcomed and well fed. Such generosity was simply part of rural life, leading McBride to conclude, "Sometimes I think that cooking is what counts most in making people feel friendly."[10] For the rest of her life, her mother's cooking set the standard: "Nothing in cookery is ever done right for me unless it's done as Mama did it. Her boiled dressing, her chicken fried with flour only, her redham gravy—these are for me patterns of perfection."[11] A sentimental convention to prize your mother's cooking, to be sure, but one that many of her listeners probably shared.

Raised on farm-style cooking that featured plenty of eggs, butter, and cream, all her life Mary Margaret gravitated toward high-calorie, high-cholesterol foods. As a result she struggled with her weight at least from the time she came to New York in the 1920s, and perhaps earlier. When she ate out, which she did almost every night, either in restaurants or at dinner parties at the homes of friends, she often would indulge in multiple tastings, "all in the interest of science."[12] Once when speaking to a local women's club, she was confronted with six different kinds of cake, all delicious. Retelling the story on the air, she looked at her skeptical announcer and said, "Why, Vincent, how you do look at me! You know it wouldn't have been polite to have refused any." This entirely unself-conscious admission of her voracious appetite contrasted with her lifelong abstinence from alcohol, a legacy of her Baptist upbringing. To certain things, it seems, she could say no.[13]

No one would ever call Mary Margaret a sophisticate ("She's the kind of woman who would look out of place with a cigarette because she wouldn't know just how to hold it," noted one magazine review),[14] but she did show increasing concern about her appearance once her radio career began to prosper. When she first came to New York, her hair had been hacked off in a mannish cut, and it often was quite untidy in her early radio days. Gradually she began styling her wavy hair in a soft pompadour, which flattered her face and set off her expressive eyes and smooth skin. Her style of dress improved, too. Gone were the "shapeless sacks with the limp white ruches [pleats] which used to give her the air of an old-fashioned farm wife decked out for a tour of the big city,"[15] replaced by nicely tailored outfits, usually in dark, slenderizing colors, topped off by an amazing array of hats made by her French friend Madame Nicole.

Publicists loved to ask well-known personalities for their favorite recipes, and as a supposed homemaking expert (despite her demurrals), the radio host was an easy target. As an example of her tastes, in the 1950s Mary Margaret shared her all-time favorite recipe with the readers of her Associated Press column. The recipe, which was for the charlotte russe her mother used to make for her birthday, was simple and easy to follow, ending in this way: "Line a brown crock—my mother's crock was always brown—with slices of sponge cake and pour the custard in the center. Put in the refrigerator for an hour or longer—and then eat with zest."[16]

Perhaps it was this recipe for charlotte russe that inspired the comedy routine by Bob Elliott and Ray Goulding (better known as Bob and Ray) featuring Mary McGoon, a regular character clearly modeled on Mary Margaret McBride, rhapsodizing about a concoction of frozen ginger ale salad. First, Mary McGoon takes a huge crock and fills it with the contents of a quart bottle of ginger ale, lettuce, marshmallows, and chocolate with almonds.

> Then I swish it together. When it's completely swished and settles down a little in the crock, I pour it off into a mold made in the likeness of a dear friend of mine. Then I take it up and put it into the freezing compartment of my refrigerator. After it's hard, and you can tell when it's hard because it will be hard when you touch it, you take it out and chip into individual servings. Serve it with Argyle sox sauce and garnish with pimento.[17]

Touché!

Another famous takeoff involving Mary Margaret McBride and food appeared in "Job Switching," an episode of the *I Love Lucy* show that aired on September 15, 1952. This is the classic show in which Ethel and Lucy, tired of doing unappreciated housework and convinced that it would be simpler to work outside the home, convince their husbands to trade places for a week. The women take on a variety of jobs, culminating in the hilarious scene in which they desperately try to keep up with a fast-moving assembly line by stuffing chocolates into the pockets and folds of their uniforms and eventually into their mouths. Meanwhile, their husbands take responsibility for the housework and cooking, with predictably disastrous results. In a reference that audiences in the 1950s certainly would have caught but that slips past most viewers today, Fred smugly says to an aproned Ricky, "You're a regular Ricky Margaret McBride."[18]

Ironically, Mary Margaret (like Ricky and Fred) was not terribly proficient in the kitchen. As more than one of her friends observed, she was not a good cook, just a good eater. Sometimes she fantasized about opening her own restaurant, but the more time she spent interviewing restaurateurs like Gene Leone (son of Mama of the famous

Leone family), the more she realized what hard work running a restaurant was. "I guess I'll just go on dreaming of writing the great American novel," she once said. "It will at least be easier on the feet."[19]

When Mary Margaret first left Missouri to come east to make her name as a writer, she had been in despair over the food in New York City, which she found so unappealing in comparison with her mother's fare that she feared she would just wither away. "New Yorkers appeared to take it for granted that food should be dull, insipid and unflavored when it was not downright bad," she recalled. "And the prices you paid for it! The unappetizing way it was served!"[20] Stella Karn, always able to find cheap and exciting places to eat ethnic and foreign specialties, introduced her to the wonders of New York City restaurant cuisine. Although McBride never lost her taste for the comfort food of her childhood, she proved remarkably broad-minded in her ability to embrace, enthusiastically, new tastes and culinary cultures. She would try anything—from shark fin soup to snails to boiled eels to tamales—at least once and often ask for seconds. As she once said of Paul Whiteman, with whom she coauthored a book on jazz in 1925, "He was a mighty trencherman and I wasn't so bad myself at putting food away."[21]

In today's world of fusion cooking, fresh ingredients, and innovative presentation, it is hard to imagine how bland American culinary tastes were in the mid-twentieth century. One of the reasons that McBride was so grateful for the original chance to appear on the radio as Martha Deane was "the opportunity to campaign for a cause that I believe in from the bottom of my heart—the cause of better food in America." In the 1930s when she went on the air, many Americans outside a major metropolitan area like New York City had probably never sampled such delicacies as Suki Yaki (as she spelled it), Hungarian goulash, crêpes suzettes, Swedish meatballs, or chicken divan, but she enthused about all those dishes on her radio programs. Listeners no doubt felt encouraged, indeed emboldened, to sample new cuisines precisely because of her effusive endorsement. There is little evidence, however, that the radio host approached these meals in any kind of anthropological sense, such as providing a bridge between cultures. She just loved the new tastes.[22]

Mary Margaret became especially fond of Chinese food after having been introduced to it in a lavish Chinese New Year feast. Any banquet that lasted for hours was all right with her, especially when it contained so many different and succulent foods to taste. She became so close to George Lee of Lee's Chinese restaurant in Chinatown that she agreed to serve as the American godmother of his three children, Calvin (who took over the restaurant after his father's premature death), Bo-Lum, and Lily. Her favorite outfits, suitable for lounging around home or even for wearing when being interviewed on national television, were a succession of colorfully embroidered Chinese silk jackets, gifts from the Lees, which became almost a trademark fashion statement for the radio host.[23]

The advantages of those loose-fitting Chinese pajamas should be obvious: all these forays into international cuisines made Mary Margaret McBride a rather stout woman. At the height of her career, she weighed at least 170 pounds, possibly more, on a frame that was less than five and a half feet tall. As a journalist friend remarked, "She's overweight, but she lives with it gracefully."[24] Another friend put it this way: "Her figure isn't perfection—maybe it's the desserts. But she's a meticulous dresser."[25]

Mary Margaret's fondness for food and her full-figured appearance were as much a part of the McBride persona as her Missouri accent and the elaborate hats created for her by the French milliner Madame Nicole. Sitting in front of a microphone day after day, combined with a lifelong abhorrence of physical exercise, proved to be a poor way to burn off all the calories she consumed in the line of work. When she gave one of her frequent lectures or made a public appearance, she often would put audiences at ease by referring explicitly to her weight. "I know you're looking me over," she would say self-deprecatingly. "I know you're saying to yourself, My, she is plump—only maybe plump isn't the word you're using. I don't mind. Take a good look."[26]

At times Mary Margaret must have felt that she was living in the wrong century. Plumpness or a hefty girth in both men and women had once been a sign of material success and personal contentment, but by the 1890s when she was born, that equation was already beginning to change in the United States. The new cultural model for the white middle class was a more slender physique, an ideal that ironically took hold as the American lifestyle became more sedentary in the shift away from agricultural and industrial labor to white-collar occupations. In addition, the inability to control one's weight was increasingly defined as a personal flaw, a sign of laziness or a lack of self-discipline, whereas the ability to maintain one's proper weight was presented as a sign of good character. While these new cultural standards of appearance initially applied to both genders, by the 1920s women bore the brunt of the emphasis on slimness. New fashion modes, such as the rise of ready-to-wear clothing and a shift away from heavy corseting, made imperfections in the female figure more noticeable. If you were fat, it was increasingly hard to hide from what Kim Chernin later tagged the "tyranny of slenderness." Since women were more often defined by their appearances than men were, they had less leeway to deviate from the new norms. Thus, many women found themselves entering a lifelong battle with their weight.[27]

Mary Margaret McBride never embraced the twentieth-century cultural imperative to be thin, although she did make periodic (and unsuccessful) attempts to go on diets, especially in the late 1940s and early 1950s when she frequently was a guest on television. She once called dieting "about the most horrible, depressing thing in the world," adding dejectedly, "and I suppose I'll be dieting to the end of my life."[28] (Her realization that being on a diet made her perpetually short-tempered anticipated Naomi Wolf's insight in *The Beauty Myth* that dieting was "the most potent political sedative in women's history; a quietly mad population is a tractable one.")[29] Even when Mary Margaret once lost ten pounds, the only thing she could think about was how hungry she was: "I'd like to go to sleep, but I keep seeing before my eyes tantalizing chunks of rich dark chocolate cake covered with buttery fudge frosting, three inches high." Or lobster Newburgh, or baked beans cooked with brown sugar and molasses, or strawberry shortcake. Pretty soon it was midnight, and she was on her way to the kitchen to whip herself up a batch of fudge.[30] The radio host frankly admitted that the only time she voluntarily abstained from food was when she had to speak in public: "That's because I'm too scared to swallow."[31]

Mary Margaret made no bones about her size, accepting that she was overweight and that there really wasn't much that she could do about it. When she discussed her weight in public, she did so with a humorous and self-deprecating edge that used comedy to cover up or deflect any private feelings she might have had about her poor body image. (This is still a common strategy for overweight women today.)[32] For example, she blamed her overweight on her ancestry, specifically "some Irish ancestor for whom emotional mountains were high but valleys abysmally low" who passed along his temperament to her. "As a result I'm a sufferer. And when I suffer, I repair to the kitchen where I substitute cooking for wound-licking." While other friends managed their moods through such pastimes as fishing, gardening, or shopping, she would "crack eggs, cream butter and sugar and recklessly fling in cinnamon and nutmeg," with predictable results in the poundage department.[33] She once confessed that if she ever ran a dress shop, she would simply mark all the dresses and shoes two sizes smaller than they really were "and let men, who increase their fish weights and decrease their golf scores at will, make what they like of that."[34]

Mary Margaret's weight was the cause of what is probably the most widely remembered moment in her broadcast history: the zipper incident, which is still recalled fondly by her surviving fans.[35] At showtime one day in March 1948, Vincent Connolly went on the air with an unusual opening: "It's one o'clock and I can't say 'Here is Mary Margaret McBride.'" He told the audience that the host had had a slight accident and would be joining them shortly. The accident turned out to be that she had zipped a chunk of her ample flesh into her corset, and the zipper would not budge. When the janitor's pliers wouldn't do the trick, she had to be cut out of her corset and then bandaged by a doctor whose office was in her Central Park South apartment building.

When she finally got to the studio about ten minutes late, she unself-consciously shared the story with her listeners: "This is probably the most ridiculous thing that ever happened to a woman, and since you'd wonder forever, I can't bear to have you wondering."[36] She knew they would understand; probably some of them had even been in a similar predicament, or close to one. When *Life* magazine and columnists like Walter Winchell picked up the story, McBride was somewhat taken aback. "You know," she told Stella, "I didn't think it would get out." It was almost as though she had forgotten she had told the story on the air to millions of listeners.[37]

In exploring the reasons why listeners bonded so firmly with the radio host and vice versa, it seems likely that Mary Margaret McBride's appearance and body type worked to her advantage just as much as her superb radio technique and stimulating program content did. To put it simply, she looked like the middle-aged housewives in her audience, even if she wasn't middle-aged or a housewife, and her listeners embraced her as one of them. Unlike Hollywood stars whose physiques reflected the slim, streamlined look of athleticism and youth, Mary Margaret's body type was more of a throwback to the older matronly woman, fortified by undergarments like corsets, which encased a woman's body in fabric and whalebone rather than releasing it for easy movement and play. Eleanor Roosevelt and Dorothy Thompson conveyed a similar no-nonsense solidity with their style of dress, as did former suffragists, early women politicians, and women professionals. While one can speculate whether a popular heroine like Amelia Earhart would have been as famous if she had been short and dumpy, it is just as easy to reverse that equation and ask whether Mary Margaret would have been so convincing and beloved to her radio audience if she had been tall, thin, and gorgeous.[38]

The figure from popular culture with whom Mary Margaret is best compared is the popular singer Kate Smith, who was at the height of her popularity in this period and a frequent presence on radio.[39] Like McBride, Kate Smith was full figured and proud of it, unapologetically incorporating public awareness of her large size into her popular persona. During World War II the singer raised more money for war bonds than did any other Hollywood or radio star. A 1946 study of wartime propaganda broadcasts documented Smith's incredible success over the airwaves and offered this tentative reason: women reacted positively to Kate Smith's appeal in part because her large body didn't conform to popular stereotypes of beauty, glamour, and personal worth. Because she looked like them, she must be a good person with values like theirs, the audience reasoned.[40]

Mary Margaret's listeners, many of whom probably also struggled with their weight, might have reacted in the same way to the radio host. To them, Mary Margaret's full figure was a symbol of maturity and tradition and a blunt counter to the svelte, agile body that was the newest symbol of modernity for twentieth-century women. After all, there still were plenty of people around in those years, including many members of her listening audience, who remembered real hunger, from either their childhoods or the hard times of the Great Depression, and who did not admire abstemiousness at the table.

That is one significance of Mary Margaret's lifelong love affair with food. The other is the role of food in assuaging her perennial insecurity. At nearly every low moment in her life, Mary Margaret ate her way out of her depression. Often this was with the help of Stella Karn, who became a master of what she called the "chocolate ice cream" technique of transforming despair into normalcy: "Often, in the middle of the night, Mary Margaret has phoned me to announce, between sobs, that she is a failure and will immediately retire to a small country town." So Stella gets out of bed, grabs a quart of chocolate ice cream, and hurries over to her apartment. "Please," begs Mary Margaret, "take that awful stuff away—how horrible to think of eating in the face of black despair." Meanwhile Stella has opened the ice cream and pointed out that since she has been aroused from bed in the middle of the night, the least Mary Margaret can do is have some. "Tearfully, she picks up a spoon . . . and one quart of chocolate ice cream later she is discussing a wonderful new idea for her NBC program."[41]

Yet Mary Margaret didn't turn to food only when she was depressed—she also turned to food when she was happy. Food brought her great joy—nothing could match the euphoria of being full after a good meal—and she loved to experiment with exotic cuisines and new culinary experiences. "One woman I know collects key-holes," she once wrote. "Another goes in for epitaphs gathered in churchyards all over the world. A third saves up every gorgeous sunset she sees to pore over when she is old. My own collection of memories of good meals in New York restaurants takes up no more space than the sunsets." More than a hobby, food was one of those things—right up there with books—that made life worth living.[42]

This equation of ice cream and positive mental health may be just a bit too neat to accept at face value, however. It certainly seems possible that some of the radio host's self-doubt and depression was linked to her weight and appearance, not just her failed attempt to become a great writer. Medical and popular literature provide many examples of people, especially women, who eat because of insecurity or an inner emptiness, eat because they don't feel loved (or, in some cases, to avoid sex), or eat to make themselves feel better. Food is a refuge, with sweets (one of Mary Margaret's favorites) being especially gendered as a female indulgence. The failure to control these cravings in turn sets in motion feelings of self-loathing and inadequacy, as the overweight person realizes that the rest of society sees her weight as a terrible character flaw. As Hilde Bruch, a pioneer in the treatment of eating disorders, noted in 1973, "Our social climate praises slenderness to such an extent that it is astounding that not all fat people suffer from disgust and self-hatred from being fat."[43]

Although these pressures were not as strong in Mary Margaret's day as they are now, it would have been hard for such a visibly overweight and public personality like her to ignore the popular cultural imperatives that privilege thinness over girth. After all, even in 1940 the etiquette expert Emily Post pronounced fat as a drawback for women, pointing out that "it is hard for an overweight woman to be dignified." But there also is something quite refreshing about the way in which Mary Margaret was so open and accepting about her weight—it is almost as if she anticipated a group like the National Association to Advance Fat Acceptance, which wasn't founded until 1969.[44]

Some people are blessed with a metabolism that burns up calories like a furnace. But Mary Margaret McBride wasn't, and she made her peace with her size. By sharing her love of food with her listeners and allowing them to empathize with a woman who did not have the figure of a Hollywood starlet and was proud of it, Mary Margaret McBride found yet another way to bond with her listeners.

6

Doing the Products

Bohack's

Dromedary Gingerbread Mix

Dolly Madison Ice Cream

Cut-Rite Waxed Paper

Icy Point Salmon

E-Z Cut Ham

IF YOU INSTANTLY RECOGNIZED the preceding constellation of names and products, chances are you were one of Mary Margaret McBride's loyal listeners. Just saying those names out loud has an almost Proustian way of transporting a listener back five decades to a world in which Dolly Madison ice cream was available at your local drugstore; newly introduced convenience products like waxed paper or sliced ham could be purchased at small supermarket chains; and old standbys like Dromedary Gingerbread might be the featured item at a luncheon for friends.

Hearing those evocative brand names also transports listeners back to a time when they valued those products precisely because they heard about them on Mary Margaret's show, indeed associated them with the talk show host herself. Journalist Louis Gordon, just back from India in the late 1940s, made this revealing comment while talking about his experiences there: "You know, Mary Margaret, the whole time I stayed with Gandhi I thought I would starve, and all I could think of was those Gingies you talk about."[1]

How many of Mary Margaret's products can you find in this picture? *Reprinted by permission of Library of Congress, Prints and Photographs Division.*

In the phenomenal bond formed between Mary Margaret McBride and her listeners, nowhere was the loyalty more evident than in "the products," which is how the various sponsors who made her show possible were always described. Rather than just a necessary evil, "doing the products" was a central and creative part of every show. Hard as it may be to believe today, listening to her do the products was actually fun, sometimes as fun (and funny) as the guests themselves. Would she be able to get them all in, or would Vincent have to hurry her along in the middle of an interview with a gentle lead-in to the day's featured product? Would she do a chunk of them in the middle of the show or leave them all to the end? What amusing or timely stories would listeners have to share about their experiences with individual products? Mary Margaret managed to make commercials interesting, suspenseful, timely—and persuasive. "That woman can sell anything" was the comment of more than one prospective advertiser.[2]

Mary Margaret's affinity for commercials and the enthusiasm with which she threw herself into this part of her radio show were all the more amazing since they directly contradicted her experience as a journalist in the 1920s. Newspapers and magazines kept editorial content and advertising distinct, with several floors often deliberately separating the advertising staff from the reporters and writers. Because she was such a neophyte at radio when she was hired, it never occurred to her that she would have to do anything but provide content for the show. When informed that she would need sponsors to stay on the air, she initially reacted to the prospect with horror. The only way she made her peace with it, and the key to her ultimate success, was this pledge: "I made up my mind though, then and there, that no matter what happened, I would never take anything that I couldn't stand back of."[3] How many other performers today would be able or willing to take such a stand?

Mary Margaret's embrace of the advertising imperative came at an interesting moment in the commercialization and commodification of twentieth-century American life. By the 1920s many Americans had the income and the inclination to participate in an emerging mass culture that increasingly substituted values like consumption, leisure, and self-realization for earlier standards like frugality, hard work, and self-denial. The Great Depression and wartime shortages slowed these impulses but never erased them completely. As citizens increasingly defined themselves as consumers rather than producers, the range of products available for their consumption jumped dramatically. Given the ongoing proliferation of products and styles, consumers faced multiple choices about what to buy. Advertisers stepped in to give expert advice, pegging their ads to helping consumers differentiate among all the new products. With so many new branded, standardized products now on the market, consumers had to find "new ways of relating to the objects of everyday life."[4]

Much of the work of navigating the new consumer-based economy fell to women. True, men still made most of the decisions about "big ticket" items like automobiles, refrigerators, phonographs, or radios. But women did most of the shopping for their families' everyday needs. Accordingly, housewives had enormous power to make choices and decisions about which products to buy for the home. Of course, the question of everyday needs was relative. What might have been seen in the past as a decadent luxury, such as mass-produced soap, a factory-made bedspread, or a store-bought apple pie, might now be seen as a necessary part of a family's lifestyle, a reflection of how consumers were upping the ante of what products and services were now considered central to modern life.[5]

Mary Margaret played an important role in helping her listeners, who were primarily homebound women, negotiate this new terrain. "Doing the products" (the inevitable by-product of the American system of commercial rather than state-sponsored broadcasting) kept her show on the air, and it also allowed her to act as an intermediary between the emerging mass-consumption economy and several generations of women learning how to participate in its complexities. Almost all the products advertised on her show were directly related to the home, with the majority being packaged convenience foods. With her endorsements and descriptions of these products, many of which were fairly new to the market, Mary Margaret was educating (and reassuring) her audience that it was all right to open a can of soup for lunch rather than make it from scratch and that it was a good value in terms of the housewife's time saved. By the 1930s and 1940s there were lots of cans of soup on the grocery store shelf; Mary Margaret could point her listeners to those brands that she felt were superior.

McBride also helped her listeners negotiate the change from shopping in local "mom and pop" stores to the larger grocery chains that began to proliferate in urban areas in the 1920s and spread steadily over the next several decades. The new chains had several advantages over the small local stores, and not just lower prices and broader selection. Housewives appreciated the ability to choose and inspect products for themselves, rather than have them handled only by a clerk, and also appreciated not having to go through sometimes tense negotiations with the owner over price or credit. In the new "cash and carry" or "self-help" stores, housewives knew exactly what they were getting and at what price.[6]

But buying and spending couldn't be too pleasurable—it had to be good for their families and homes. These women were frugal housewives after all, often on a strict budget, and if they were going to try a new product, they had to know it was a good buy for the money and would not be seen as self-indulgent or frivolous. Even though much of twentieth-century advertising has been aimed at convincing consumers that whatever they have is not enough, Mary Margaret was not pushing products so that women could escape the dreariness of their homes or the emptiness of their lives through extravagant (and unnecessary) purchases. Instead she was trying to help them fulfill their traditional gender roles more efficiently and effectively through new food-related products, an appeal to which her audience could relate. That is why the Mary Margaret seal of approval was so important.[7]

There also was something else at work here: if Mary Margaret had not loved food so much, she would not have been half so convincing at helping her listeners negotiate the new consumer economy. As we have seen, food was a critical component of her radio success and a key component of her radio persona. This enthusiasm extended directly and effortlessly to the products. "To eat her sponsors' products while on the air," noted one journalist, "and smack her lips from time to time, is one way of bringing their goodness home to the audience." To that end, when Mary Margaret broadcast at her usual time of 1 P.M., Stella would make sure that she had only toast and tea before going on the air, so that a hungry host could emote about the products in an especially convincing manner.[8]

From the beginning, McBride took a rather unorthodox approach to her sponsors. Only after she had determined through personal experience (she was always ready to try the taste test) or through a laboratory that the product or service did indeed live up to its claims would she accept it as a sponsor. She and Stella exercised complete veto power over which sponsors they would accept, a by-product of their power as independent brokers producing the show. In the early years of the program, when money was tight and sponsors not as plentiful as they were later, a sponsor once objected to an appearance on the program by First Lady Eleanor Roosevelt. Incensed, Stella returned his contract marked canceled and told him that he could never buy time on the show again. On the other end of the spectrum, long-term advertiser Henry Sell, maker of the eponymous liver paté, became such a good friend that he was considered part of Mary Margaret's radio family, invited to birthday celebrations, and given a prominent place on the dais at events like her fifteenth anniversary at Yankee Stadium in 1949.[9]

McBride's first real sponsor, a cleaning powder named Oakite, set the pattern for later sponsors. After overcoming her initial dread, she threw herself wholeheartedly into learning about the product and sharing this information with her listeners. Since it was her only sponsor at the time, she could devote as much time as she wanted to it, with interesting results. Her reportorial training helped her discover that Oakite was used to clean the steel wires of the cables on the George Washington Bridge, to scour the inside of the Lincoln Tunnel, and also at the New York Public Library and the laboratories of the Johns Hopkins Hospital, all of which she spun out into interesting stories for her listeners.[10]

Like the rest of Mary Margaret's show, these plugs were unscripted—in fact, they were completely spontaneous—which caused heart palpitations among nervous sponsors and advertising executives until they got used to her approach. (On other radio programs, commercials were read from a script, often prepared by an advertising agency, and they sounded like it.)[11] She wasn't trying to be high-handed or uncooperative, she claimed, just practical: "The truth is that there is only one way for me to manage the program, commercials or otherwise, and that is to do and say whatever seems natural and sincere at the time."[12] An article in *Life* noted that she might interrupt a conversation with "Ah, the Alpes-Maritimes! Do they have Glaubenfaust's pumpernickel there?" and launch directly into a commercial. She never read from a text, only allowing herself scraps of paper or listeners' letters as prompts. It was left to Vincent to supply the continuity that got her off one product, whose charms she might be stuck enthusing about, and on to the next and the next.[13]

This interplay between host and announcer added to the appeal and enjoyment of the potentially onerous task of doing commercials, which were integrated into the program so well as to be nearly seamless. For example, Mary Margaret once did a series of impromptu Shakespearean soliloquies ("To Blue or Not to Blue") tied to her products. Another time Stella and Vincent plugged products by linking them to books: somewhat incongruously, *Strange Fruit*, the novel by recent guest Lillian Smith protesting racial inequality, became the prompt for a brand of bananas. With gimmicks such as riddles, promotions, and games, the commercials bore a certain resemblance to popular radio quiz shows, which further added to their entertainment value.[14]

As part of her general commitment to never talk down to her listeners (a radio critic once observed, "She doesn't assume that the listener is an escaped idiot who flunked out of kindergarten"),[15] Mary Margaret McBride believed that they would be interested in things beyond just the household, and that applied to products as well as guests. When, for example, the makers of a well-known brand of shelf paper suggested that she should stick to how it could be used in the kitchen or pantry, Mary Margaret countered that listeners would also be interested in hearing about how the product was made and about the workers who produced it. She settled the disagreement in her usual way, "by going directly to my listeners and asking them to tell me how they felt about it. They backed me up and expressed themselves forcibly."[16]

As the Martha Deane program became more successful, the task of handling the logistics of multiple sponsorship for a six-times-a-week radio show fell to Stella Karn, who functioned as the show's business manager.[17] A forty-five-minute show had twelve sponsors, and sixteen for an hour-long program. If this seems like a lot of sponsors, it was, which explains why a good chunk of each show—at least one-quarter, perhaps one-third—was given over to the products. Every product was mentioned on every show, although sometimes just in passing, which was quite a feat. Each product received more prominent play two or three times a week when it was a "major" or featured product, when it might get several minutes (or more, if Mary Margaret really got going) of airtime. The cost at the height of the program was $275 a week for the radio time and $150 for the talent, a total of $425. Advertisers quickly learned it was worth it and usually dropped their sponsorship only if a business reversal made it impossible for them to continue. On at least one occasion, the radio host offered to carry a sponsor for free until his business improved after an unexpected budgetary shortfall. So loyal were her sponsors that when Mary Margaret jumped from NBC to ABC in 1950, every single one of her sponsors followed her, as did her entire waiting list.[18]

Who were these loyal sponsors? Since the core of Mary Margaret's listening audience was in the metropolitan New York area, they tended to be more often local products than national name brands. While products like Johnson's Wax, Pepsodent, and Maxwell House coffee sponsored prime-time radio shows like Fibber McGee and Molly, Bob Hope, and Burns and Allen, respectively,[19] Mary Margaret drew from a somewhat less prestigious and more varied corporate base, mainly related to food items or other small products to be consumed in the home. For example, Bohack's was a local supermarket chain in the New York metropolitan area. Some of her products eventually developed into successful national name brands, like Birds Eye frozen foods, but most remained local. When her programs were syndicated, as with the cooperative agreement she had with WGN in Chicago in the early 1950s, she would simply cut out the segment with the New York–based products and, before the show was broadcast on a time delay, substitute sponsors geared to her Chicago audiences (like W.H. Nahigian Oriental Carpets on Wabash Street).[20] By having multiple sponsors rather than a single sponsor associated with her show, Mary Margaret prefigured the direction that radio, and later television, took, one of the many reasons she is so important to broadcast history.[21]

One of her earliest and most faithful sponsors was Dolly Madison ice cream, which stayed with her program for almost twenty years. Ice cream was one of Mary Margaret's basic food groups, if not her all-time favorite, and certainly a big attraction of this sponsorship was that the company would regularly deliver to the studio a pint or two of ice cream before the show, which Mary Margaret and her hungry guests would often consume on the air, complete with lip-smacking sighs of satisfaction for whatever flavor was being featured or introduced that month. Store-bought brand-name high-quality ice cream was still somewhat of a novelty when Dolly Madison began advertising in the mid-1930s, so it was up to Mary Margaret to convince her listeners that this ice cream was as good as the ice cream that families used to produce laboriously at home and was worth the cost.[22]

Dolly Madison is also a good example of the kinds of tie-ins to local communities that gave the program such a homey feel. As part of her weekly plugs, Mary Margaret or Vincent would read the names of two or three local drugstores where Dolly Madison parties were being organized, complete with addresses and directions. The idea was that listeners could go by for a free sample and meet other similarly inclined fans of the show. Even if there wasn't a drugstore selling Dolly Madison products in their area, listeners enjoyed knowing that somewhere not too far away Mary Margaret's fans were getting together over a dish or cone. One of the most popular foods for Martha Deane parties (when listeners got together to chat and listen to the show) was, not surprisingly, Dolly Madison ice cream.[23]

This highly personalized, idiosyncratic approach to radio sponsorship got results. "She has sold more merchandise than any other woman in this age or any other age," declared *Sales Executive Weekly* in 1950.[24] H. C. Bohack ran a butter contest and received a "terrific" response of more than forty thousand entries, when they stopped counting. "Mary Margaret sure can pull them in," wrote their advertising manager,[25] with whom Goodman's Soup Company would agree, having received fourteen thousand requests for a sample of a noodle soup.

The all-time high, however, was the 92,824 listeners who wrote in for details about a bread promotion.[26]

Mary Margaret sold products, not just promotions. When Winter Garden Carrots started advertising on her show, their daily sales jumped from two to ten carloads daily, despite a glut of carrots in the market.[27] The Bedford Food Market in Stamford, Connecticut, noting that its customers now insisted on the Winter Gardens brand, began to feature them in its advertising to tie in to her programs. In the future, the store manager promised to "stock every food item that you advocate in your broadcasts."[28] Gristede's grocery stores in New York City had a similar epiphany. When they learned that Mary Margaret had accepted OXO beef cubes as a new sponsor, they immediately arranged to place OXO on sale in every Gristede store. "We knew that your listeners would be coming to our stores for OXO, as they do for the other fine things you recommend, and we wanted to be ready for them." The end of the story? "They came . . . and we were ready. As many as eighty-four women have bought OXO in one store in one day!"[29] Pity the local grocer who did not carry the products that Mary Margaret so lovingly and convincingly plugged every day on the air.

In a profile of the McBride phenomenon for *Life* magazine, writer Philip Hamburger noted, "In many homes a recipe from Mary Margaret has the majesty of law."[30] When the radio host was hired as a spokesperson for Florida citrus, 97.3 percent of her listeners polled in a national survey could identify the sponsor.[31] Henry Sell claimed that ten times as many people recognized his brand of liver paté as a result of advertising on her program than in any other medium.[32] And it wasn't just food products that sold, as bookstores quickly found out: when an interesting author or book was promoted on the program, the book usually sold out that day.[33] In her 1942 profile in the *New Yorker*, Barbara Heggie wrote only slightly tongue-in-cheek: "It certainly is just as well that she draws the line at tobacco and liquor; otherwise, undoubtedly, the housewives of the Eastern seaboard would be lying about their houses in an alcoholic stupor, smoking like chimneys."[34]

Mary Margaret threw herself into the products each day, but even she admitted that the task of getting so enthusiastic about twelve to sixteen products daily was a "challenge to my ingenuity." She often had a lot of help, mainly from Vincent, always ready with the slip of paper containing the nearest Dolly Madison promotion or the address for the free Metropolitan Life Insurance pamphlets or, if necessary, correcting her mistakes on air. "Did I forget anyone today?" Mary Margaret would ask. "Well," Vincent would answer smoothly, "you forgot to tell about the special sale of Baldwin apples at all the Bohack's stores this week." By the end of the day all the apples would be gone.[35]

What was really fun for listeners was when the guests pitched in, too. Bennett Cerf was one who found himself drawn in while making a guest appearance: "I found myself emoting over Bruce floor wax although until ten minutes before I had been firmly convinced that all wax came from bees."[36] Historian and biographer Carl Van Doren, a favorite guest as well as a loyal listener, often arrived with plugs for various products. Sample: "May I tiss oo?" "Yes." (*Yes* was the name of a tissue.)[37] Poet Langston Hughes composed an on-the-spot jingle about cake mix,[38] and Eleanor Roosevelt confessed that she had become so engrossed in listening to the commercials on one show that she had trouble getting back to the United Nations matters they had been discussing before the break.[39] After Betty Smith had the heroine of *A Tree Grows in Brooklyn* wash a horse with Sweetheart soap, she cheerfully inscribed Mary Margaret's copy, "With love from one of your products, Betty Smith."[40]

In a class all by herself was Tallulah Bankhead, who made a memorable appearance on the show in 1952. Bankhead was so entranced watching Mary Margaret doing the products that she didn't want her to stop. "But, darling, do go on, yours are the first commercials I ever enjoyed, because you are telling the truth. Listen, you out there [addressing the listeners], she's not reading. She just has a few little notes she glances at." Tallulah then grew worried that Mary Margaret wouldn't have time to get them all in, "and, after all, that's what we're here for." By the time Tallulah finished enthusing, and interfering, the program was almost over.[41]

Of course, not all guests were so obliging. Once when interviewing an opera singer who was discussing the importance of fruits and vegetables to her diet, Mary Margaret jumped in brightly, "I suppose you eat lots of broccoli?" (Andy Boy broccoli was one of her current sponsors.) "I loathe broccoli," the singer stated firmly.[42] Another time when actress Florence Reed was a guest, Mary Margaret launched into a Florida grapefruit commercial, one of her major sponsors. "Broiled grapefruit!" Reed interjected. "It's the most horrible thing I've ever heard of!" followed by "Hot grapefruit—gives me the willies just to think about." Gamely carrying on and unable to shut up her guest,

McBride asked whether perhaps she preferred fresh grapefruit, but Reed would not budge. "What could I do?" Mary Margaret remembered. "I laughed—a little hysterically—but I went on talking about the virtues of grapefruit, accompanied by quite audible rumblings of disapproval from my guest."[43]

The most telling fiasco occurred in the early days of the program and concerned a sponsor for soda pop, except that Mary Margaret refused to see it as a fiasco. She had recently signed on with the new product, its having passed her personal taste test, and she decided that it would be amusing to drive out to Long Island on a summer Sunday afternoon and observe people drinking the soda at various picnic grounds. The only problem was that after visiting almost a dozen picnic areas, she could not find anyone drinking the product, even though the sales charts showed it was a popular item on Long Island. Instead of merely covering this up, she decided it was a good joke on herself and shared it with her listeners the next day. As she later realized, "a trained advertising expert would have been horrified at my candor." Luckily the advertiser was based in Chicago and didn't hear about the episode for a few days, after a pile of letters had come in from listeners promising to buy so many bottles of the soft drink that this experience would never happen again. McBride proudly claimed that sales of the drink increased that summer from 6,000 to 600,000 cases without other advertising.[44]

Even if those numbers may have gotten more than a little inflated in the retelling, that story tells much about the bond between Mary Margaret and her listeners. "We believe in you and your products because you have the courage to tell us the truth no matter what it happens to be," wrote one.[45] A listener from New York City always waited until after the broadcast to telephone in her grocery order to the market because she knew that she would be tempted by at least one of the products. McBride recalled, "I always figured that I had a solid base of listeners who would try at least once anything I recommended and, better still, would attempt to get it the very day I spoke about it, or at least the next day." Her truth-in-advertising meshed perfectly with her listeners' need for comprehensive information about all the new consumer products crowding the grocery shelves.[46]

As in all aspects of the program, the listeners were an important part of doing the products. Almost every show contained letters from listeners about certain products, how they had been used at a special party or perhaps as the source of an amusing anecdote. For example, because McBride regularly advertised dog and cat food (presumably she didn't taste it herself, although it was never made clear how it passed the rigorous scrutiny of all new products), she often had funny stories from pet owners to share. Many programs offered recipes or coupons if listeners wrote in, entitling them to a special discount or product if their letter was read on the air; sometimes prizes went to listeners who had written the most creative letters about a certain product. All these things helped tie the listener directly to the products that Mary Margaret endorsed and, by extension, to the show itself. "I would do anything I could to keep your program on the air," wrote K. D. from Nyack, New York, "so I am going to drink twice as much coffee, Savarin Coffee, as I ever drank before."[47]

Since the millions of letters that came into the radio host were not kept systematically, it is impossible to determine how many of them actually mentioned the products, but circumstantial evidence suggests that the number was quite high. "Your products are all so tempting sounding (which is very bad grammar but good sense) that I am sure no one could resist them," wrote a listener from Kingston, New York:

> This afternoon I naturally had grocery shopping to do after my weekend in New York City, so I went to my favorite store and the very first thing I looked for was Dromedary ginger bread mix—and I found it, too. So just as soon as I try it (which will probably be tomorrow) I am going to write to you and tell you how I like it.

From H. S. in Brooklyn: "This is from one of your devoted listeners. I'm right on the job listening as always. On my pantry shelf are Dromedary Ginger Bread Mix, Date and Nut Bread. Thank you again for your wonderful tips on food—really all one could want for a very delicious meal."[48]

Once advertisers were put onto Mary Margaret's sponsor list, they were almost guaranteed results with this established and highly motivated audience. As a magazine writer once said, "Admission to the McBride program is the commercial equivalent of admission to Groton."[49] On holidays like Thanksgiving or other days when she decided that the show was "too important to be associated with products (though goodness knows they were pretty vital to me) I would just list the clients and add that I depended upon every listener to buy twice as much of everything as usual."[50] What it all came down to was the formula that McBride had settled on at the start:

> The reasons the listeners did what I asked them was because they knew I never recommended a product unless I had not only tested it but proved to myself that I really liked it. That was my invariable rule, though it took considerable doing to persuade advertising agencies that I meant what I said.[51]

Advertisers quickly learned that this "stamp of approval pays out for you."[52] When McBride was asked to address the organization of the nation's top sales executives at their annual Valentine's Day luncheon, she did her entire NBC program from the event. One of the featured guests was a listener named Mary Hastings who astounded the assembled ad executives by not only knowing the entire list of Mary Margaret's sponsors but also being able to ad-lib stories about how she used the products. "Mary Margaret's honesty in selling over the years is proof enough to me that anything she recommends is the best," announced Hastings, adding, "and I have never been disappointed in following her advice."[53]

Mary Margaret managed to make her commercials work for her listeners, even those who initially had been dubious about the products' increasingly large role in the shows. "I was disappointed when you first began to interrupt your program with commercials," wrote one. "But when I happened to notice a box of your cleaner at a store where I traded, it seemed the most natural thing in the world to buy it. I like it so much that I feel differently about the whole commercial idea."[54] That listener's response confirms a pattern identified in the 1946 survey *People Look at Radio*. While a small minority had strong feelings against advertising on the radio, most listeners accepted the idea of commercials themselves without comment, as long as the advertisements were well integrated into the program and not in bad taste (no ads for alcohol, laxatives, or deodorants, please). And if the commercials offered constructive or useful advice or had human interest value, listeners regarded them as a positive contribution to the radio experience.[55] It is doubtful that a survey would find such support for commercials today, but back in the 1930s and 1940s when radio was still new and many homes quite isolated from other forms of mass media, radio really did bring new products and ideas into homes.[56]

Over the years Mary Margaret did her fair share of endorsements in the print media as well, allowing her name to be used in connection with products such as Instant Tender Leaf Tea, Murine eyedrops, and Fleischmann's yeast.[57] But it is unlikely that those ads had anywhere near the impact of the endorsements she offered on her radio show. It was one thing to see an ad in *Life* or *Time* featuring a favorite personality—a boost to the prestige of certain products but rather removed, almost lifeless. To hear their favorite radio show host talk every day in mouth-watering, sincere, and totally convincing terms about products for which listeners could find an immediate use in their homes was a different matter, almost like having a neighborly recommendation over the back fence. It took the intimacy forged over the radio to make this work. It also took Mary Margaret's sincerity and her listeners' faith in her recommendations.

It was this bond that caused *Printers' Ink* in 1939 to take note of what it called "perhaps the most outstanding example of reliance upon the word of a human being in the commercial field": "the enormous following among women of the recommendations over the radio of Mary Margaret McBride." She had been on the air for only five years when *Printers' Ink* singled her out, but she had already mastered the medium's commercial possibilities. Calling her "a commercial asset of untold value," it pointed out that to her audience "she is friend, neighbor, one of us, whose word about any product from ham to smoking gadget is believed because she recommends it and they have found that the products she recommends are, upon test, exactly as she has said they were." *Printers' Ink* was clear about the moral of the story. "Do women want the truth about the things they buy? The commercial success of the Martha Deane program would seem to prove that they do."[58] A listener from Media, Pennsylvania, summed up this symbiosis perfectly: "I try to buy all your products whenever I can and know that they are all you say. I have never been disappointed in one product yet, and know I never shall."[59]

That is one of the larger significances of Mary Margaret's "doing the products." Another is how, as far back as the 1930s and long before the advent of call-in radio or other audience-participant devices, she managed to make her listeners a central part of her program. True, it might take a day or two before a letter reached her from a listener about a new idea for how to use a favorite product, but once it arrived, it could be shared over the air. The connection was still there.

Sometimes the bond came close to the instantaneous interactions that we have come to take for granted in live shows or Internet chat groups. One day when McBride was broadcasting from Westchester County, she promoted Dolly Madison ice cream, adding, "If the Larchmont Pharmacy is listening, please, please send me six quarts." Within two minutes, the pharmacy's phone lines were jammed with listeners relaying the message, and the ice cream was on the way within five minutes. Another time she put out a call, again instantly answered by the Larchmont Pharmacy, for Merri-mints, which caused her to quip, "if the FCC doesn't go after us, we may have originated a new shopping service."[60] On another broadcast, a guest suggested that she retell the story of how she had climbed under a table during a certain show, but Mary Margaret could not remember the details. "Immediately the NBC switchboard began to get calls from listeners who remembered exactly what had happened." Finally, on a December 28, 1950, broadcast, when the host and guests got stuck on a sports statistic, one guest quipped they should ask John Kieran of *Information, Please.* Almost immediately the phone ran in the control room, and it was Mrs. Kiernan with the answer from her husband.[61]

Always a forward-looking pioneer, Mary Margaret McBride managed to make radio interactive long before the technology even existed.

PART II

BECOMING
MARY MARGARET MCBRIDE

"Tell about it," Mary Margaret has probably just said to her author guest.
Reprinted by permission of Library of Congress, Prints and Photographs Division.

7

Listening to Lives

WHEN MARY MARGARET MCBRIDE'S LISTENERS sat down next to their radios on January 16, 1940, for their afternoon session with their favorite radio host, they were greeted by a somber announcement. Instead of Martha Deane's chatty voice, they heard a very subdued Hilda Deichler, the show's producer, who sadly informed the radio audience that Mary Margaret's mother had died away the night before and that the radio host and Stella Karn had flown down to Florida to be with her family.[1]

This news would have come as a terrible shock to most of her faithful followers: to them, Elizabeth Craig McBride was as much a part of their lives as Mary Margaret. Listeners had been hearing her daughter tell stories about her on the air for years and had enjoyed the numerous shows on which Mrs. McBride was a featured guest.[2] She was one of the family, everybody's mother. So when something so traumatic happened, it had to become part of the radio show itself. Years later, on each Mother's Day Mary Margaret still received hundreds of letters from listeners in honor of Mrs. McBride's memory: "Apparently she represents a kind of symbol of motherhood to everybody who came even as close to her as the receiving end of a broadcasting system."[3]

There never was any question of canceling the show or rebroadcasting a show that had aired previously. That would have been too abrupt, too harsh, for the listeners, who needed to find their own ways to come to grips with the loss, just as Mary Margaret was doing. So in the finest show-business tradition, the show did go on. For the next forty-five minutes, members of the radio family who had assembled with only hours notice did the program. Herman Smith pulled himself out of a sick bed to come in, and Missouri friend Jane Rogers composed rhymes on the train down from Connecticut to promote the products. Substitute announcer Dick Willard and Mrs. D. asked listeners to be patient as they tried to fill Stella's and Mary Margaret's shoes. They all told stories and reminisced, but mainly they settled on doing the products. That is what Mary Margaret would have wanted, they concluded, and they happily latched on to this task to fill the time. The next day they filled in again.[4]

During these impromptu programs, listeners gradually learned more about the circumstances of Mrs. McBride's death. Mary Margaret had originally planned to go to Florida at Christmas, but her mother had asked her to postpone the trip until February because then the orange blossoms would be in bloom. Mrs. McBride had recently had a stroke and was somewhat feeble, but her nurses were not especially concerned when she caught a cold. But then her condition began to deteriorate rapidly, and she died before Mary Margaret could arrive from New York by plane. So it was up to her friends to break the news over the air, friends who had loved her mother almost as much as Mary Margaret herself did.

Two days later, barely forty-eight hours since her mother had died, McBride returned to the air. Her voice flat and exhausted, Mary Margaret told her listeners that she wanted to talk to them as if they were having a conversation, just the two of them, in their own home. She warned any one who might have just casually happened to turn on the show that day not to listen. This was going to be a very personal show, and she wanted to talk to her audience "alone" (her revealing word).[5]

She began by apologizing that she hadn't been able to tell them about her mother's death herself because she knew how much they had cared for her. She reassured them that her mother's final days had been calm and peaceful, and she hoped this would be a comfort to them, as it had been to her. She did not hide her grief but focused on her feelings of peace and serenity to give them a sense that she was all right and so was her mother. At one point she almost cried (and I almost did, too, listening to this sixty years later) when she talked about her mother's voice coming back to her from beyond the grave, to say, "Yes, daughter, I'm all right." She profusely thanked her friends for filling in for her when she was away. Friends meant even more to her now, she realized, and she would always remain grateful.

By now, perhaps fifteen to twenty minutes into the show, McBride's voice was getting stronger and more animated as she switched into radio gear. She even managed to do the products, including a plug for the George Washington brand of broth that sustained her when she was

too exhausted to eat anything else. She read letters from listeners prais-
ing the broth and then moved on to Wesson Oil. Perking up even more,
she tackled a guest who had been lined up for the show before tragedy
struck, even though she protested that she didn't know whether she
could do an interview without breaking down. She performed well, although she let the guest talk a little more than usual. Then she did more
of the products, realizing that this was easier and avoided a "situation"
in which she might break down. Now it was full steam ahead for a new
flavor of Dolly Madison ice cream and Kitchen Bouquet. After a little
more time with her guest and another round of heartfelt thanks to her
listeners for all their telegrams, cards, and messages, the time was up,
and she signed off with her usual "Good-bye, y'all." Even though she
had admitted that "my brain isn't as good as usual today" and that she
felt a "consuming weariness" inside, she had survived the show. It was
a bravura performance.

Actually there was a precedent: Mary Margaret McBride had done
a similar show after her father died unexpectedly in Florida in 1937.
That time, too, she had worried whether she could do the show without
choking up, but she wanted to tell her listeners how important to her
their messages of sympathy and support had been. She told them that
this was the first time she had lost anybody really close to her, except
her little brother as a child, and that now she felt like a member of a secret organization. She confessed that she was sorry she had never had
her father on the program but that she had been afraid that he would
brag too much about his famous daughter. Knowing that her listeners
would wonder how her mother was faring, she reassured them of her
strength and courage and then segued into a commercial for a new
sponsor, Swift's, saying that it was one her father would have liked.
And after she had done the products, her voice now strong and full, she
started talking about Florida as if it were just a normal trip to be shared
with her listeners.[6]

If there ever was a question that Mary Margaret's life was her radio
program and that her listeners were a surrogate family, these very public but also surprisingly intimate ways of dealing with grief and loss
provide the ultimate proof. Connecting with her audience over the airwaves, sharing bad times as well as good, was her way of drawing
strength from the unseen but hardly anonymous millions who listened
to her every day. She felt she could turn to them in times of distress and
need in large part because she knew that she was there for them when

they needed her, as the thousands of letters that poured in each week confirmed.

It was more, however, than just reaching out in extreme moments like the loss of a parent. In many ways Mary Margaret's whole life was an open book to her listeners. They knew almost every aspect of the host's personal history—because she told them. On a regular, almost daily, basis Mary Margaret would refer to some aspect of her life, past or present, and weave it seamlessly into the show.

Listeners enjoyed hearing about her daily life in the city, but they especially loved hearing stories of her childhood and growing up on a Missouri farm. America in the 1930s and 1940s was still not that far removed from the small-town, agrarian-based world of the turn of the century when she was born. Listeners might or might not have grown up on a farm, but this familiar, if fast disappearing, aspect of American life continued to delight them. These stories were reassuring, comfortable, easy—what she called a "record of a time that is gone." In some ways they were comparable to the late twentieth-century nostalgia for the United States in the 1950s, with its strong, stable, nuclear families; traditional gender roles; and a prosperous economy dominating the world. Of course the world of the 1950s was far more complex than that mythology, as was no doubt the turn-of-the-century world that Mary Margaret evoked from her memories. But the allure remained.[7]

Other radio commentators traded on nostalgia for a lost past, but Mary Margaret did not stop with her rural childhood. Her listeners knew all about her life before radio, too: spending her first Christmas away from home, sharing a tiny apartment with Stella in Greenwich Village, being broke, and still finding ways to eat out and enjoy it. They knew how proud she was when she had earned enough money to invite her mother to visit her in New York and, later, to take her to Europe. They heard her stories about getting shabbier and shabbier as the Depression dried up her income. Few details of her life before radio weren't at one time or another shared with her listeners. Of course the nonexistent line between the private and the public continued once she had her own radio show, when basically everything that she did, ate, or saw was fodder to be recycled for the on-air enjoyment of her listeners.[8]

"At the risk of being misunderstood," the radio host said after being on the air for only two years, "I must say here that my listeners are most interested of all in what I am doing personally—to them my life is a sort of continued story. And I hold nothing back, goodness knows."[9] Yet it is hard to escape the feeling that she was not always quite so open or forthcoming as she let on. No telling of a life ever is. She repeated the story of her Missouri girlhood and her desire to be a great writer in New York so many times that it took on a scripted, almost formulaic quality. She spoke openly and often about Stella Karn, but the true meaning of their relationship remained illusive. She alluded to periods of deep depression and despair but never probed their roots. That is, Mary Margaret shared her life, but only up to a point.

Although these stories and memories might have lacked spontaneity or depth, they proved enormously popular with listeners. These shared confidences and reminiscences became key elements of the McBride radio persona, their details well known to even the most casual listener. Not only were these stories a staple of her radio shows, but they also appeared in her volumes of memoir and autobiography as well as countless articles, which invariably contained phrases like "as almost any of her listeners could tell you" or "almost every Mary Margaret fan knows." In order to fully understand the Mary Margaret McBride phenomenon, it is necessary to look at not just her radio technique but her entire life story, because it is impossible to separate the two.[10]

Biographies often unfold in a fairly formal, almost ritualistic way. Details of childhood and youth open the book, followed by the development of a career path and whatever challenges or struggles needed to be overcome along the way, and culminating in success (or occasionally failure) and then a gradual tapering off as the subject grows old and dies. That is one way to tell a life.

Evoking Mary Margaret McBride's on-air presence and radio's encouragement of active listening, I now invite you to use your imaginations and "listen" to a recital of her life as if you were one of her faithful fans. Listen to the stories of her father losing the farm by betting on a horse, how she got a scoop when she was a college reporter by seeing who ordered extra ice cream at the local drugstore for parties, or the dish named "Chaos" that her penniless roommates invented in Greenwich Village in the 1920s. Think about how McBride grew up in an atmosphere that validated conversation—the neighbors who dropped by for a chat, a style that profoundly influenced her later interviewing technique. Pay attention to how Mary Margaret may have sounded like a naïve, unsophisticated country girl on the air, but underneath that exterior lay a seasoned reporter and writer whose hard-won experience was critical to her success on the radio. Note how close she was to her mother, whom she idolized, but more distant from her father, whose mercurial personality was just a bit too close for comfort to her own. Think also about the roots of her crippling insecurity and need for approval in her failed attempt to become a great writer. In other words, listen to a life that not only served her well as preparation for her radio career but also provided her with some of her best—and most revealing—material.

8

A Missouri Childhood

IN A TRIBUTE TO AMERICAN DEMOCRACY called *America for Me* (1941), Mary Margaret McBride claimed three states as her own: her native Missouri, her adopted state of New York, and the "step-state" of Florida, where her parents moved in the 1920s.[1] Her radio career took her a long way from Missouri, but in many ways she never left the state of her birth. She constantly talked about her childhood and upbringing on her radio show and never missed an opportunity to bring the conversation around to her home state. Until the end of her life, her most popular lecture was titled simply "I'm from Missouri."[2]

"Missouri is not just a state to me," Mary Margaret McBride once said. "It is my childhood."[3] Paris, Missouri, population 1,500, where she was born on November 16, 1899, is located in Monroe County, not far from where Samuel Clemens (better known as Mark Twain) had been born sixty years earlier. Commentators sometimes referred to her "Ozark" accent, but this section of the state is much closer to Illinois and the Mississippi River than to the Arkansas foothills. There is no denying the state's strong southern heritage, however, in both speech (she always pronounced it "Missour-ah") and migration patterns. In the *WPA Guide to Missouri*, this area is called Little Dixie, as most of its settlers were families transplanted from Kentucky or Tennessee.[4] Her father's family, originally from Ireland, ended up in Missouri after leaving South Carolina for Tennessee; her mother, whose Scottish ancestors arrived around the time of the American Revolution, was descended from a slave-owning family in Virginia that migrated to Missouri by way of Kentucky.[5]

Mary Margaret was the first of five children born to the former Elizabeth (or Lizzie) Craig and Thomas Walker McBride. Their only daughter thought that their match was one of "an attraction of opposites,"[6] he the fun-loving, joking, almost irresponsible life of a party and his wife the solid rock that held home and family together, no matter what the

The spit curl and the middy blouse that Mary Margaret wore when she left Missouri for Washington, D.C. *Reprinted by permission of Library of Congress, Prints and Photographs Division.*

trials or challenges he put them through. In this household the father's word was law. He was always served first, and he always insisted on a bottle of ketchup and a bowl of syrup to go with whatever meal was being served, even if there were guests, which wasn't very often. Living in isolated farmhouses where other children were miles away, Mary Margaret was especially close to her next youngest sibling, Tommy, who was her co-conspirator on the few childhood pranks that she allowed herself. She proudly considered herself a tomboy and reveled in the freedoms of a childhood lived primarily outdoors.[7]

The family moved often, almost yearly, in her early childhood, because her father was, in her words, "a born trader." He would trade anything—a horse, a mule, a buggy, even a farm. "No sooner were we settled in one place with the orchard bearing, the corn and wheat doing well and Mama making the house look a little better, than Papa was at it again, swapping our farm for a bit of cash and another piece on the prairie."[8] Later Mary Margaret remembered a series of homes that were "bleak and unpainted with not even the grace of age to give them beauty. There were no bathrooms, no electric lights, no conveniences at all and everything had to be done the hardest way." Every time the family moved, Mrs. McBride would immediately plant some pansies and sweet peas to bring cheer to their new home.[9]

Without a doubt Elizabeth Craig McBride was the dominant influence in Mary Margaret's childhood, indeed her entire life. No matter how bleak the family's surroundings, her mother's love and hard work redeemed them in her daughter's eyes. The life of a farm woman at the turn of the century was physically demanding and emotionally harsh. Mrs. McBride got up every morning at four o'clock, winter or summer, to get the fire going, haul water, and prepare breakfast for her family. Then she had a full day of housekeeping, plus food preparation for her family and whatever hired hands were working on the farm at the time. She worked seven days a week, and neighbors recalled that she always had a broom in her hand and never sat down. She juggled her household chores with the responsibility of watching her growing family of young children who arrived quickly and regularly "like little stair steps." As the only daughter, Mary Margaret had her chores, too, including making the featherbeds (her least favorite) and drying the dishes (not much better), but she always felt that she should be doing more to protect her overburdened mother.[10]

Mary Margaret drew an important lesson from her mother's life:

It was an accepted way of life for women and Mama asked nothing better. Yet like so many American mothers she hoped her daughter wouldn't have to work so hard. She didn't mind that her own hands got stained and calloused and so swollen that she couldn't wear her wedding ring, but she wanted my hands to stay smooth.

Wanting to give her mother things that she never had was a prime motivation for Mary Margaret's desire to leave Missouri and make something of herself.[11]

Her relations with her father were much more complicated. When his Irish temper flared, the children learned to stay out of his way. He also had a reckless streak, with horses as his passion. When a beloved horse won a red, not a blue, ribbon at the county fair, he became so incensed that he stormed out of the ring and never showed a horse at the fair again. Mary Margaret always blamed him for not being a good provider and causing her mother to have to work so hard: "I thought him often unjust to his children, inconsiderate of my mother, and although it was wicked to my training to judge a parent, I felt he was not as 'good' as my mother and grandfather." Ironically, even though she wanted to be a selfless, kind individual like them, she found herself much more akin to her hot-tempered father: "I was, alas, my father's child. He was a man of extremes and I inherited his temperament. I never admitted this to myself, though."[12]

Two other important influences on her childhood were her maternal and paternal grandfathers. Her grandfather McBride taught her Greek and Latin poetry, and her grandfather Craig, always referred to as "Pa," taught her religion. Pa, who lived with them until his death when Mary Margaret was twelve, was an itinerant Baptist preacher who covered thousands of miles ministering to the needs of his far-flung parishioners. Pa's was a harsh religion, without much room for doubt, but his emphasis on the Golden Rule stayed with Mary Margaret for the rest of her life. So did his confidence, often articulated, that she would someday be a famous writer, which was just what this little girl desperately wanted to hear.[13]

It is nearly impossible to write about Mary Margaret McBride's life without giving food a starring role, and the genesis of this love affair came, like so much else, from her childhood. While growing up, Mary Margaret was far too active to be a chubby child, but she was never thin.

Although she fretted about her size, nothing could ever diminish her ravenous appetite for the fattening food of her youth.[14]

The other constant in her childhood besides food was books. Mary Margaret read everything that she could get her hands on, including her family's well-worn copy of Dr. Chase's *Recipes or Information for Everybody*, which dispensed household advice, etiquette, and hints about that vexing mystery (never addressed in her household) of where babies came from. But it was fiction that captured her fancy, especially works like *Alice in Wonderland, Ivanhoe*, and the collected works of Shakespeare and Dickens. "I loved books so much that I can still see whole pages from some of them and the very type in which they were set."[15] Her love affair with reading, like that with food, was a lifelong obsession that served her well with the thousands of authors she interviewed on her radio program. As she once said, "I can always bury myself ostrich-like in a good book when life is too much for me." Years later the dominant memories of friends visiting her New York penthouse or her converted barn in the Catskills were of the overflowing bookcases with personally autographed copies from friends or favorite guests.[16]

For all its warmth and strong family ties, however, there was an undercurrent of fear and bleakness that shaped Mary Margaret's childhood. Much of this uncertainty centered on her father's often irresponsible habits. As a child, Mary Margaret remembered lying awake at night, hearing her parents talk about the mortgage in hushed and worried tones. "They spoke of 'The Bank' in the same apprehensive way and I got the idea that the mortgage was some kind of monster with fiery eyes and a gaping mouth that lived in the Bank."[17] At the peak of her career, McBride still had not put these fears behind her: "Well, because we were poor when I was a child, I still feel insecure. I suppose I always see the poor farm just around the corner. I worry about being poor and alone and unloved."[18]

The family suffered from a certain emotional poverty as well. Sometimes Mary Margaret had headaches so severe that only being close to Mama would bring relief, yet she was so concerned about burdening her mother that she hesitated to ask for help or special comfort herself. These emotional symptoms shaped her whole life: "It seemed to me that many of my problems as an adult—my personal uncertainty, my passion to be approved at any cost—were hangovers from experiences in my childhood."[19] But even if she had sought help for her problems then, what kind of psychiatric help would have been available to farm girls in turn-of-the-century Missouri? All she could do was internalize her feelings.

Especially upsetting were the rapid-fire pregnancies that her mother endured, none of which were explained to her oldest daughter, who suddenly was confronted with one, then two, and yet another baby who competed for her mother's attention. Mary Margaret's reaction to one of her mother's confinements was so extreme that she brought on a relapse of the measles and, for a time, seemed to be near death. The local doctor prescribed a shot of brandy, but the eight-year-old had already taken the temperance pledge and she refused. She did recover, a confirmed teetotaler for the rest of her life, but later looked back at this episode as a rather dramatic way to get her mother's attention.[20]

Another cloud on Mary Margaret's childhood was an incident of attempted sexual molestation by a hired hand when she was probably four or five years old. (She discussed this only in a published memoir, never on the air. Talking about such predatory sexual practices on the radio would have been taboo then.) Who knows how often this happened on isolated farms, which depended on the labor of roving hired hands, especially at harvest and slaughter times. The incident occurred after they had moved to a particularly ramshackle old farmhouse, whose upkeep took up so much of Mrs. McBride's time that she had less energy to see what her children were up to. One day George, the hired hand, lured Mary Margaret to the loft of the barn with an offer of candy, which "greedy little girl that I was," she accepted eagerly. Speaking to her in a low, husky voice very different from his usual voice, he reached toward her, only to be interrupted by Mrs. McBride's voice calling from afar. Mary Margaret had not been afraid up to that point, but she suddenly realized something was terribly wrong. Sobbing and shaking, she ran back to the house and her mother's arms. When she was a little quieter, her mother asked, "George didn't hurt you, did he, Mary Margaret?" and she answered no. George was never seen again.[21]

Those bad memories were soon replaced by what Mary Margaret remembered as a truly idyllic, special summer when she was six. "Perhaps every human being in his lifetime cherishes one memorable period that stays clear and shining, its colors intermeshed, its fragrance unfaded. My memorable period is that summer on the Old Home Place," the farm where her mother had in fact been born and raised. Mary Margaret remembered her mother singing in the kitchen, and a "brief season of content and plenty" after "some very stormy financial times." Even the food was specially enchanted at the farmhouse, with her mother's cooking at its zenith.

> Even if I knew exactly what we did to make that summer so happy, I suppose nobody could ever duplicate it, any more that I can take Mama's simple recipe for charlotte russe and emerge with anything as delectable as the crockfuls of creamy custard perfection that glorified all our birthdays.

One ingredient was the good health of a child "who ran barefooted and bareheaded from morning to night. Another may have been the quantities of milk expertly conveyed by my father straight from the cream-colored cow into my little silver mug." And finally there was "the joy that fills a child when all is well with family and home."[22]

Then two events shook the family's calm. One night the dogs started barking, neighbors turned up, and Mary Margaret and her brother Tommy overheard that a man had been lynched on the bridge they crossed when they went into town. (No further details of this episode survive.) The second event struck much closer to home. One morning Addie, "the colored woman who did our washing" (probably a measure of the family's temporary affluence) was working in the yard, with Mary Margaret pestering her to help. Buford, her two-year-old brother, was underfoot as usual. Addie thought Buford was with his mother, Mama thought he was with Addie, but he had followed his older brother Tommy down to the creek to wait for their father to come home. It had rained the night before, and the creek was high. Buford slipped on a rock and drowned in the current. "If only we had never come back here," her mother moaned repeatedly. Soon afterward, the family moved into town, ostensibly so that Mary Margaret could go to school but really to escape the memories of that awful tragedy.[23]

There is a postscript to this story, which says much about a writer's ability to reshape memories. In retirement in 1966, McBride wrote a children's book called *The Growing Up of Mary Elizabeth*, which is a very lightly fictionalized account of her childhood. Paris, Missouri, became Rome, Missouri; Mary Margaret McBride was Mary Elizabeth McDonald, also known as Sister or Sis, her childhood nickname. Whole incidents and episodes were lifted practically verbatim from her nonfiction writings. But when it came time to tell the story of Buford, he was saved by the intervention of his older sister.[24]

Moving into town relieved some of the burdens on her mother and also gave her more opportunities to socialize with other women, including the extended family networks that connected that part of Missouri. But her child-care responsibilities hardly diminished, as she bore two more children, Milton and Boone. The family's precarious financial situation had not really improved, either. When her father stopped being a farmer, which he had been all his life, he got involved in a venture to fatten up cattle and pigs to ship to the markets in Chicago and St. Louis. Something was always guaranteed to go wrong—prices would dive before the stock reached the market, or the animals would succumb to drought or illness along the way—and the hoped-for money never materialized. Just the thing for a speculator at heart.[25]

Not all the McBrides were so crossed when it came to making money, however. Great-Aunt Albina, a wealthy relative whom Mary Margaret used to butter up with fawning letters designed to produce a gift or a bit of cash, offered to pay her niece's tuition at a small girls' school in Fulton, which later became William Woods College. In 1910 when she turned eleven, Mary Margaret took her first train ride, and her father deposited her at school, the first of many changes in her life as she left her family of origin.[26]

Boarding school was a big adjustment for a young girl who had spent most of her life on a farm. To her, the small town of Fulton probably seemed as strange and foreign as New York City. At home she had basically been allowed to do whatever she pleased, but now she was subjected to strict rules of deportment, such as being expected to wear an awkward uniform of flowing black robes and a mortarboard cap. Her response to this new environment was to try to fit in, that is, until she began to fear that she was being too much of a goody-goody. A few acts of minor rebellion ensued, but she settled down to be a fairly good student. "That was the trouble with me, I reflected. I wanted to be a spirited creature like my cousin Margaret, known as one who could look authority in the face without quailing, but I didn't want to pay the price." For the rest of her life she often yearned to be wicked but was too timid to rebel.[27]

Another disincentive to misbehaving was that good conduct earned students the chance for a monthly visit to a bakery called Frank's, and the prospect of food invariably squashed any thoughts of mischief or rebellion:

Always hungry, my idea of an earthly heaven was . . . enough cash for several rounds of McIntyres (named for a local gourmet and composed of ice cream in a tall glass smothered in pecans and butterscotch sauce), fried oysters with plenty of pickles, and enormous soft buns stuffed with ham. The order in which I have mentioned these viands is just about that in which I ate them, too.

Some of her food orgies, including one in which she downed thirteen ice-cream sundaes and then did not eat for three days, became part of William Woods legend.[28]

"I sized you up as the crying kind," said principal Fannie Willis Booth later, "but you turned out better than I feared."[29] It also turned out that Aunt Albina had ulterior motives for footing the bill for Mary Margaret's tuition: she wanted someone named McBride to serve as the next "lady principal" of the boarding school, and she was grooming the teenage Mary Margaret for that position. Instead of the expected college education in her chosen field of journalism, her aunt wanted her to prepare to be a teacher. All summer she and Aunt Albina went back and forth on the question of her future, and in the end her aunt said no to her plans for a nonteaching career. It was, as Mary Margaret said later, "the great crossroads of her life."[30]

With the McBrides' chronic money problems, it was clear that her family would not be able to send her to college, even to a relatively inexpensive state school, and yet Mary Margaret was convinced that a college degree was necessary to realize her ambition to become a great writer. So the plucky sixteen-year-old decided to earn some money and then to work her way through college. First she got a part-time job on the local newspaper, the *Paris Mercury*, which was founded in 1837 and has been published continuously since that date. "There was no salary and I was the only reporter. It was apprenticeship with a vengeance."[31] She covered everything: courthouse proceedings, social events, baby contests, whatever. The paper's editor, Tom Bodine, whose influence reached far beyond Paris through a widely quoted column entitled "The Scrap Bag," proved a great influence on Mary Margaret's life. At one especially low moment on New Year's Eve, she despaired that she would never get out of Paris. He took her aside and gave her a bit of advice that she never forgot: "Don't let them stop you—don't even let me stop you. If you want to do it, you can do it. Resolve now that you will!"[32]

With that boost of encouragement to launch the new year, within a few months she left home for Columbia, sixty miles away where the state university was located, and enrolled as a student. Based on her clippings from the *Paris Mercury*, she finagled a job on the local newspaper. She worked at night and went to school during the day, proud "that I'd worked my way through college on that paper instead of waiting on tables or washing dishes."[33] She survived on a ten-dollar-a-week salary, paid irregularly, and the kindness of local merchants, who often took pity on this college student with a healthy appetite by plying her with leftovers and free food. It was these same merchants who often gave her the equivalent of a small-town scoop: she figured out who was having parties by who had placed larger than normal orders for ice cream or rolls, then called the hostess for confirmation, and printed the details of the social affair. Like her stint on her hometown paper, McBride gathered an enormous amount of practical experience in the newspaper trade that she later carried over into radio. A fellow student remembered her as "very determined and kind of a loner. She always was going after the choice assignments." Mary Margaret remembered her college days more humbly: "I think I took the assignments they gave me."[34]

Mary Margaret never wrote or talked much about her college years, one of the few periods of her life she didn't exploit and recycle repeatedly for her radio audience and the reading public. There were no descriptions of favorite classes or professors, no nostalgic portraits of social events and football games. Nor did she mention any national political events, such as World War I, the proposed League of Nations, or the women's suffrage campaign that was building toward a successful climax. Probably she was just too worn out working full time while trying to keep up with her extra course work (she completed the requirements for her degree in two and a half years) to have anything close to a typical collegiate experience. She may also have been afflicted with one of the periodic bouts of depression and self-doubt that always seemed to accompany her ambitious professional aspirations. Still, it must have been a moment of intense personal satisfaction when she graduated in 1918 with a B.A. in journalism.[35]

There was no question about what she planned to do next:

> Every since I was five years old I'd been determined to go to New York
> and get on a newspaper. . . . There was even more to my ambition: I in-

tended after an apprenticeship on a newspaper to become a great novelist and so rich that I could take my mother on a trip to Europe.[36]

Careers for women were still unusual, and she was intensely aware that this kind of determination was "fairly new for the Middle Western female" and certainly for women in her family, who had never aspired to be anything but farm wives or, at most, teachers. Not totally ruling out marriage but certainly putting it on indefinite hold, she proudly labeled herself "a young woman WITH A PURPOSE," adding, "I was just engrossed in myself and my ambitions."[37]

Her first job was as a cub reporter at the Mexico, Missouri, *Ledger*, a paper that had strong links to the journalism school at the University of Missouri. Mary Margaret was one of a long string of reporters, male and female (her graduating journalism class counted twelve women out of twenty-seven), who gained invaluable experience working on the *Ledger* until they were ready to move on. Her biggest story was the lead coverage of the Ringo Hotel fire that destroyed the town's main hotel and several surrounding businesses on April 19, 1918.[38]

After working at the *Ledger* for less than a year, Mary Margaret was offered a job through a newspaper colleague in Washington, D.C. She had never been out of Missouri and had never slept overnight on a train. In fact, she was so terrified to have a man in the lower berth of the Pullman car that she never undressed for the night. She arrived for her job as a lowly assistant in the Office of the Sergeant at Arms at the U.S. Senate dressed in a middy blouse and pleated skirt, an outfit whose unattractiveness was enhanced by the spit curl that graced her forehead. It took some not-so-subtle hints from her boss to get her to upgrade her schoolgirl apparel. Within a year or two, the spit curl and long hair were gone, too, cut into a more fashionable bob.[39]

After only a few months at the Capitol, Mary Margaret was offered a job at the *Cleveland Press* at $35 a week. (The job offer came through her Missouri journalism buddy Pauline Pfeiffer, soon to be the second Mrs. Ernest Hemingway.) She received this brusque welcome from the editor on duty: "We are paying you $35. It's probably more than any woman reporter is worth. And if you aren't worth it, you will have to go!" She called her time at the *Cleveland Press* "the severest and most effective training I've ever experienced." One invaluable lesson she learned was how to meet the *Cleveland Press*'s standard of writing in words that could be understood by an imaginary foreign-born reader named Mike Zabosky. (She later put this training to good use in her radio show.) Working at a big city daily was an excellent apprenticeship, but she missed her family dearly, especially on her first holiday away from home when her expected Christmas package did not reach her in time. She spent the day in tears, watching a Mary Pickford movie at a local movie house and drinking chocolate ice-cream sodas.[40]

One of her local assignments unexpectedly offered her the ticket to New York that she had been waiting for. Her editors assigned her to cover an interfaith religious convention meeting in Cleveland, which turned quite fractious over the question of labor unions. "I had been brought up in a very strict Baptist home and was still close enough to my early training to believe that religion was something to treat very reverently,"[41] she recalled, so she left out the details of this unseemly fight in the story she filed. Her editor was livid, but the organizers of the interfaith movement (which included John D. Rockefeller Sr.) were so pleased with her "sober" coverage that they offered her a job in New York doing publicity for the group. The pay was $10 a week less than her newspaper job, but she snapped at the opportunity. "At last I was really on my way. Once I was actually in New York City, that great novel I was going to write would be only a matter of time."[42]

The great novel never was written, and the job at the interchurch organization didn't last long, but at least it introduced her to her lifelong companion, Stella Karn. Soon Mary Margaret landed a job at the *New York Evening Mail*. Like so many ambitious and talented young people who flocked to New York in the 1920s, once she finally got there, she never left.

9

Stella

A RADIO REPORTER once asked Stella Karn what she would want to be if she had her life to live over again. Her reply was quick and to the point: "The manager of Mary Margaret McBride."[1] Mary Margaret returned the compliment, pronouncing Stella Karn "the best manager a radio program ever could have." She added tellingly, "If we had not met in our early twenties, I am convinced I would have been out of radio forever before my first six months were ended."[2]

Mary Margaret and Stella first met in New York in 1920 when they both were doing publicity work for John D. Rockefeller's Interchurch Organization, a short-lived group set up to encourage interfaith cooperation and religious unity through missionary outreach. Stella had been brought in to revitalize the publicity wing. "I can see her now, a tiny creature, well under five feet, heavy red-brown hair in a great bun, brown eyes eager," Mary Margaret recalled. "Stella blew into our loft like a cyclone, overflowing with vitality and ideas."[3] Stella's last job had been managing publicity for a circus, and she did not bother to change her style in her new position. To Stella, the missionaries under her charge were simply "the mishes" (as in "My mishes have a lot of pep and zing"), and she treated them in much the same manner she had her charges at the circus. At first Mary Margaret was a bit put off by her brusqueness and big-city ways, but she and Stella soon became good friends and then roommates.[4]

Stella was six years older than Mary Margaret and much more worldly, an orphan who had run away from her guardian's home in San Francisco in her teens and who had been on her own ever since. Estella Hattie Kahn (she later changed her name to Karn, possibly during the anti-German hysteria of World War I)[5] was born in 1893 in Mansfield, Louisiana. Her mother died when she was quite young, and her father soon after, leaving Stella and a younger brother orphaned. The children

The dynamic duo: Mary Margaret and Stella. Who do you think is going to win this argument? *Reprinted by permission of Library of Congress, Prints and Photographs Division.*

were not kept together, and Stella was raised by relatives in San Francisco, where she had a miserable childhood dominated by an aunt and uncle who were "mean to her."[6] To support herself after she left home, she took various jobs, including cutting clippings for United Press, a time-honored start to a journalism career. After a stint as a press agent for an amusement park, she "joined out" with the circus. Ironically she had never even seen a circus because her aunt did not believe in such frivolities. "I sought the job because I wanted to travel. I had always wanted to go places, being eternally curious about the world and the people in it."[7] Years later on Mary Margaret's show, she kept the audience in stitches as she described taking a baby elephant named Pearl out for a stroll. "And from the back you couldn't tell which was Pearl and which was Stella!"[8] Much as Stella relished telling these stories after the fact, Mary Margaret knew better. "I often thought that she'd rather talk about being a circus press agent than to have to do it all over again."⁹

Stella never aspired to a career under the big top, but she was a crackerjack press agent. She crisscrossed small towns in the West several weeks in advance of the circus and sometimes would go as far east as Michigan and Maine. Was she ever lonesome?

> Of course I was—ahead of the show most of the time, and meeting only strangers every day. I used fairly to ache to have somebody call me by my first name. But I was interested in my work, and there was so much of it to do that I had little time to mope.¹⁰

Besides she had Cora and Ben to keep her company, Cora being her portable typewriter and Ben her alarm clock, necessary to make the early trains that would speed her on to her next assignment. Stella loved to hang out in the caboose, making friends with the brakemen and exchanging stories about life in wartime America. Less appealing were the traveling salesmen who came on to her, a single woman traveling alone. Finally she had a tramp printer make calling cards to hand out whenever a man tried to win her sympathy by launching into a familiar story. One read: *Yes, I know. Your wife doesn't understand you.* Another said: *I'm sorry that your wife is an invalid.*¹¹ End of conversation.

Press agents developed quite a feel for what made for a successful gig, and one of the first rules was that most communities could not support two major events in the same season. One year the circus's main competitor was a band of traveling evangelists, who in a spirit decidedly lacking in brotherhood, spread rumors that the circus was carrying smallpox, which caused the health authorities in one town to refuse to give them a permit. Stella got even. When she spied bundles of the evangelists' posters and promotional material on a railroad platform, she promptly rerouted them to another town in the opposite direction from the planned next stop. "The revival had to skip that town," Stella concluded smugly, "but we did very well there." When Mary Margaret first heard this story, she was appalled, but she gradually came around. Lightening up Mary Margaret and keeping her on an even emotional keel was a job that Stella had for the rest of their lives together.¹²

Circus folks have a phrase—"winging with the bluebirds"—to describe leaving their winter quarters and hitting the road with a new show in the spring. Over the years Mary Margaret noticed that each spring Stella would suddenly invent an emergency that necessitated a trip somewhere, her years as a circus press agent still giving her a seasonal urge to roam and escape the humdrum of ordinary life.[13] The same pattern affected Stella's choices of where to live. For a while she would take an apartment and throw herself into domesticity. Then she would begin to get restless, and "that old winging-with-the-bluebirds look would come into her eye." Soon she would escape to the impersonality of a hotel, which suited her temperament better. She loved to be able to order room service, have her bed made, her clothes cleaned and pressed by the staff, and generally be taken care of with only the responsibility of paying the bill. Given her insatiable curiosity for people and situations, she relished getting to know the hotel staff, from the desk clerks to the maids to the elevator operators, as well as her all-time favorites, the house detectives. (Stella would have made a fantastic house dick.) For the last decade of her life, she made her home at the Waldorf-Astoria.[14]

"Life was never dull where Stella was," Mary Margaret pointed out with probably a bit of awe and envy, adding she "enjoyed life more than anybody I've ever known and got more out of it."[15] Stella always had at least three telephones, all of which might be in use simultaneously—amazingly she was able to keep all the conversations straight. She also was well known for keeping every telephone book that ever was delivered to her office, not just for New York City but for other cities as well. She claimed that someday she might need to find an address that was not in the current phone book.[16]

Hoarding telephone directories was part of a pattern: Stella hoarded everything. Wherever she lived or worked was crammed to the gills with stuff. Her radio partner thought it "undoubtedly went back to the time when she was starting out, a poor little girl at sixteen, depending on her own efforts and never having enough of anything." A batch of unsent Christmas cards, vintage unknown and lacking only stamps, shared space with piles of newspapers waiting to be clipped. She loved getting Christmas gifts but usually didn't bother to open them. Once when dining out with a friend, she admired a set of steak knives. Taken aback, the woman pointed out that she had given Stella a set of steak knives the previous Christmas. When she was shamed into tracking down the gift in some obscure corner of her office, she found not one but three sets of knives from friends, along with boxes of decaying chocolates and some truly ancient fruitcakes. She bought dresses by the dozen, liked to have multiples of everything in case she ran out, and especially loved sales and auctions (a ten-foot-long jousting pole, of absolutely no use whatsoever, was one triumphant purchase). She never could resist a bargain and was especially partial to anything to do with elephants, no doubt a relic from her circus days.[17]

Stella also spent at an indiscriminate rate whether or not she had money and lent money in the same spirit, offering cash and a shoulder to cry on to an odd variety of lame ducks and sad souls, rarely getting anything in return. Like her impulse buying, Mary Margaret attributed this to her manager's hard luck growing up. Whenever she had a financial windfall, she would surprise friends with special gifts like a mink coat, a new refrigerator, or some other "trifle." But she made Mary Margaret buy her own mink coat before they journeyed to Mexico, Missouri, for "Mary Margaret McBride Day" in 1940. Stella was planning to wear hers, and if her partner did not have one, too, she reasoned, the fans and McBride family members would assume that her manager was stealing from her. Mary Margaret was so taken with that reasoning that she shared it with her listeners on the air the next day.[18]

Stella Karn was a woman of strong convictions. In 1945 she went to San Francisco to cover the opening of the United Nations, sharing her experiences and impressions with Mary Margaret's listeners back east. On her way home, a stop in Texas to see a nephew caused her to lose her priority for air travel back to New York. Taking this exclusion from the airways as a personal challenge, she discovered a loophole that allowed live freight to be sent if it met the airline's specifications. She then matter-of-factly informed the airline employees that she planned to travel in a specially constructed five-foot-square crate. Faced with that prospect, a seat on the next plane to New York miraculously opened up, first class no less.[19]

As the airlines luckily did not have to find out, Stella could be (in her partner's words) "terrifying when aroused." Once a New York police officer tried to give her a ticket for driving too slowly, but she was so incensed at his wasting his time on such an inconsequential matter that she announced that she was taking him to the station in her car to have him arrested. Another time she had a run-in with a live bear that was appearing on Mary Margaret's show. When he entered the control room of the studio, she shouted at him to get out. When the bear failed to respond, she punched him and he ripped her dress. His trainer said apologetically, "He had a cold and was scared of Stella."[20]

Stella did not just fight with bears: her battles with Mary Margaret were legendary, on everything from driving directions to specific sponsors to plans to have Mary Margaret enter Yankee Stadium on an elephant for her fifteenth anniversary celebration, one of the few times Stella didn't prevail. Stella told an interviewer that of course they sometimes quarreled—"Don't sisters and the closest of friends have their differences at times? But we always make up"[21]—but that benign rendering camouflaged the intensity and frequency of these tiffs. Usually these battles were in private, but occasionally they occurred in quite public venues, like on a live, transatlantic hookup from Norway in 1946. Stella was back in the studio in New York, so that she could tell Mary Margaret when to cut for the commercials. They began to run short on time, and Stella desperately prodded Mary Margaret to sign off. Finally she said, "If you in Norway don't shut up, you won't have any sponsors left when you get back." Replied the host, "Well! You can't tell me to shut up, and you can't tell the Ambassador's wife to shut up. She's here and she's going to talk—and if you want to know what I think about you—well, I think you ought to be lynched." Deadpanned Stella later, "It was probably the first time two women ever conducted a personal argument over an international network."[22]

Another passion of Stella's, somewhat surprising for such a confirmed urbanite, was country living. "I have never know a person who wanted to live in the country so much," recalled Mary Margaret,[23] and the two women often spent weekends driving around rural New Jersey, Pennsylvania, and New York checking out real estate for sale. In the spring of 1939, Mary Margaret was asked to judge the local apple blossom queen contest for Ulster County and she and Stella drove the ninety miles up from New York City for the event. They immediately fell in love with the area.[24]

Stella didn't find her dream property right that weekend, but soon afterward she found an old farmhouse on 185 acres of land that had formerly grown potatoes and supported an apple orchard. Hundreds of years earlier it had been part of the estate owned by Robert Livingston, the second governor of New York, who had received it as a land grant from the Dutch. Located in West Shokan, it had a view of the Ashokan Reservoir (a source of New York City's drinking water), the Hudson Valley, and the southern Catskills. Mary Margaret burst into tears when she first saw the property ("In the rain-soaked piggery, chicken house and other out-buildings that dismal day, I saw the dreary ghosts of rented farms in Missouri"),[25] but Stella bought it on the spot, and they used it as a weekend retreat whenever their hectic schedules allowed. They gardened, entertained, and shared their beautiful view with friends. The house wasn't fancy, nor was it winterized, but it suited them fine. Stella christened it "Dunrovin," a somewhat ironic name from a woman who literally never could stay still.[26]

Mary Margaret often broadcast her show from the farm during the summer months, with memorable results for host, guests, and listeners alike. "Some of my happiest broadcasts away from the studio were done on the stone terrace of Stella's farm in the Catskills with a view of mountains and water that reminded almost every guest of his favorite scenery wherever located—Scotland, Switzerland, Italy."[27] Sometimes she had guests up from New York. Other times she interviewed her West Shokan neighbors. Often she and Stella and their friends would simply sit around and reminisce. Her radio fans loved these shows. "I've never *really* been there," wrote one listener from New Jersey, "but I guess the happiest weekends of my life have been spent with Mary Margaret and Stella, up at the farm."[28]

Other than their similar shapes ("round and butterballish"), Mary Margaret and Stella always made a rather unusual couple. Remembered Mary Margaret, "No two people were more unlike. My reaction to a crisis was to dissolve in tears; Stella's was to charge into battle."[29] There really was no question about who was the stronger force in the relationship. "People say Stella bossed me, and I guess it was true," Mary Margaret admitted. "I did nearly everything she told me to, and the reason was that after I'd worked with her awhile I knew she was probably right." It is also just as possible that Mary Margaret liked being dominated and ordered around as long as it meant that she still had someone truly looking out for her needs.[30]

Nowhere were the differences between Stella and Mary Margaret more evident than in their attitude toward entertaining and guests. Stella loved to entertain and, in later years, often would invite "great crowds" to her farm for weekends. The more people who came, the happier she was, and she would make sure that they had a good time and were well taken care of. After a hard week in the city and probably facing a weekend's worth of reading in preparation for the next week's shows, Mary Margaret was not amused to find that she would be sharing her weekend with hoards of guests. "I loved people out there at the receiving sets and I loved the people I interviewed, but I didn't have time or inclination to be gracious and hostesslike every weekend."[31]

Given their personalities, one might have thought that it would be Mary Margaret who would bottle things up and Stella who would let fly, but in fact it was the reverse, as McBride remembered: "A month or six weeks would sometimes go by and she'd be rather cross with me the whole time, resenting something I had done or said, yet she'd never tell me what." When Mary Margaret was angry, she always had to do something to let off steam right away, and then she felt no more anger, just "remorse for my display of temper." Stella saw it differently: "Just because you say you're sorry doesn't mean that the other person isn't hurt." Yet just as often as not, it would be Stella who would arrive at Mary Margaret's apartment at midnight with a quart of ice cream to break her out of her despair, a technique that always seemed to succeed.[32]

This friendship forged on ice cream and a phenomenally successful radio show had its ups and downs, but it was life affirming for both women, each of whom would have been lost without the other. Not surprisingly, the depth of such a relationship between two unmarried women raises questions about whether there was a sexual undercurrent in or dimension to their long association. New York City (especially Greenwich Village) in these years was home to many female couples, often professional women who shared lives of varying degrees of intimacy.[33] Although the word *lesbian* would have appeared only rarely in the national press in this period, nonetheless Mary Margaret and Stella's relationship (which was widely reported in the news media) drew no special comment. Moreover, it is highly unlikely that in the 1920s, or even later, either woman would have chosen that description of herself. Although colleagues sometimes speculated about Stella's sexual orientation, Mary Margaret always presented herself as a single heterosexual woman who chose an exciting career over what she perceived as the constraints of marriage and motherhood.[34]

It is hard not to be struck by the ways in which their relationship did in fact replicate the patterns of long-term commitments between women in this era. These bonds were far deeper and more emotionally significant than just a substitute for marriages that never happened. Mary Margaret's and Stella's lives were intertwined for almost four decades. After their Greenwich Village days in the 1920s, they generally preferred to maintain separate residences, but their ties to each other were far stronger than to any members of their families, indeed to anyone else. When Stella faced a serious operation in 1946, Mary Margaret confessed to a friend that she was "frantic with worry about her." And when Stella died in 1957, she was devastated.[35]

The world of the 1920s and beyond was dotted with friendships like Mary Margaret and Stella's. They never felt any need to conceal or hide their relationship from their listeners or friends and openly (if testily) affirmed its importance. Mary Margaret presented her partnership with Stella as yet another open book, sharing its good times and bad with her listeners as a regular part of her radio show. But like so many other aspects of her life, especially in regard to her emotions, she didn't share everything. Mary Margaret McBride had invested an enormous amount of personal capital in creating a radio persona that connected with the lives and concerns of ordinary women. Even though she wasn't a housewife, wasn't married, didn't have children, and lived in the most cosmopolitan city in the country, she still was one of them. The facade of presumed heterosexuality served her well, allowing her to create a personal life with Stella that was potentially far more complex and unconventional than she let on.

Hometown girl makes good: Mary Margaret returns to the *Ledger* in 1940.
Reprinted by permission of Library of Congress, Prints and Photographs Division.

10

The Journalist and the Writer

"HOW I DO HOPE that French woman journalist who made the front page a while ago because of her parachute-jumping coverage of the war in Indo China hasn't started a trend," Mary Margaret Mcbride wrote in her nationally syndicated column in the 1950s, because "I don't believe I could bear to go through a second period of feeling as inadequate as I did when I was a cub reporter."[1] After the Interchurch movement folded soon after her arrival in New York, Mary Margaret dutifully made the rounds of the city's daily newspapers, but with no luck. New York was the Mecca for aspiring journalists in the 1920s, and there were at least sixty applicants for every job. Her finances became more and more desperate, her spirits lower and lower. And then an old contact offered her a job at $40 a week at the *New York Evening Mail* with this captivating pitch: "We need a girl who can cover fires dramatically and I thought of you at once."[2] Who could resist a job offer like that?

The ghosts of sensationalist stunt journalists Nellie Bly and Winifred Black were still very much alive when Mary Margaret broke into the field in 1921. "I've always thought that my permanent inferiority complex stems from the damaging fact that I could never get up the courage enough, even in the face of their examples, to pretend to be a criminal, an insane person or even a chambermaid for the sake of my by-line." She concluded, "I think now I was probably born too meek to make a really good reporter."[3] As usual, she sold herself short. As Ishbel Ross, herself a pioneering female journalist, wrote in her 1936 survey, *Ladies of the Press*, Mary Margaret McBride was "as smart a newspaper girl as ever scaled a ship ladder before dawn to listen to the bubblings of visiting celebrity."[4]

"Women reporters were not popular in city rooms in the early twenties when I got a job on the *New York Evening Mail*,"[5] Mary Margaret McBride announced sanguinely, but that did not stop her, and many other young women in the 1910s and 1920s, from choosing journalism as a career. Journalism promised more stimulation and rewards than did the traditional fields usually open to women, such as teaching or social work. Being a journalist offered a glamorous and exciting way to see the world, or at least to get out of one's home town, plus the chance to work side by side with men. "It's hard to explain the fascination of newspaper work," McBride later admitted. "I am sure that men feel it as much as women, and once you've had it, no matter where you go or what you do, no matter how much money you make or how famous you become, your proudest boast is still that you were once a newspaperman."[6]

Note that she did not call herself a *newspaperwoman*. Women who entered the field of journalism in the 1920s wanted nothing more than to be treated like regular newspaper folks—as individuals, regardless of sex. They asked for no special treatment and wanted no special attention. All they wanted was the chance to do their job as well as anybody else, men included. A 1924 editorial in *The Matrix*, the organ of the journalistic sorority Theta Sigma Phi, exhorted, "All we can do is to decide what we want to do, regardless of our sex, and keep on demanding and achieving the right to be treated as human beings, not as women, when we seek a job and when we fill one."[7] Ishbel Ross noted that the highest compliment that could be paid to a woman reporter was "the city editor's acknowledgment that their work is just like a man's."[8]

This stance was very much in keeping with a moment in postsuffrage women's history in which women, having won the vote in 1920, now believed that it was up to their sex to go forward and succeed as individuals, eschewing much of the gender consciousness that had united activists in the women's suffrage campaign. This rising generation of women, who did not necessarily consider themselves feminists and often assumed that an organized women's movement was no longer necessary, wanted to live, love, and work alongside men in an increasingly heterosocial world that was a far cry from the settlement houses, women's colleges, and women's voluntary associations that had shaped earlier women's contributions to public life. Women like Mary Margaret McBride were proud of women's accomplishments and defended women's rights to do whatever they pleased, but on a case-by-case basis. This emphasis on being treated as individuals, not women, was probably best captured by what Connecticut politician

Chase Going Woodhouse proposed for her tombstone: "Born a woman. Died a human being."[9]

The problem was that the workplace of the 1920s was not quite ready for gender equality, even if individual women were. As an area of women's professional employment, journalism grew steadily in the 1910s and 1920s: the 1930 census counted 14,786 women in the category of editors and reporters, up from 7,105 in 1920.[10] Even though women comprised approximately one-quarter of the journalism field by 1930, they still often found themselves confined to certain segments of the profession, especially the dreaded women's pages. The women's pages were often called "hen coops" for their out-of-the-way location, and few women reporters willingly ended up there. (In the 1950s McBride pointedly told the convention of the Managing Editors Association that women's pages should be abolished.)[11] Somewhat better off in pay and prestige were the so-called sob sisters, the derogatory (male) term for general women reporters on daily papers who were automatically expected to have a natural feminine talent for writing sad, heartbreaking stories. But at least they got to participate in the camaraderie of the city room rather than be relegated to the hen coop. Other women journalists excelled in feature writing and dominated the syndicates, a measure of their inroads into the profession, but in the 1920s it was still a rare woman like Lorena Hickok or Emma Bugbee who had a front-page byline and regular assignments to cover hard, fast-breaking news.[12]

Freshly hired reporter McBride was quickly put in her place. "I functioned as the *Mail's* sob sister, a title I vaguely resented but seemed to be able to do nothing about."[13] Although most sob sisters didn't in fact sob, Mary Margaret often did cry on the job, such as when she wrote stories about poor children in the tenements or when she was thrown out of a courtroom in the middle of a murder trial for reading a newspaper:

> The assumption that I was only good for one type of story made me feel like a sort of second-class citizen, but I was still unmodern enough to like the fact that even in this busy, noisy news factory the men behaved with considerable chivalry. They never told dirty stories or swore when I was around—often I'd see one gesture to another to warn him of my approach—and they often took me out for coffee or a sandwich.

Showing her prefeminist consciousness, she added, "They would have been shocked, I'm sure, if I had offered to pay my share, and it would never have occurred to me."[14]

As one of only two women on the *Evening Mail*, it was automatically assumed that McBride would cover mainly stories relating to her sex. She recalled being "hustled out to interview female firsts whenever they came along" because these stories rated as front-page news: "Thirty years ago, a woman who tried a case in court or became head of a business or ran for any public office, even dog-catcher, was a sort of seven-day wonder and was made the most of in adjectives and headlines."[15] She interviewed Viscountess Rhonnda, a British feminist and political leader who talked to her about her favorite theme: woman's political progress. Nevada feminist Anne Martin, the first woman to run for the United States Senate, told her that American women had to get over their inferiority complex before they could influence politics. McBride also covered the League of Women Voters and various women's peace organizations.[16]

Feminism had not been part of Mary Margaret McBride's vocabulary when she was growing up. One reason is that the word had come into general use only in the 1910s, replacing earlier phrases like "the woman question" or "women's emancipation."[17] More fundamentally, the young, naïve, but ambitious girl from Missouri did not connect her individual strivings with the wider cause of women: "I knew all about the pioneers in the field I hoped to enter—Dorothy Dix and Winifred Black, front-page sob sisters—but not much about that group of dedicated crusaders, Jane Addams, Carrie Chapman Catt and the rest who were making a new world for women."[18] Once she arrived in New York, however, she found feminism and women's issues impossible to avoid. An interview with Anne Morgan of the American Woman's Association challenged her to connect what she was covering as a reporter and her life as a woman. When McBride began to ask questions, Morgan turned the tables on the cub reporter, pointedly asking

> what I thought about life and my sex and I believe she was horrified to find that I had very little knowledge or appreciation of what had been done for my generation by the women who had gone before. I hadn't known I was taking it for granted until she scolded me.[19]

Eventually McBride did break out of the sob-sister mold, and yes, she did get to cover a big fire, which got her her first front-page by-line. From 1921 to 1924, her name constantly appeared in the paper, where she was under contract for $100 a week. Her favorite assignment was meeting the celebrities as they disembarked in New York Harbor after an ocean journey from Europe. Emotionally she had her high and low points, mainly fueled by her ongoing insecurity about her talent, her personal life, and her ambition as a writer, but she could take pride in the successful launch of her journalism career, in New York City no less.[20]

During her time on the *Evening Mail*, Mary Margaret had not given up her childhood dream of writing the great American novel. Indeed, no theme looms larger in Mary Margaret McBride's personal autobiography than this ambition. What this great work of fiction was supposed to be about she never said, although since most of her writing drew heavily on her Missouri background, it probably would have been based on her early life. Perhaps she saw herself as a female Sherwood Anderson writing the equivalent of *Winesburg, Ohio* or another Sinclair Lewis, although she never showed any evidence of the kind of biting satire with which Lewis dissected small-town life in books like *Main Street* and *Babbitt*. In many ways McBride was closer to the writings of Laura Ingalls Wilder or the early Willa Cather. But all those writers had a gift, and she, rather abruptly, realized that she didn't.

Her epiphany came during her newspaper days. At first Mary Margaret convinced herself that she was just marking time on the *Evening Mail* and that her New York experiences were exactly what she needed for this as yet unformed piece of great literature. Then one otherwise ordinary day as she was reading a story that was going to run in the next edition of the paper, she suddenly began to feel dizzy. Always one to dramatize her situation, she claimed a voice inside her was saying: "This is all you're capable of. This is the best you can do. You are a third-rate writer and you'll never be anything else." She continued, "The worst was that I knew instantly that it was all true." Her colleagues rushed to help her as she collapsed at her desk. Stella found her crying in front of the Western Union office, about to send her mother a telegram announcing her imminent return to Missouri. But Stella wisely steered Mary Margaret to the nearest Schrafft's for some cake and ice cream, and the crisis passed.[21]

In the multiple retellings of this epiphany, her near breakdown oc-
curs fairly close in time to when the *Evening Mail* was sold to Frank
Munsey in 1924, which caused her to lose her job. The 1920s was a period of intense newspaper consolidation, especially in New York City,
which had fourteen major dailies at the turn of the century but only six
by 1931. Between 1916 and 1924 Frank Munsey, who had earned the
nickname "Grand Executioner" by steadily buying and combining a
string of New York dailies, merged seven papers, including the *Evening
Mail*, into three—the *Herald*, the *Sun*, and the *Telegram*. In 1924 he sold
the *Herald* to Ogden Reid, who merged it with the *Tribune* to create the
New York Herald-Tribune. Two by-products of these consolidations were
extensive layoffs and fewer jobs available for editors and reporters. *Editor and Publisher* estimated that six hundred people were likely to be
fired as part of the *Herald-Tribune* merger, including as many as one
hundred reporters.[22]

Mary Margaret McBride was twenty-five years old when the
Evening Mail folded. She wondered whether she would ever have a by-
line again. (Her last story in the *Mail* was headlined "Chicken Raising
Catches Millionaires and Mechanics Alive.")[23] She could have sought a
job at one of New York's three tabloids: the phenomenally successful
Daily News, founded in 1919, or the *Graphic* or the *Mirror*, both established in 1924. As Ishbel Ross noted, women "were welcomed with
warmth in the city rooms of the tabloids."[24] Instead, McBride used the
liberation from the demands of a daily newspaper job and, more specifically, a generous severance package, to forge a much more lucrative career as a freelance writer of magazine articles.

Once again it was Stella who prodded and spurred Mary Margaret
to rethink her career by exhorting, "This is your great chance. You have
nothing to do, so you can write for magazines."[25] After the Interchurch
movement folded, Stella had found a niche doing promotional work in
the music field through the Leo Feist Music Corporation, and one of her
clients was the white bandleader Paul Whiteman, who called himself
(or perhaps Stella did) the "King of Jazz." Out of that association came
a four-part series of articles, under the joint byline of Whiteman and
Mary Margaret McBride, that chronicled the new phenomenon of jazz
for the readers of the *Saturday Evening Post*. To Mary Margaret, the by-
line on the cover "seemed like the most magical thing in the world. The
Post ranked with the Bible and the Sears, Roebuck catalogue where I
came from. To have my first stuff in it was like a dream."[26] Perhaps be-

cause of that intended audience, the articles (and the book that followed) somehow managed to talk about jazz without mentioning that
this was a field pioneered and dominated by African American artists.[27]

Fulfilling Stella's expectations, over the next few years Mary Margaret prospered as a freelance writer, becoming one of the top (and best-
paid) feature writers of the decade and gaining invaluable experience
for her future career on the radio. Her nonfiction appeared regularly in
Harper's Bazaar and *McCall's*, as well as the upscale *Country Gentleman*.
None of this writing was terribly erudite or serious, however, and one
wonders whether she regretted how far she had strayed from her earlier literary ambitions. An especially light piece of fluff was a book entitled *Charm: A Book about It, and Those Who Have It, for Those Who Want
It*, coauthored with Alexander Williams. Mary Margaret later found it
such an embarrassment that she claimed it had been written only because she desperately needed money during the Depression. Actually it
was published in 1927.[28]

McBride was especially in demand as a ghost writer or, as she referred to herself, "a demi-ghost," since she received byline credit, writing "as told to" articles about people like Prince Christopher of Greece,
opera singer Marion Tally, and David Sarnoff (her first introduction to
the new medium of radio). Ghosting took special skills as an interviewer and a writer, especially the ability to extract a story and then
retell it in words that sounded like the subject and not the writer. When
the article sounds "more like me than the ghostee," it is fatal to "a good
ghost style."[29] In many ways, McBride's success in ghostwriting foreshadowed her success as a radio interviewer: she kept the focus on her
guests and was dedicated to drawing them out and making them the
focus of the program while she performed the role of facilitator by moving the conversation along. Doing that required a great deal of skill,
plus a willingness to cede the limelight, exactly the skills that had made
her so successful as a ghostwriter. In contrast, this inability or unwillingness to develop a personal voice of her own hampered her efforts to
grow and develop as a writer.

Whether she was writing journalism, fiction, or autobiography,
Mary Margaret's approach never really changed. "As for my writing
methods, I put everything off until the last possible moment, then I go
to it like an insane person and work night and day." She was a strong
believer in writing multiple drafts of an essay and did not think there
was such a thing as overrevision. Her tendency to keep reworking a

piece, plus the procrastination that led her to put it off until the last moment, meant that her agent often had to literally tear the manuscript pages from her hands in order to make deadlines.[30]

Before her radio days, McBride went back and forth between magazine articles and books, although many of her books read like extended magazine articles. In the late 1920s she arrived at a successful formula with her friend and fellow journalist Helen Josephy, who had been her travel companion on several trips to Europe. At the time it was still somewhat unusual for Americans to go abroad, especially women traveling alone or with other women. They pitched that idea to publishers, and the result was a series of travel books, like early Fodor guides, which talked about shopping, where to stay, local customs, and interesting things to do. The first of these collaborations to appear was *Paris Is a Woman's Town* (1929), followed by *London Is a Man's Town (But Women Go There)* (1930), *New York Is Everybody's Town* (1931), and finally *Beer and Skittles: A Friendly Guide to Modern Germany* (1932). The first two books were best-sellers, but the New York and Germany guides failed to find a market, hardly surprising in light of the deepening worldwide depression and Hitler's rise to power. In fact, the worsening political situation in Germany was never even mentioned in the final guide, which in retrospect made its light tone even more incongruous.[31]

During this time McBride and her agent also tried to place several pieces of fiction, but with little success. A story called "Pastorale," which chronicled the burdens of a farm wife and mother, was rejected by *Country Gentleman* because it lacked a strong plot and by *Pictorial Review* because it was "too slight."[32] A fragment of a story about a young girl who goes to the city to become a social service worker has sentences like this: "She had been too indolent all her life to argue and as she grew older, her luscious girlish curves turned into rolls of fat and her china-blue eyes glazed from pouring over the bad print of cheap love stories." Another story called "Prudence Studies Harmony" is a vapid tale of a snooty girl who excludes a schoolmate from her birthday party. What all these attempts at fiction have in common is an overreliance on a farm childhood fairly similar to Mary Margaret's and an inability to draw meaningful characters or to move the plot forward in a credible manner.[33]

Was anything really lost by Mary Margaret's realization that she was never going to write the Great American Novel? Surviving evidence suggests not. Over the course of her career, she wrote three autobiographical memoirs, two nonfiction books, countless articles, and several fictionalized children's books. Her prose is workmanlike, and her stories are mildly interesting, but nothing jumps off the page. Since she was not an adventurer or gambler, she rarely took risks, either personally or in her writing. She certainly had plenty of emotional crises to plumb for material, but her analysis never got below the surface. So she let it go.

But she never overcome her nagging sense of failure. "I once wanted to be a great writer," she told an interviewer in the 1940s, but "I'm an eighth grade one."[34] In 1960 the final words of the third and final installment of her autobiography return to this theme:

> I do have to acknowledge that life has defeated me in one particular. I wanted to be a good writer, and now I never shall be. The trouble was, I suppose, that I wanted to be a writer but I didn't especially want to write, and, anyway, I had nothing of consequence to say. So I was far better off as a day-to-day talker than as a would-be creative writer breaking my heart trying to reach the stars.[35]

She's right, of course, on all counts. Luckily she had talents in other directions which she had the sense (and the opportunity) to pursue.

Mary Margaret in her version of urban sophistication, 1920s. *Reprinted by permission of Library of Congress, Prints and Photographs Division.*

11

Men, Marriage, and Sex

"A YOUNG MAN KISSED ME AT HIS PERIL. I either slapped him or assumed he wanted to marry me."[1] As a young woman recently arrived in the big city, Mary Margaret McBride was not exactly an adventuresome participant in the supposed sexual and social revolutions of the 1920s. Raised as a strict Baptist and a teetotaler since the age of eight, she found the new mores of Greenwich Village confusing, even sometimes offensive. "Imagine my genuine horror, then, to find that nearly all the girls and women I met in the city both smoked and drank. And, what I thought worse, they did it as a matter of course, with no apologies and no indirectness. They even offered them to me!" The only time she tried smoking, she "expected lightning to strike me for the deed, but nothing happened except that the cigarette tasted terrible."[2] One memorable afternoon Stella, who had a cigarette practically permanently attached to her lips and did not share her roommate's temperance sympathies, came home to find Mary Margaret at the sink, self-righteously washing the liquor off the expensive brandied peaches that Stella had splurged on for dessert.[3]

Stella referred to this period of their lives as their "F. Scott Fitzgerald recipe for the twenties": "You know, a Greenwich Village apartment, Bohemian friends, long nights of talk about books to be written and pictures to be painted."[4] Mary Margaret painted a much tamer picture of Greenwich Village as "a nice country town where you were trusted at the corner grocer and where the iceman would take the mice out of the traps."[5] According to cultural historian Caroline F. Ware's 1935 study of Greenwich Village, they both were right. Ware's study showed a changing neighborhood in the 1920s, where Italian and Irish immigrants lived in densely knit ethnic communities alongside native-born professionals, often young and single, who saw Greenwich Village merely as an interesting place of residence. In fact, one of the attractions for these new residents besides affordable rents was the ability to go about their business, to keep to themselves, freed from any notions of enforced neighborhood conformity. As more of these young professionals moved in, the old ties that bound the ethnic neighborhoods weakened. In a telling statistic, by 1930 Greenwich Village housed proportionally more single people than did the rest of Manhattan and New York City as a whole: 48.2 percent of the men and 40 percent of the women were single.[6]

As to Greenwich Village's reputation for bohemianism, Ware concluded that it was "imposed from without" and did not really reflect those who lived there. Instead of fixating on its image of unconventional behavior, she placed Greenwich Village in the context of changing cultural values after World War I. "Many who were drawn to the Village came to seek escape from their community, their families, or themselves. Others who did not altogether repudiate the background from which they had come sought to reconcile new conditions with whatever remained of their traditional ways." She subsequently divided the population into those who upheld traditional values, those who totally repudiated them, and a "great mass" in between.[7] Mary Margaret and Stella belonged in the great mass in between category.

Happy to live in a neighborhood where they could take advantage of its reputation for bohemianism, even though their lives were more humdrum than daring, these two young women joined thousands of others who flocked to Greenwich Village in that decade. They often were broke, but that did not stop them from enjoying their urban adventure. Stella was an inveterate party giver even when their finances did not allow for entertaining, being of the school of thought that when you didn't have much money was precisely the time to be spending it. But sometimes Mary Margaret would get into what Stella called her "solitary mood" stage, during which she would shut herself in her bedroom and refuse to come out. Given the layout of the apartment they shared with one other friend, this produced some odd situations, as when Mary Margaret emerged in the middle of a dinner party that Stella was giving (and which she had refused to attend), stomped out, and returned ten minutes later with a stack of ripe bananas. No explanations were offered to the somewhat startled guests.[8]

Like so many other of Mary Margaret's memories, this period in her life is associated with food. When they couldn't afford to eat out, Mary Margaret and Stella indulged in creative cookery at home, with their most noted improvisation being a dish called "Chaos," which was composed of whatever happened to be left over in the icebox. Their favorite version consisted of canned tamales, canned corn, green peppers, pimientos, chili sauce, and (if finances permitted), a slice or two of bacon on top, all cooked in one pot for easy eating and cleaning up. Mary Margaret told this story on the radio so often over the years (and also gave out the recipe) that many of her listeners probably improvised their own versions of "Chaos" on numerous occasions.[9]

Soon after she was settled in her new job, Mary Margaret realized her ambition of bringing her mother to New York City for a visit. The trip was not without complications: Mrs. McBride arrived on a different train than the one her daughter met and promptly, though she had never been in a taxi before in her life, arranged for one to take her to her daughter's apartment. Mary Margaret had been worried about how her mother would react to her new life and how her friends would interact with a woman who had spent her whole life on the Missouri prairie, but her friends soon were fighting to show her around the city, especially Stella who considered her something of a second mother. Mrs. McBride proved herself absolutely unflappable when it came to big-city ways. For example, after a trip to Coney Island where she happened to see the scantily clad vaudeville dancers, her only comment was "Poor girls. How glad I am that Sister doesn't have to do that for a living." Thereafter Mrs. McBride made yearly visits whenever her daughter's finances allowed.[10]

In some ways Mrs. McBride fared better at accepting New York on its own terms than did her daughter, who described herself as "abnormally unsophisticated and serious even for my time." Compared with the talented urbanites she met when she arrived in New York, Mary Margaret realized that "in truth, I might as well have been a South Sea Islander come among them for all I knew of them and their ways." At least that is how she always presented herself, never sharing in print or interviews a less starkly black-and-white picture of her behavior. It wasn't just a question of learning new ways; the real difference was in moral standards: "Right and wrong ran in widely separated parallel lines and never the twain could meet. But no one in the city seemed to care about right and wrong as I knew them. These people used a different yardstick." As a result, her initial tendency was to classify everyone she met as "downright wicked, even depraved," even when on further acquaintance they turned out to be decent, friendly souls who didn't fit her old notions of sinners.[11]

Accepting that friends might smoke, drink, or (heavens) even be divorced was difficult, but the general openness about sex in mixed company was the most shocking to the country girl, who remembered when she was growing up that there were certain things you would never discuss in front of your father or brother, let alone a casual acquaintance. She quickly realized it was more than just sex: "The doctrine preached everywhere I went was freedom—freedom from taboos, from old established loyalties such as religion, patriotism, and monogamy. . . . I was fascinated and shocked. My first impulse was to bolt out of the room, my second to linger as inconspicuously as possible and hear more of this." In the end she lingered and grew more tolerant but never strayed all that far from her country ways. Or if she did, she wasn't telling.[12]

Mary Margaret finally felt so dissatisfied with her inability to make peace with this new behavior that she saw a psychiatrist. (Of course even the fact of seeking out psychiatric help, which would have been unheard of back home in Missouri, was a sign of increased urban sophistication.) His not terribly profound diagnosis was that she was "the victim of a clash between my old and new environments" and would eventually adjust, which of course she did. Just as important to her increasing tolerance was Stella's steadying influence. In the end Mary Margaret accepted that "I probably would be—had been—influenced by my new environment, but I did not need to be coerced by it."[13]

Despite all her protestations and self-flagellation, Mary Margaret kept up a fairly active social life and even had a blind date on the first day that she arrived in New York. For a time she kept company with a married man who worked in her office, although she was the last to know about his marital status and immediately broke it off when she found out. She had come to New York to have a career, not find a husband, and that remained her top priority.[14]

Actually there was someone who wanted to marry her, the only time that she seriously doubted her ambitions to remain single, have a career, and become a writer. His name was Richard (Dick) Dorris, and he had been a classmate at the state university. "As much as I loved him," she later told an interviewer about this college romance, "I can remember thinking to myself, 'I'll never marry you. I'm going to New York to become a great writer.'"[15] For a long time after she left Missouri, she wore his ring as a token of their mutual affection and informal engagement, although she kept putting him off when he mentioned marriage. Sexual experimentation was definitely not part of their courtship: "Caution, aspiration, the protectiveness of the young man and luck got me through this period without my becoming, in the parlance of my world, a fallen woman."[16] More than thirty years later, McBride astonished a young television writer assigned to preinterview her for *Night Beat*, Mike Wallace's popular television show, by asserting, "You know, I am in my late fifties and I'm still a virgin." He told his boss that she would never repeat that on the air, but sure enough, she did, to great and general astonishment.[17]

Although she never engaged in premarital sex, Mary Margaret came awfully close to succumbing to Dick's proposal of marriage. At one point when she was feeling especially maladjusted in New York, she convinced herself that where she really belonged was home in Missouri with a husband. When Dick told her that he was still "cherishing an unattainable ideal," she hinted that she was open to his proposal. But the more time she spent in Missouri (and away from New York City), the more she realized that her "vision of a nice little house, with me in a pink apron presiding over everything and never thinking of using a typewriter, except maybe to make out the housekeeping accounts" was totally unrealistic.[18] In the end she let him down gently and returned to New York. He married another Missouri woman not long afterward.[19]

For women of Mary Margaret's generation, marriage and career were often seen as either/or choices. "Why, the fact is I gave up the idea of a husband and child, before I had them, for New York!" she exclaimed after she started on the air as Martha Deane.[20] Thinking back about her decision not to marry her suitor, she summarized her reasoning in this way: "I suppose it was the fear of settling down too, of never knowing first hand what was going on in the world, that kept me from marrying him. . . . I know that I would always have felt a lack if I had chosen that life."[21] Reflecting on marriage in general, she concluded, "If I'd married the first man that came along and settled down on a farm with children, I'd have made him miserable."[22] She added revealing, almost as an afterthought, "I have been in love."[23]

As supportive as Mary Margaret was of modern women's desire to break new ground, she harbored no illusions about the difficulties of such choices. A 1929 piece for *Scribner's* entitled "Marriage on a Fifty-Fifty Basis" was a cautionary tale of five marriages in which the wife's new freedom of expression and professional advancement dramatically undermined the husband's "masculine pride." Only if the wife was "tactful enough to permit masculine dignity to assert itself," McBride argued, which basically meant putting her career on the back burner, did the marriage have a chance to survive.[24] The next year she set out to interview women who were ten years or so younger than herself, women the age (early twenties) she had been when she first came to New York. "In my role of feminist and professional woman, I had expected to create a little sensation of my own by telling them that the best career the average woman can have is marriage," and yet the pendulum had already swung so far in that direction that she ended up calling the piece "Husband Hunting: The 1930 Girl Has Her Own Ideas about Woman's Best Career."[25]

Given the difficulties of combining marriage and career in the 1920s (and later), the choices of women like Mary Margaret and many of her friends to stay single make more sense. The writer Edna Ferber once observed to Mary Margaret that people often asked her why she never married, but she never regretted it. McBride continued, "She feels she was kind of born for work and that work had been enough. My dream of writing was like that."[26] But Mary Margaret did not argue that the life of singlehood was total bliss. Her "Husband Hunting" piece concluded pessimistically, "I know intimately a good many successful women who have never married, and with a few exceptions I think it fair to say that they are less happy than those women of my acquaintance who have married and had children."[27]

Perhaps part of this unhappiness came not from being unmarried but from remaining childless, which in the 1920s (although not today) were usually synonymous. Because she was so devoted to her mother, Mary Margaret set very high standards for herself as a potential wife and parent, standards that she realized would have been impossible to meet if she had kept up her career. But she never gave up the dream of having children, especially a daughter. In her autobiography she quoted this exchange with a fellow newspaperwoman and self-described "spinster," Nell Snead of the *Kansas City Star*, who once said to her half-jokingly, "Every woman ought to be allowed one baby and no questions asked." Added Mary Margaret parenthetically, "I agree with her whole heartedly."[28]

Once she even flirted with the idea of making the dream a reality. On a trip to Italy in the late 1920s, she had a fling with an Italian referred to in her memoirs as both Caesare and Tony. Her Neapolitan flame, "dark-haired, dark-eyed and ardent," was a career civil servant who took her on wonderful excursions around the city and its neighboring environs. She actually considered marrying him in order to get pregnant, have his child (she wanted a daughter), and return alone to New York where she could raise her child far from the fascism that already was gripping Italy. Nothing ever came of that idea, and she soon concluded that she had been seduced (only figuratively) by his "making her feel like an 18th-century heroine" or, she added tellingly, "perhaps it was his taste in restaurants." (With Mary Margaret, food and love were always intimately connected.) Much later she retold the story on television, and it was picked up by the wire services, causing much chagrin back in Missouri. "If only someone had asked I would have told them I intended to marry him FIRST." From the perspective of thirty years or so, she could now treat the whole episode flippantly: "Besides my love lasted as long as my command of Italian—I don't speak it, you know."[29]

There must have been some point at which Mary Margaret realized that she was not likely to marry or have children. In an Associated Press column from the 1950s, she set thirty as the age when an unmarried woman would be considered a spinster, and she would have reached that age in 1929.[30] Fortuitously she entered radio soon afterward, and her work became her life, her radio audience her family. Plus there were always her friends, her beloved mother, and her complicated but immensely rewarding relationship with Stella. Over the years she would say at regular intervals, "When I retire, I am going to marry a nice old-time newspaperman and run a nice country newspaper,"[31] and maybe she really did think that. And yet once she was safely settled in West Shokan, she admitted, "I'm glad I don't have a husband to clutter my converted barn home."[32]

Mary Margaret and Pierrot, a souvenir of a European vacation. Unfortunately, U.S. customs officials were not so charmed, and the goat was sent back to France. *Reprinted by permission of Library of Congress, Prints and Photographs Division.*

12

Affluence and Depression

MARY MARGARET McBRIDE once referred to the 1920s as the "nonsense era," which she linked to "people trying to shake off the memory of a frightening war."[1] In retrospect the whole decade had an air of unreality to her. Freshly arrived from Missouri and determined to make her way in the big city, she landed a job, lost it, was hired by a newspaper, lost that job, and started freelancing. For extended periods of time she was broke or just barely getting by. Then, when her magazine career took off in mid-decade, she had the first glimmerings of affluence: a bigger apartment in a fancier neighborhood, nice clothes, entertaining and travel with friends, money in a savings account. She enjoyed her newfound luxury, but it was all so foreign to her that she didn't really have time to become accustomed to it. Showing the lingering effects of her impoverished and uncertain childhood, she believed deep down that it was "too good to last and not right anyway."[2]

One of the manifestations of her newly acquired affluence was her ability to travel abroad. On assignment in 1926 to interview exiled royalty in Europe, Mary Margaret was able to fulfill her lifelong ambition of taking her mother to Europe. It was a very sentimental journey for her. Traveling with Stella, the three women set sail for Le Havre, whereupon Stella promptly produced a shot of brandy disguised as cherry bounce as a remedy for the teetotaler Mrs. McBride's seasickness. Mary Margaret was never much of a sightseer (Stella accused her of preferring to settle into a nice hotel with a stack of American magazines and a box of chocolates), but Mrs. McBride saw more than her share of the sights in France, Switzerland, Germany, and Spain. She especially enjoyed Marie Antoinette's play dairy at the Petit Trianon at Versailles, although as a lifelong farm woman, she was a bit perplexed as to why a queen would want to churn butter for her own amusement.[3] It is revealing that Mary Margaret's father was not included in this excursion to Europe paid for by his now prosperous daughter, nor was he in any

other of the earlier trips to New York City. Mary Margaret always resented what her father had put her mother through, and she seemed to
see no reason to reward him for his past behavior.[4]

Just around the time of this European trip with her mother, Thomas
McBride came into a small inheritance, which he used to settle all the
debts he had accumulated over the years in Missouri and to move his
family to Florida. But his old ways quickly returned. Mary Margaret
wasn't fooled:

> Florida in the mid-twenties was full of men like my father who,
> though they had never been conventional speculators, had really fol-
> lowed that kind of life from the time they began to work, for certainly
> nothing is more speculative than farming. . . . With his impulsive Irish
> temperament it was inevitable that once in Florida he should have em-
> barked with zest upon the boom.[5]

Although Mr. McBride bought an orange grove near Orlando, he devoted most of his energies to speculating in the real estate mania sweeping across the state, putting down small amounts of money on lots, $50
or $100 at a time, and expecting to resell them for large profits—with-
out telling his family what he was up to. When a hurricane hit Florida
in 1926, it destroyed his speculations, and those of many others in this
get-rich-quick state.[6]

Mary Margaret had to come down to sort through his sorry financial affairs, a humiliating prospect for her father. She later described the
effect on him in more revealing language than usual:

> Though my father could still rise to heights of the old childlike enthu-
> siasm, the Florida catastrophe had a sobering effect on him. Perhaps it
> also made him less confident that whatever he decided was right. In
> the old days it seemingly never occurred to him that he could be
> wrong. Also, with his old-fashioned ideas about woman's place being
> in the home, it was galling to have me a witness to his humiliating fail-
> ure. Apparently, too, he began to realize that he was no longer a young
> man.

In the end she sold off the orange grove (the real estate was worthless)
and bought her parents a small house in Winter Park.[7]

As Florida goes, so goes the nation, or to put it another way, like father, like daughter—Mary Margaret was about to duplicate her father's folly. "Like millions of other Americans, I too had become a speculator. I was playing the stock market on margin."[8] In fact, it was her paper profits that made it possible for her to take her mother to Europe and then settle her father's financial difficulties. Of course, she could have cashed in her stocks and paid off the two mortgages right then and there, but the rich acquaintance who was her stock market mentor convinced her that her money was much better invested in the stock market than in a house. "I didn't agree with him then and I certainly don't agree with him now," she later recalled. "If I'd paid completely for the house as I had the money at the time to do, I would have been spared many agonizing hours later."[9]

It is impossible to describe the next five years of Mary Margaret's life without the specter of the 1929 stock market crash and ensuing depression hanging over the story. At the time, of course, she and millions of others had no inkling that the much vaunted prosperity of the 1920s was about to evaporate and that the country would soon be plunged into a decade-long economic contraction that would be the worst in its history.[10] Personally, however, she was probably more open to a sense of foreboding than most Americans were, since she had always been subject to extreme ups and downs in her emotional life. She was flying high in the late 1920s, as her travel companion Helen Josephy pointed out on one of their last trips abroad: "You have life licked at last. Everything's just the way you want it. I'll bet you never again go through all those awful downs."[11] But now she was ready to crash, in both senses of the word. As she concluded in her characteristically pessimistic frame of mind, "You never 'succeed' for keeps. Reach your goal and rest on your laurels, and before you know it the props will be knocked right out from under you."[12]

In her 1959 memoir, A Long Way from Missouri, McBride left a detailed and sobering account of how smart people got taken in by the stock market frenzy and literally lost their shirts. It started when a male acquaintance who had quite a lot of money established credit for her and Stella at his broker's. Soon the small initial purchases on credit became so valuable that they had enough paper profits not to need guaranteeing by their benefactor. Then the stocks were sold, and they started over again with new stocks purchased by their initial profits. "Nobody seemed able to lose," Mary Margaret remembered, "at least nobody who had the kind of 'expert' advice we were getting."[13]

At the beginning of 1927 she had already earned paper profits of $21,000, which were quickly reinvested in the bull market, where they had quadrupled by year's end, despite her having used some of the money for a down payment for her parents' house in Florida. Then with one stunning deal, she and Stella made enough to take a two-year lease on an elegant Park Avenue apartment. "At least it *would* have paid our rent for two years if we had then and there taken it out of the market, labeled it 'rent' and socked it in the bank. Of course we did nothing of the kind." They were hardly alone. Stella was a born gambler, but Mary Margaret had always regarded the stock market as somewhat sinful, the money made there as not quite real. Yet she proved unable to resist the temptation of what seemed like a harmless pursuit at a time when even the cashiers at Schrafft's talked about their stock purchases with customers.[14]

Stella and Mary Margaret were on an extended European vacation in the late summer and early fall of 1929 when the stock market peaked, their trip no doubt financed by their still-growing paper profits. When they arrived home on October 21, financial analysts were talking about a "nervous market," and their rich investor friend asked if they wanted to get out. Mary Margaret wavered but decided to hold firm. When stocks plunged on October 24, they had to start withdrawing real money from their bank savings to cover their losses. That day Stella and Mary Margaret had planned a book party for their friend Inez Haynes Irwin, and they tried not to let their despair show to their guests. "The strange thing was that if I'd pulled out as the broker advised, I should still have had a tidy little sum of money. This I couldn't seem to realize. Apparently my idea—everybody's idea—was to save all or nothing." In the end every cent that she could raise went into covering her losses in the market, and it still wasn't enough, so all her stocks were sold, Stella's too. They were completely broke.[15]

Mary Margaret turned thirty several weeks after the crash, and instead of celebrating her success, she now she had to start over again almost from scratch. Later she tried to put the experience in perspective:

> While the years between 1930 and 1934 were certainly the most difficult of my life, I'm glad I had them. From being a moderate success as a newspaper and magazine writer, from having a reasonable amount

of money to spend, from summers in Europe and a Park Avenue apartment with maid, I was suddenly plunged into complete poverty. Beginning all over again is tough when you have lost considerable of your youth and excitement.[16]

One thing that helped was that most of their friends were in the same predicament.

Compared with what was to come, 1930 was not such a bad year. They were able to get out of their expensive Park Avenue lease and find a cheaper apartment. Stella never lost her publicity job, and the stock market crash hadn't yet affected the world of New York magazine publishing, which was still full of advertising from manufacturers and industries trying to build consumer confidence to spend their way out of the economic downturn. In the first year of the Depression, Mary Margaret was able to earn close to $40,000 with her freelance writing.[17] But she was carrying heavy family responsibilities, especially her parents' mortgage in Florida, as well as her own expenses, and these ate up her entire salary. She started accepting new kinds of assignments. In 1930 a short-term job in Washington handling the promotion and coordination for the White House Conference on Child Health and Protection convened by President Herbert Hoover brought her into contact with child welfare experts from around the country. An offer to write a campaign biography of Dwight W. Morrow, the U.S. ambassador to Mexico (and father-in-law of aviator Charles Lindbergh) who was running for the U.S. Senate from New Jersey, was another welcome assignment.[18]

Then suddenly in 1931, magazine editors stopped buying, and her main source of income, articles that her agent had previously placed for $1,500 or $2,000, dried up completely. Referring to both the Great Depression and her own personal problems, she sighed, "There were days when I felt I'd raised it myself from a pup to an oversized wolf at the door."[19] Reluctantly she was forced to resort to doing publicity work ("the worst possible way to make a living in the writing field," in her opinion),[20] even if she was lucky and found photographer Margaret Bourke-White as a client. Finally she was reduced to writing pulp biographies of Hollywood movie stars that sold in five-and-ten-cent stores.[21]

A trip to California in connection with those books produced one of the few funny moments in her Depression saga. She had interviewed thirty-two stars in three weeks and was relaxing in her nightgown ("a fragile, diaphanous affair that had been a going-away gift for Holly-wood") in her hotel room. A dressmaker who had been there earlier in the day called to say she had left her rubbers outside the door and would McBride please bring them into her room. Stepping into the hall in her nightgown to retrieve the rubbers, the door slammed behind her, leaving her locked out of the room in flimsy lingerie holding a pair of rubbers. Desperate, she rang the bell of the door across the hall, shout-ing wildly, "If you're a man don't open this door." Luckily it was an eld-erly woman, who burst out laughing when greeted by this outlandish spectacle. At least she got Mary Margaret out of her jam without further embarrassment. Later this story proved an oft-repeated favorite with McBride's radio audience, but at the time it was just one more thing gone awry.[22]

"In the three and a half years of my private depression my clothes got shabby and my confidence in myself followed suit."[23] For someone whose self-esteem went up and down like a yo-yo, this experience was devastating and resulted in what she called "a complete nervous break-down" at the beginning of 1931. She offered few details of her collapse, other than that she did seek help from a neurologist and eventually pulled herself out of it, as she had all the other emotional crises she had faced. But this one was more extreme than any of those that came before or after, and the experience left her "almost morbidly sympathetic to women with mental burdens to bear."[24]

For the rest of her life, Mary Margaret McBride divided her life into two parts: before and after the crash. After working her way up to a place of professional stature, "then came the crash, right on top of me, so it seemed." She had to either give up or start over. "And that's when the miracle happened," she remembered. "It was after the depression, after my own personal panic and despair, and then the finding of a brand-new niche, that some of my wildest dreams came true."[25] Enter radio.

13

"I Murdered Grandma"

"Just then the door opened and in ran Penny and Jenny—they're my son Johnny's twins, his youngest. He has three girls besides—Judy, Josie, and Jessie." [Pause, then a flat discouraged voice] "Oh, what's the use? I can't do it! I'm mixed up again with all those grandchildren I've invented. I'm not a grandmother! I'm not a mother. I'm not even married. I made that up and it doesn't sound real because it isn't. The truth is I'm a reporter who would like to come here every day and tell you about places I go, people I meet. Write me if you'd like that. But I can't be a grandmother any more!"

—Martha Deane

MARY MARGARET McBRIDE had been on the air less than three weeks when, in her words, she "blew up" and "committed mass murder."[1] Hired to host a daytime radio show that appealed to women, she tried to dispense chunks of homey philosophy and household hints as a fictional character named Martha Deane who devoted herself to her large family. (Martha had nice biblical connotations, and Deane was a lucky name at station WOR, where she broadcast.) One day she just snapped. Her candor so shocked the radio producer that he was certain she had committed "radio suicide."[2]

That is, until the letters started to come in from listeners who said they liked, indeed preferred, this new format. "I didn't even wait for the end of the broadcast," remembered one excited listener:

I wrote to you that very minute to say "hooray, at last a woman's program that isn't all about making jelly and dusting behind the clock." Go ahead—see all of New York for us, tell us about Broadway, what the Waldorf is like, and the Stock Exchange and the Zoo.

No birthday or anniversary ever went uncelebrated: the bigger the cake, the better. *Reprinted by permission of Library of Congress, Prints and Photographs Division.*

Mary Margaret McBride stayed on the air, and this story became a treasured part of her radio biography, trotted out in interviews and profiles for the rest of her life.[3]

When McBride landed the job as Martha Deane in the spring of 1934, her career was in shambles. When her agent called about a possible audition at WOR for a woman's program, she had to ask what an audition was. Later she claimed she got the job because she was the only one of the applicants who didn't ask about the salary. Stella, pegging her friend as too shy ever to succeed on radio, saw this primarily as something to tide her over until her freelance writing career picked up again.[4]

But Mary Margaret took to radio, and radio took to Mary Margaret. She brought her reporter's curiosity to the mike, transferring her journalistic skills to this new (and still evolving) medium. Unlike most other radio programs at the time, day or night, from the start Mary Margaret's was totally spontaneous and ad-libbed. She assumed that her listeners, male or female, young or old, would be interested in any subject, domestic or otherwise, if it was presented in an interesting or stimulating manner. This was a far cry from the traditional daytime programming geared toward women, which McBride dismissed as giving out recipes and telling them "how to make pants for little Johnny out of the old curtains."[5] Her listeners could tell that she took them seriously, and that bond cemented an amazing loyalty between the radio host and her listeners that often stretched over decades. "You're not like some of these women on radio," listeners wrote in. ""You don't talk down to us."[6]

With hindsight it is clear that McBride could not have sustained the fiction of the grandmotherly Martha Deane indefinitely, but there is some question about whether the break was quite as dramatic as the oft-repeated "I murdered Grandma" anecdote. In a 1936 potboiler called *Here's Martha Deane* commissioned to capitalize on the popularity of the show, McBride presented the shift as much more gradual:

At first I was a kind of Mrs. Dooley person, more colloquial than I am naturally and endowing myself richly with children and even grand-children in the first few days. . . . The children and grandchildren died off gradually from neglect. After the first broadcasts, I insisted the station would have to permit me to be myself, to say what seemed natural in a way that seemed natural, to talk as I might to my friends about anything that seemed interesting.[7]

Another version lays the epiphany to a flea circus. One night fairly soon after she had gone on the air she visited a flea circus on Forty-second Street where she was fascinated by a talented performer named Oscar. The next day, instead of the usual household hints and family goings-on, she told her listeners about the flea circus. When her producer and a prospective sponsor complained about the deviation, she appealed directly to her listeners:

> Do you want me to give you household talks when you know more about dusting than I do? Or do you want me to talk about the things that I do and see and find interesting, in other words, to bring as best I can, the outside world into your homes?[8]

When the return mail brought hundreds of letters from listeners, with only one exception, asking her to tell them more things like that, the station realized they had a good thing on their hands and gave McBride full rein to develop her show.[9]

Whether it was mass murder or a flea named Oscar is impossible to determine, since there are no recordings of the early Martha Deane shows. In later years listeners were more likely to cite the flea circus story, some even claiming to have heard the actual broadcast. Because this story and its variations were told on the radio so many times over the years, it is quite likely that many listeners remembered hearing the retelling of the story rather than listened to the actual broadcast. (The same is true of the "zipper" incident.) In the end it doesn't really matter. The most important thing was that McBride discovered a formula that worked.[10]

Mary Margaret McBride debuted as Martha Deane in what was generally considered to be dead time on the air—from 2:30 to 3:00 in the afternoon—a time of the day, in her words, "when tired young mothers nap with the children, suburban matrons are on the way to the bridge club, and older women are gadding to matinees or shopping." How hard was it to build an audience at that hour? "I soon began to wonder if anybody would listen even if Clark Gable courted Greta Garbo at such an hour."[11]

The show aired on station WOR, one of the largest independent stations in the New York metropolitan area, with a potential listening audience of more than ten million people in New York, Connecticut, New Jersey, and Pennsylvania. WOR promoted the program as "not just another woman's hour," promising that noted newspaperwoman Mary Margaret McBride would bring her perspective and experience to the show. Highlighting the program's mix of traditional women's programming with something extra, WOR called McBride

> a woman who is qualified to talk about every phase of home making—
> a woman who knows women and their special problems and interests—who is constantly scouring the highways and byways in search of material of definite interest to women—a woman with a personable personality—in short, *a woman's woman.*

Capturing a key to her success that was apparent from the very start, the station noted, "Martha Deane chats with her audience as though they were actually in the studio with her."[12]

The Martha Deane program was initially under the supervision of producer Scott Lucas, who had hired Mary Margaret in the first place. Lucas earned $200 a week for his efforts, and his on-air talent, a meager $25. With memories of her Depression-induced unemployment still fresh in her mind, McBride settled for the certainty of steady work over a good salary, not that she had much bargaining position. She quickly learned that nobody in the studio was going to give her any kind of training or preparation for her new role and that she would have to learn by doing it herself. Lucas, who turned out to be an alcoholic, was so unreliable that he was soon fired from his job. The station manager knew that McBride couldn't handle all aspects of the show herself and wondered whether she had any ideas for a business manager to handle them. She did: Stella Karn. One of the first things Stella did was to get her boss a tenfold raise. Once the business aspects of the show were in Stella's capable hands, the show was on sound financial footing. Mary Margaret and Stella worked as a team for the next twenty years.[13]

The *Martha Deane Show* ran six days a week, Monday through Saturday. Mary Margaret always insisted that her listeners were the heart of the show: "Martha Deane's listeners are expected to take an active part in each program. It is truly 'our hour.'"[14] Listeners organized Martha Deane parties at which they got together to listen to the show or tried out recipes that had been mentioned on the air. They also conscientiously supported the sponsors (her "fairy godfathers") whose financial support kept Martha Deane on the air.[15]

From the start there was a real bond between Martha Deane and her listeners, one that grew stronger once she abandoned the charade of being a grandmother. When the radio host planned her programs, Mary Margaret often had in the back of her mind a picture of what her life might have been like if she had married Dick Dorris and settled down:

> I'd have been tied down, and yet maybe fascinated, too, by the routine duties of a wife and mother, but very likely I'd still have ached with the frustrated desire to be doing interesting things, meeting well-known people, taking part in the excitement of the biggest city on the globe. I figure there are lots of such women who listen to the radio, and I plan my programs chiefly for them.[16]

That simple insight laid the foundation for a phenomenal broadcast career.

One way to think about the Martha Deane program is as a kind of "My Day" of the air.[17] Like First Lady Eleanor Roosevelt's syndicated column, which she started writing in late 1935, McBride's early programs covered a variety of subjects that were unified mainly by the personality of the host herself. Although by the 1940s and 1950s Mary Margaret featured prominent writers, well-known politicians, and famous performers, in the 1930s the show was more low-key. "Before I began to have daily guests," McBride recalled, "I depended a great deal on a group of friends and employees who appeared on holidays and special occasions or sometimes for no reason except that we felt like having a jam session, as our very informal unrehearsed gatherings around the microphone were called."[18] Several of these close friends developed distinct radio personalities of their own, quickly ranking among her listeners' favorites. In addition to the radio family, many of the early guests who appeared on the show were simply human-interest types in odd jobs that she had heard about. Such curiosities always held a special spot because "these are the things, too, that many women tell me furnish them with convenient dinner table talk. I pick them up everywhere."[19]

It actually was Stella who pushed the developing radio star to alter the format of her program to include more guests. As always, she offered the advice in her blunt, no-nonsense style. "But they want to hear *me*," Mary Margaret protested. "That won't last," Stella predicted grimly, and she was right.[20]

Noticeably absent from these early shows is any sustained attention to the Great Depression, which was still gripping American society despite the New Deal initiatives coming out of Washington. Later in her broadcast career Mary Margaret was more attuned to larger questions of democracy, social justice, and equality, but in the 1930s she pushed a smaller, more localized vision, one focused on getting through life one day at a time rather than changing the world. That perspective was shared by many of her listeners, who were struggling with the challenges that the economic downturn had forced on their families. Even though they probably weren't doing without (after all, they still had their radios), they most likely still were worried about getting by. Life was tough, and the good cheer, humor, and conversation that Martha Deane brought them each afternoon helped them get through hard times.[21]

There are no reliable figures for audiences in the 1930s, so it is hard to gauge how many listeners Martha Deane was actually reaching, but the numbers were sizable and growing. Ben Gross, radio critic of the *New York Daily News*, was one of the first to praise her in print.

> When Martha Deane first appeared on the radio, I was irritated by her self-conscious tittering and other mannerisms. She has overcome these and now her half-hour is one of the most interesting on the air. It's far more than a mere woman's entertainment. . . . It's a lively commentary of life, literature, health and the art of good eating. Martha's becoming one of our outstanding microphone personalities.[22]

In 1936 her home station WOR touted her as "the most popular woman on the air today . . . despite the fact that there are sections of the country which do not even get a chance to hear her." The station attributed her popularity to the programs' "naturalness and sincerity," adding, "The listeners get the impression that Martha Deane is speaking to them just as she would if she were holding a personal conversation with each across a tea table."[23]

Mary Margaret McBride played the role of Martha Deane on the radio for more than six years. This was not a question of a hidden identity, as she was identified by her own name in promotional material and news accounts. Whenever McBride referred to Martha Deane when she wasn't on the air, she used the pronoun "she" rather than "I," and she continued to publish magazine articles under her own name. The 1936 quickie book *Here's Martha Deane*, subtitled *Presented by Mary Margaret McBride*, even had a preface by a psychiatrist talking about these dual personalities. The two did, though, make rather an odd couple. "I don't think Mary Margaret McBride really enjoyed Martha Deane at first," she later confessed. "The truth was this strange poised woman frightened me. I didn't frighten her, though. She wasn't afraid of anything."[24]

It is testimony to Mary Margaret McBride's rapid rise in radio popularity that a publisher would bring out a book targeted to her loyal audience just two years after her show started. *Here's Martha Deane* was "affectionately dedicated to you all, my listeners, who make doing a radio program the greatest happiness I have ever known." Basically it rehashed the radio show in print format: its beginnings, favorite guests, embarrassing moments, funny stories about the sponsors, and so forth. (Many of these stories were in turn recycled word for word in McBride's later writings.) Confirming the radio host's propensity to hold little back from her radio audience, the final chapter began like this: "Because my listeners and I are so close, I tell them all about my family and myself. Here are extracts from two very personal broadcasts to end this memory book."[25]

This final chapter, "When I Was Very Young," no doubt was the genesis for *How Dear to My Heart* (1940), the first of three linked autobiographical memoirs that McBride published over the next twenty years. The memoir tells stories about her childhood and family, her aspirations and disappointments, ending when she went off to boarding school at the age of eleven. ("The timid little country girl was growing up" was its pedestrian last line.)[26] The central character is not Mary Margaret but her mother, and the book really is a daughter's extended love letter to the most important person in her life. Sadly, Mrs. McBride died shortly before the book was published. For Mary Margaret McBride's radio career, this crisis could not have come at a worse time.

14

Citrus Follies

WHEN MARY MARGARET McBRIDE started out as Martha Deane, she was given a half hour, but after a few years, she won an extra fifteen minutes, and that always remained her preferred time slot. For most people, filling three-quarters of an hour with conversation and talk five or six times a week would be a challenge if not a chore, but that amount of time perfectly suited a radio host who refused to be rushed or hurried. Anything shorter just didn't allow enough time for the kind of digressions and tangents that made up a good radio conversation for her—what she called "time to turn around in." It took her a "year of heartache" from 1940 to 1941 when she was limited to just fifteen minutes on the air every day to learn that lesson.[1]

In 1937 Mary Margaret had decided to take on a second program in addition to *Martha Deane*. This nationally syndicated show, which was promoted under her own name, was part of the CBS network and was broadcast daily from 12 to 12:15 P.M. The prospect of being heard all over the country, including back home in Missouri and in Florida where her parents now lived, was just too strong to resist. But this program caused a certain amount of confusion among Martha Deane's loyal fans. One woman wrote to her, "There's a woman imitating you but she's not as good as you are, darling." Other fans rushed up to the radio host on the street to tell her about the supposed imposter, oblivious to the fact that they were in fact the same person. In 1939 she even received two invitations to an event in upstate New York, one addressed to Martha Deane and another to Mary Margaret McBride, each one assuring her that she was the best female broadcaster on the air. Playing along with the joke, Mary Margaret cordially replied to both invitations in separate letters, saying she would be delighted to come.[2]

Under the sponsorship of LaFrance and Satina (bluing agents), Mary Margaret compressed her usual potpourri of conversation, stories, products, and guests into a fifteen-minute broadcast three times a

Mary Margaret's sour relationship with the Florida Citrus Commission may or may not have influenced her taste for grapefruit. *Reprinted by permission of Library of Congress, Prints and Photographs Division.*

week.[3] (Forty-five minutes on a nationwide hookup would have been prohibitively expensive for any sponsor.) Trading national exposure for time, she and Stella gamely took on the responsibility of producing two different shows every day. Fairly quickly Mary Margaret realized that she could do a fifteen-minute show successfully—if somewhat breath-lessly—if she also had another program at a different time to talk about all the other things that had to be left out, so this arrangement was not as crazy as it sounds. But when she learned in 1939 that CBS wanted to give her time slot to another show and move her to later in the day, she balked and, against Stella's advice, decided to drop the shorter show and once again concentrate on Martha Deane. She signed off with "Keep on being fond of me, don't forget me, and write to me."[4]

Then in the spring of 1940 Stella told her about a feeler from the Florida Citrus Commission to sponsor another fifteen-minute network show. Mary Margaret had just gone through the trauma of losing her mother that January, and she had been listless and off her game ever since. The thought of being responsible for two shows again was more than she could contemplate in her diminished state. When the sponsors matched her financial demands, she impulsively decided to go with the citrus offer and drop Martha Deane, forgetting her earlier experience with Satina and LaFrance. Stella was dismayed that Mary Margaret was planning to give up the show that had been her lifeblood for the last six years but glumly went along with the decision.[5]

The next task was to break the news to the executives at WOR, who were understandably upset at losing a proven audience draw but had no choice but to accept her decision. McBride would never have turned over her show to just anybody, however, and for the next host, she or-chestrated the selection of Bessie Beatty, a writer and editor who had been an occasional guest of hers. Beatty was a close friend of her dear friends Elmer and Berta Hader, and McBride had heard she was having some family financial problems that could be helped by a steady job. It was a generous gesture, but once Beatty was on the air and doing well, McBride was so envious of her success that it almost destroyed her friendship with the Haders.[6]

Martha Deane's loyal listeners were abruptly informed of the news after Stella and Mary Margaret came back from a six-week summer trip to Alaska, and the last show took place on September 20, 1940.[7] It was broadcast from Town Hall to accommodate all the listeners who wanted to be there, handkerchiefs ready, to say good-bye. Rather than have any guests, Mary Margaret and Stella treated it like a jam session and in-vited the members of the radio family to reminiscence and tell stories about their favorite moments on the show. Mary Margaret told a few stories about herself, such as the time she gave ingredients for a rice pudding that would have turned it into cement or when she had to deal with the guest who said "I loathe broccoli" just as she was launching into a commercial for that product. Hattie Silverman recalled the show when the radio family went on the air after Mary Margaret's mother had died. Stella told about once pinch-hitting for the host who was de-layed while taking a ride on a dirigible, and Hilda Deichler and Janice Devine reminisced about what it was like to be employed on the show's staff. Mary Margaret even did a few of the products, proudly announc-ing that at her insistence, sponsors like Dolly Madison would continue with the show after she left. "Will you stick to my products, will you?" she asked the audience, and of course they said yes.

Mary Margaret then turned serious. She took great pains to explain to the assembled audience and all her listeners that this change had been her idea, that she had not been fired, and that they should not take out their anger on the station. She briefly introduced her successor but warned them, "Don't you dare like her better than me!" As usual, she miscalculated the airtime left and could only say in haste her usual "Good-bye, y'all." The open mike caught a final "Oh, boy" as the show faded out. She was already regretting her decision.[8]

Two weeks later she was back on the air with her fifteen-minute program, called *Columnist of the Air*, under the sponsorship of the Florida Citrus Commission. (These were the same folks who later chose Anita Bryant and Rush Limbaugh to pitch their products.) But the show never found its rhythm, and even Mary Margaret admitted that the broadcasts had "lost their old-time flavor." She felt constrained by the length of the show and, after years of cordial relationships with her sponsors, was unhinged by the displeasure of the citrus growers, who did not know much about radio and could not understand why she did not spend more of the program talking about citrus products and the beauty of Florida. Somehow it escaped their attention that she had signed the contract with the understanding that she would have the bulk of the time to offer her trademark conversation and chatter, with the commercials relegated to less than three minutes of the overall show. Instead the commission expected more grapefruit and less Mary Margaret.[9]

In addition to her problems with the sponsor, Mary Margaret had another reason to regret her decision to give up Martha Deane: Bessie Beatty was doing quite well as her replacement, and Mary Margaret found herself insanely jealous. She later analyzed her reaction in this way:

> I had sincerely wanted Bessie Beatty to make good. After all, she was my choice and I had fought for her, but I hadn't dreamed she could really take my place. And on top of that, I was, for the first time since I had begun radio, wretched in my work . . . I was inwardly bleeding.

Distressed at her feelings of bitterness and jealousy, miserable with her new sponsors, and fearful for her career, she began to realize that her move to going "completely network was the beginning of disaster."[10]

One of the few high spots in this interlude was the designation of November 22, 1940, as Mary Margaret McBride Day by Governor Lloyd Stark of Missouri.[11] The honor came in conjunction with a reunion of former journalists who had worked at the Mexico, Missouri, *Ledger*, at which Mary Margaret had gotten her start. The event snowballed into an all-day celebration of the *Ledger's* most famous alum, featuring a parade (organized, she later learned, by Stella, with her usual publicist's flair), speeches, and seven different parties at which she was the guest of honor. Faced with mounds of her favorite foods prepared in her honor, she confessed, "I ate it all!" The forty-one-year-old celebrity took special joy in pounding out the story of her reception at her old desk at the *Ledger* office where she had worked as a green teenager. The festivities were broadcast, of course: nationally in her Florida Citrus time slot (unfortunately she forgot to mention grapefruit in all the excitement), as well as on local stations, including a replay later that evening. *Life* magazine even sent a photographer to cover the story. The pride that she must have felt at her triumphant hometown return was palpable, but her joy in the event was no doubt tempered by fears that her whole radio career might be floundering after her decision to give up *Martha Deane*.[12]

Things just got worse with the citrus growers. McBride tried doing the broadcasts from Florida, but this just put her in the middle of all the supercharged political recriminations. One day while walking through the lobby of a hotel, she heard a man say loudly to his wife, "There goes two million dollars of our money," incorrectly assuming that the entire budget for the promotional campaign was going straight into McBride's bank account. "Every night I would go to sleep worn out from another day of strain and after two or three hours jerk awake to face bleak reality."[13] Being back in Florida so soon after her mother's death also must have added to the pain. Her last broadcast was on July 4, 1941, thirteen weeks before her contract officially expired. It seems the citrus growers decided that their money would be better spent on print and advertising campaigns than on the cost of sponsoring the final weeks of this unsuccessful program.[14]

Seeing financial ruin and failure right around the corner again, Mary Margaret was convinced that her career in radio was finished. She hadn't been fired from anything since the *Evening Mail* had closed in 1924, and the debacle forced her to rethink her priorities and the chain of decisions that had gotten her into this mess in the first place. (She entitled this chapter of her autobiography "Pride Goeth before a Fall.") Stella told her that she could easily get another fifteen-minute slot with a more supportive sponsor, but Mary Margaret yearned for the luxury and leisurely pace of three-quarters of an hour. She no longer coveted coast-to-coast exposure. "What did I care about a national audience? I just longed to feel warm and snug around me again the approval of listeners who had been with me from the beginning."[15]

Once again Stella came to the rescue, although it wasn't easy to find forty-five minutes a day on a major station. On September 21, 1941, Mary Margaret debuted on station WEAF, the NBC flagship in New York City, at 1:00 P.M. , the time slot she would dominate for the rest of her radio career. The first broadcast was staged at the Vanderbilt Theater before a live audience of listeners culled from an index that McBride had kept of fans who had written to her over the years, with the NBC ushers passing out cookies made from Dromedary Gingerbread Mix, one of her new sponsors. Mary Margaret was practically beside herself to be back on the air. "I guess there's no two ways about it," she told her friends afterward. "My tempo is the forty-five minute tempo."[16]

15

The War Years

THREE MONTHS AFTER Mary Margaret went back on the air, the Japanese bombed Pearl Harbor. The radio host was visiting friends on Long Island, and they all had just finished supper when they heard the news flash. (This being Mary Margaret, she of course had to share what they had eaten: fried chicken, hot biscuits, and chocolate icebox cake.) In retrospect it is lucky that Stella had been able to grab the 1 P.M. slot on WEAF when she did. If Mary Margaret had been trying to get back on the air during wartime, it might have been difficult, perhaps impossible, to win commercial and station support for a "women's program" with everyone's attention diverted by the war. Just as vexing were the as yet unresolved questions about the role that radio would play in the national emergency. But her loyal listeners probably saw it another way: with war on the horizon, they were just relieved to have her back.[1]

There are hints of the coming war in Mary Margaret McBride's *America for Me*, which was published in November 1941. Even though it must have been written during the unhappy months when she was embroiled with the Florida Citrus Commission, the book (like most of her published writing) is remarkably upbeat. Its genesis lay in her newspaper days in the 1920s, when one of her favorite assignments was meeting celebrities arriving by ship in New York Harbor. Invariably, she greeted them with two questions: "What do you think of America?" followed by "Do you plan to write a book about America?" Twenty years later, she decided she had just as much right to have her say about her country as did any visiting celebrity. In fact, with democracy under siege in many parts of the globe, she felt it was especially important for Americans to realize what this country stood for and what values made it so special.[2]

Despite that lofty agenda, *America for Me* is really just an extended love letter to New York City—its skyscrapers, its neighborhoods, its food (no surprise there), and the opportunities that it had opened to a

Mary Margaret and the flight crew that flew her around Europe, nose art and all. *Reprinted by permission of Library of Congress, Prints and Photographs Division.*

young woman like herself several decades earlier. Full of platitudes and vague exhortations to rise to whatever challenges might threaten the American way, any hopes for the book's commercial success were buried in the public shock after Pearl Harbor. Mary Margaret soon had to find other, more productive ways to help America win the war.[3]

The 1940s were a significant decade for radio as the medium—and the country as a whole—went to war. The federal government never seriously considered taking over the airwaves, and unlike the experience in Germany, American radio did not become an overt propaganda tool of the state. Censorship also was kept to a minimum. Instead, the federal government worked alongside the radio industry, leaving its commercial basis untouched but encouraging and facilitating the broadcast of programming dedicated to boosting the home front's morale and educating the citizens of a democracy in the need for wartime sacrifice.[4] Even though radio remained free of government control, it still changed quickly and fundamentally during wartime, as historian Barbara Sav-

age observed: "With its extensive official use during the war, radio re-
cast its own image from that of a source of inexpensive entertainment
to that of a civic voice of immediate importance, whether delivering
breaking news from the front or carrying politically unifying appeals."[5]
That recasting applied equally as well to Mary Margaret McBride's
wartime radio experience.

Almost immediately she found that her program changed—it simply was not possible to continue with business as usual when the country was preoccupied by war. "Whoever the guest and however we
started," the radio host recalled, "we always came to war before we finished."[6] Her program was subject to frequent interruptions by war bul-
letins and sometimes was preempted totally. For a while it even began
with a regular newscast. Events such as her birthday celebrations or
various anniversaries were invariably linked to a cause like the Stage
Door Canteen, the Red Cross, or wartime recruitment. Even McBride's
relationship with her sponsors changed. Instead of exhorting her listeners to buy more products, she now often talked to them about how
to be careful consumers and make the most of their rationing points.
When chocolate was rationed, which affected her longtime sponsor
Fanny Farmer, she used her amazing powers of persuasion to ask her
listeners to eat less of it, not more, until the crisis had passed.[7]

In response to an America at war, McBride fine-tuned her program,
trying to find the right balance between the gravity of the world situation and the need to reassure her listeners that everything would work
out in the end. "I guess I was too solemn at first," she later realized.
"Even mothers with enlisted sons asked me please to be as gay as possible." To this end she offered war news and discussion of home-front
activities but also the chance to chat, relax, share moments of lightness
and humor, and take a temporary respite from global affairs with talk
of new books or recently opened Broadway plays. This was not a question of escapism, however, because the war was threaded through
every program that Mary Margaret did until well after V-E day and V-J
day. For example, when the cast members of the new Broadway production of Philip Barry's *A Kiss for Cinderella* appeared on the program,
leading lady Luise Rainer included a pitch for her work with the U.S.
Committee for the Care of European Children, personalizing the story
by telling of her childhood memories of World War I in Europe.[8]

As part of her support for the war effort, Mary Margaret made her
program available for a variety of government officials and military

leaders who were trying to rationalize production and consumption on the home front. In addition, at the request of the Office of War Information (OWI), each Wednesday the program featured "Home Front Forum," which was designed to let listeners know what they could do to help the war effort.[9]

In February 1943, Mary Margaret was especially pleased when the OWI lined up mystery writer Leslie Ford to talk about how destructive rumors were to the war effort, because she had always wanted to snare Ford as a guest for the show. Of course, to make the point for OWI, they had to repeat some untrue rumors (like the one about a woman's being issued a clothing ration card instead of her lost sugar rationing card, even though clothing was never rationed), but they got the point across to listeners. Then Ford reverted to her role as a private citizen, and she and Mary Margaret talked about her mystery writing. An unofficial additional guest on that Wednesday show was journalist John Hersey, who told stories about spending time with the troops in the Pacific theater, personifying the reasons why soldiers were fighting by saying they were "fighting for blueberry pie," a symbol of home and democracy. At the end McBride credited Hersey's insights with making her understand what war was like from a soldier's perspective.[10]

Many of the "Home Front Forum" segments were built around the general theme of "the nature of our enemy," and one of the most memorable featured Bella Fromm, a Jewish refugee who had fled Germany under threat of death. On an earlier show to promote her book *Blood and Banquets* (1942), a diary of her days in Germany, she traced Hitler's terrible rise to power, admitting that he once (in 1933) kissed her hand, even though he claimed that he could always smell a non-Aryan. She remembered feeling poisoned, almost contaminated, and wished she had had a revolver to kill him. On this "Home Front Forum" segment six months later (her book was now in its fifth printing, perhaps because of the publicity it had received on the air), Fromm described watching as those books now designated "un-German"—including, but not limited to, books by Jews—were burned in a public bonfire in 1933. As she talked about watching the cheering, hysterical crowd from afar (she called the swastikas "Nazi rags"), she tried not to cry, which is what Mary Margaret said she would have done. The moral about the nature of the German enemy? They will do anything to get what they want.[11]

Mary Margaret McBride did not limit her patriotic activities to just forty-five minutes a day on the air. Rather, she threw herself into war work, mainly selling war bonds and making speeches for the Red Cross, the blood bank, and other causes throughout the New York metropolitan area. She estimated that she was out four or five nights a week, and following her long-standing pattern, she shared her impressions of each war-related event with her listeners the next day, multiplying its effect. Her one disappointment was that her offer to become a nurse's aide was politely but firmly turned down by Mrs. Walter Lippmann, head of the Nurses' Aid Committee. Surely Lippmann realized that Mary Margaret could do much more good by continuing her radio show and making speeches for the war effort than by working in a hospital ward rolling bandages.[12]

Although McBride continued to pick up new listeners during the 1940s in addition to her loyal base, one group of women dropped out of her potential audience: the six million women who answered the government's call to take a war job. Many of these new workers (whose numbers doubled during the war) were married women, often with children—the prime demographic of Mary Margaret's audience. The women that the media referred to as Rosie the Riveters took on a wide range of home-front occupations and jobs, and having a regular job usually meant they could not tune in to a favorite radio show each midday. (Those who worked the night or swing shifts probably were asleep when it aired.) Unlike movie houses, which stayed open twenty-four hours a day so that war workers could still catch their favorite films, if you missed a radio show, there was no way of catching a repeat.[13]

The greatest change that Mary Margaret McBride's show underwent during wartime was in its deepened relationship with the listeners who continued to tune in each weekday at one o'clock. As before, the letters poured in, but instead of talking about their homes, gardens, or the products, women wrote about their sons or husbands going off to war, and their grave fears, which Mary Margaret shared, that not all of them would come back. Because she had always shared her listeners' letters on the air, she continued to do so in wartime. When Mary Margaret visited a flower show in March 1942 (something she thought might cheer her listeners up), she noticed that many of the women waiting to get in seemed a bit weary and frazzled, which reminded her of a letter she had just received from a woman whose son was called up to active duty. As the woman explained, at the train station she remained cheerful for her son's sake but then burst into tears as soon as his train left. It could break your heart, Mary Margaret said, if her courage didn't also cheer us up so much.[14] Rather than reinforcing fear or uncertainty, sharing these letters and experiences encouraged strength and stoicism, knitting the women in the audience together in shared empathy with their host.[15]

McBride's Thanksgiving show on November 25, 1943, achieved the same result. The radio host took special care with these shows each year, knowing that her audience would be at home with their families, and she found even more things to be thankful for in wartime. This show featured Harry Maule, an editor at Random House who had compiled *A Book of War Letters*, with proceeds to go to the relief agencies of the armed services. She greeted him by saying that she was thankful for Harry Maule, because he had made her cry and laugh over the last twenty-four hours as she read this courageous and inspiring compilation. As they discussed the book (she was actually better at telling the stories than he was), the elements of humor, like one soldier who asked for bobby pins and chocolates as "devil's lures" to catch foreign girls, were outweighed by the gravity of most of the situations described, like the last dispatch before the Japanese took over Corregidor or a letter from a father to his unborn child before going into battle. (He was expecting a boy, but Mary Margaret was happy to report the baby turned out to be a girl). The most sobering moments occurred when the audience learned that the letter writer had subsequently been killed in action. The grief and shock in the studio and, by extension, the national audience, was palpable.[16]

On this Thanksgiving show, six letters from the book were selected to receive $100 war bonds as part of a wartime promotion, and two families were there to accept awards for their sons in absentia. The first family was so overwhelmed by the occasion, and Mary Margaret's kindness toward them, that the father was barely able to speak. Then Mary Margaret started reading out loud a prize-winning excerpt from the second soldier, who had been taken prisoner by the Japanese. She read aloud the part about the war and then turned over the letter to his mother in the studio, who, in halting English, read its final message of love and hope to his family. With that benediction, which occurred just as time ran out, the Thanksgiving program drew to an end.[17]

Not quite as emotional but just as uplifting were the stories Mary Margaret shared about women's home-front patriotism and activism: "I don't need a Gallup poll to tell me American women hate war. My correspondents make it clear. But I know, too, that a crisis will always find them ready with whatever kind of courage it takes to meet the troubles we have failed to prevent."[18] Throughout the war years, regular listeners of the program heard countless examples from all over the country of how women banded together in their communities to take on new responsibilities, how they held their families together, and how they managed to cope with wartime restrictions and shortages with their spirits still high. If Mary Margaret had not donated the millions of letters she received in the 1940s to wartime scrap-paper drives, they would have provided compelling documentation of the lives of ordinary Americans in this time of extraordinary crisis.[19]

Some of the most compelling programs during the war years were those that featured refugees.[20] Because many listeners were recent immigrants from the very areas in the European theater where the fighting was fiercest, this topic was of vital concern to them. On shows throughout the war, listeners met refugees who had fled occupied countries (France, Finland, Norway, Poland, Greece, Turkey, and Hong Kong), as well as French, Finnish, Italian, and Yugoslavian resistance fighters; survivors of the bombing of London; and various former political prisoners. Generally the refugees were identified by the country they were fleeing without reference to race or creed, but Mary Margaret also sometimes referred to the specific persecution of Jews (or non-Aryans, as they were often called). The stories these refugees told brought home the war through the medium of radio.[21]

Obviously the fact that these refugees were appearing on the radio in America meant that they had escaped from Europe, usually with harrowing tales of political persecution, forced relocation, or physical danger. They also came with an agenda, which Mary Margaret shared, of trying to counter isolationism in the United States so that its citizens would continue to support the worldwide struggle to restore democracy. On the shows, refugees from occupied countries like Norway and Yugoslavia, as well as Germany, repeatedly thanked the American people for joining the fight against Hitler. Often these grim tales of possessions and family members left behind, deprivation and sacrifice, as well as untold small acts of courage and heroism, were so moving that they brought Mary Margaret and the studio audience to tears. On more than a few occasions, it would have been so incongruous to interrupt these sagas to do the products that she just let the guest talk, knowing that her sponsors would understand and that she could make up the commercials at a later time.[22]

One example of what she warned her listeners would be a "very dramatic show" took place on November 26, 1942, when her guests included a man under sentence of death overseas, a woman who had survived twenty-six bombing raids, and another woman who had been expelled from Germany. McBride reassured her audience that this was not a "gloomy, atrocity program" but an example of why they should be thankful for the freedom and democracy they enjoyed in this country. (This was an annual Thanksgiving show.) The program opened with Norwegian photographer Kari Berggrav (McBride carefully spelled out her name for listeners), who talked about her country's brave resistance to the Nazi invasion, even though her political views meant that she would be shot if she returned home. (At one point Stella told her to stop hitting the table with her elbows, because it sounded like the bombing she was describing.) The next guest was a Yugoslav professor named Dr. Boris Furlan, now in exile in the United States, who also had been sentenced to death. Finally, activist Bella Fromm talked about her forced exile from Germany, a country that she described as "gangsters on the other side." As she tried to convey the horror of what was happening in her former country, she told stories about friends who dared to entertain Jews in their homes, only to be reported to the Gestapo and threatened with being sent to a "concentration camp." One of the few light moments in the show came when all three guests pledged themselves to one great world Thanksgiving ruled by brotherly love, no starvation, and optimism for the future, which someone in the audience quickly dubbed "a turkey movement."[23]

Obviously, the newspapers and radio broadcasts from abroad carried details about the horrors of war, but as historians who have studied when and what Americans knew about the Holocaust have found, these details often did not sink in, either because they were buried in the general glut of war news or because the allegations were just so mind-boggling that they were impossible for ordinary Americans to process and digest. For example, historian David Wyman documented that clear evidence of the existence of Hitler's specific plan to exterminate the Jews and other people who did not belong to the "master race" was made public in the United States in November 1942. For the rest of the war, however, coverage of the various atrocities and the disappearance of large segments of the European population rarely received concerted attention in the national press. This silence, which was compounded by the inaction of the Roosevelt administration, is one of the great moral failures of World War II.[24]

Although it is clear that most Americans failed to grasp the horrors being perpetrated on European Jews and other "undesirables," this does not mean that all citizens were totally clueless. Here radio had a huge advantage over print. Even with rare front-page coverage, how much emotional wallop does a print story pack? Compare that with real people on the radio, speaking in halting English to a host whom the listeners trust almost as a member of the family, as they talk about their flight for freedom, what they were escaping from, and the horrors of what they left behind. The immediacy and the bond created by such revelations would have made it harder to just slough off the information as war propaganda or something not germane to one's own life. In this way Mary Margaret helped bring the war into millions of homes across the country and, more broadly, the reasons why America was fighting.

The number of refugees featured as guests during wartime, their warm reception, and the credibility they acquired by appearing on the show raises the possibility that Mary Margaret's listeners might have been better prepared than most Americans for the revelations of the Holocaust in 1945. Although they may not have totally grasped the extent of Hitler's plan to exterminate the Jews until it was fatefully revealed by the liberation of the concentration camps in May 1945, the cumulative effect of four years of hearing about families separated or disrupted by death or disappearance, the forced relocation and migration of multitudes of people, and the huge numbers of refugees and displaced persons created by the dislocations of war would have given them a background and context to process this final bit of awful news. To Mary Margaret's listeners, the refugee problem was not just an abstraction: it was the voices of real people who had offered their stories over her airwaves. Mary Margaret McBride's embrace of perhaps the most wrenching human catastrophe of the twentieth century ranks as one of the most significant contributions of her radio program to American history.

Even though Mary Margaret knew that her show was helping the war effort, this former reporter may well have chafed at being stuck stateside behind a microphone rather than at the front. If only she had been twenty years younger, and fifty pounds lighter, she must have thought. In fact, several times she had raised the possibility to military officials of going to the European theater but was always turned down. Her friendship with General Omar Bradley, whose wife had been a childhood friend of hers, finally opened the door. Just a month after V-E day, NBC pages reported excitedly that a man who looked like General Bradley was standing in line with his wife waiting to be admitted to the audience for the show. Stella quickly jumped them in the line, and then Mary Margaret invited the general to the mike to talk about Germany's recent surrender and the prospects for an end to the war in the Far East. Showing her ability to humanize even the most serious of situations, she then asked Mary Bradley what she planned to feed her husband when she got him home. "Swiss steak with cream gravy," Mrs. Bradley answered promptly, "and apple pie with ice cream."[25]

When McBride broached the possibility of a trip to the European theater, General Bradley endorsed the idea, but only after the war with Japan was over.[26] In September 1945, barely a month after the end of hostilities, Mary Margaret flew to Europe on a military plane. She was accompanied by a member of her radio family, the milliner Juliette Nicole (Madame Nikki), who hadn't seen her family in France since before the war. Stella stayed behind to take care of the show. As Mary Margaret told an interviewer who covered the trip, "I wanted to see for myself what things really were like. I felt that I owed my listeners as much truth as I could give them and as much informed honesty."[27]

They landed outside London and saw firsthand the devastation to that city. It was far worse than she had ever imagined. "You don't have a chance to recover from shock," she said at the time. "You see some things so terrible you think nothing could be worse. Then you see some things more terrible next day. So you don't build up immunity and it finally knocks you out." Everywhere she went, she talked to as many ordinary people as possible, trying to get a sense for her listeners of what it had been like to live through the last six years of war.[28]

After England, McBride and Nicole went to Paris, where they met with Nikki's sister, who had spent the entire German occupation in the city. Her pantry was bare, but somehow she had managed to find ingredients to make a tiny tart without sugar or shortening. "It was the most awful and most beautiful little apple tart that ever was and forever will symbolize for me six years of sacrifice, courage, and hope," recalled Mary Margaret. Over the years she shared that story with her listeners many times, but she could never truly convey how shaken she had been at the time. For the first and only time in her life, she lost weight—fifteen pounds in two weeks.[29]

In Germany, she was assigned a B-17 and its crew to fly her around. Getting her hefty frame in and out of an airplane built for combat and lacking a gangplank provided one of the few moments of comic relief: "At first it took the whole crew to push and prod me aboard, but as I lost weight and got more agile I was able to manage by myself."[30] She spent her entire time in Germany consumed by feelings of dread and felt no desire at all to engage ordinary Germans in conversation. She reported, "Again and again our soldiers tell you the Germans don't know they are beaten. I believe this is true."[31]

On at least two occasions, she was able to broadcast directly from Europe, which must have been thrilling to her listeners. The reception for her September 19, 1945, relay from Berlin was quite poor, but she managed to introduce the airplane crew who had been flying her around and share some of the camaraderie of their joint exploits. She also mentioned visiting displaced persons' camps, wondering what would become of these families who had no countries to return to. She described bombed-out Berlin, which had not a building untouched (try imagining New York in that condition, she challenged listeners) and, without addressing whether it was right or wrong ("it had to be done"), just tried to report what she saw.[32] Mary Margaret was so overwhelmed by her impressions that she saved most of her stories until she returned to the air in New York. Memories of this trip, especially of the displaced persons' camps and their "'sweet' horrible smell of death," haunted her for the rest of her life.[33]

The Mary Margaret McBride who became a crack reporter in New York in the 1920s and then assumed the role of Martha Deane in the 1930s was not an especially concerned citizen. Her early shows and writings show very little evidence of engagement in the wider political and social issues of her times. Although the topics were interesting, they hardly were weighty. As personally isolated from world events as her country was as a whole in the 1930s, McBride ignored or sidestepped the disturbing news from Germany and Japan. Nor did she talk about politics or social movements, the accomplishments of the New Deal, or the rise of the labor movement.

Only in the 1940s did the glimmerings of a wider social perspective begin to appear. Her growing association with Eleanor Roosevelt was one factor, and she always gave the First Lady credit for helping activate her social consciousness. But just as large an influence was her firsthand exposure to the horrors of war and its unsettled aftermath. "After I saw the people and listened to them and stood for hours in their food lines I felt as if I would have no right to anything I called mine until I had made some effort to help."[34] For the rest of her radio career, she did make that effort, embracing the banner of civil rights as human rights and joining with other women to find a will to peace. World War II completed the personal and political evolution of Mary Margaret McBride that had begun back on a Missouri farm more than four decades before.

PART III

TRANSITIONS

Mary Margaret and her favorite guest, Eleanor Roosevelt. *Reprinted by permission of Library of Congress, Prints and Photographs Division.*

16

Eleanor Roosevelt, Mary Margaret Mcbride, and Postwar Politics

ELEANOR ROOSEVELT was a frequent guest on Mary Margaret Mcbride's program, and sometimes the radio host would take a taxi to Roosevelt's apartment on Washington Square Park to pick her up before the show. One day on the way back uptown to the studio, they got caught in traffic, and the former First Lady suggested that they get out of the cab and make a run for it. Mary Margaret quickly, and firmly, nixed that idea. When Bennett Cerf later recounted the story, he added this coda, "thereby depriving Fifth Avenue strollers of what would have been certainly one of the great sights of the century." When they finally arrived at the studio, breathless and just a few minutes late, Mary Margaret composed herself and explained the delay to her listeners. She then said calmly, "You know what we really need, Vincent? It's a pitcher of that delicious, economical iced Ehler's Tea."[1]

Mary Margaret was often asked who her favorite guest was, and there was never any hesitation in her reply: Eleanor Roosevelt. The two women had first met in the 1920s when Mary Margaret was a freelance journalist assigned to write an article about how famous men were helped by their wives. Franklin Roosevelt then was serving as the governor of New York, and Eleanor promptly invited her up to Albany, where she had dinner with the Roosevelts and spent the night at the governor's mansion.[2] She also got her story—the first of many acts of personal kindness that Eleanor Roosevelt sent her way over the years. In 1941 when Mary Margaret was worn out by her dealings with the Florida citrus growers, Eleanor Roosevelt learned of her troubles through their mutual friend, newspaperwoman Bess Furman. The First Lady immediately sent her an invitation to stay at the White House on her way back from Florida, an enormous emotional lift in a tense situation.[3] "I have plenty of reason to know about Mrs. Roosevelt's concern for other human beings," McBride concluded. "It has been evident in every contact I've had with her."[4]

For a while in 1950, the First Lady of Radio and the First Lady of the World actually had competing radio shows, and the press had a field day. When Mary Margaret decamped to ABC from her longtime affiliation with NBC in New York, NBC signed Eleanor Roosevelt to do a show, with her son Elliott as the announcer. The *New Republic* judged the shows in this way: "Both bring to their microphones people of prominence; both touch frequently upon important matters; neither talks down to her audience; Mrs. Roosevelt has a slight edge as far as serious topics are concerned." But Mary Margaret had a definite edge when it came to commercials, being far more convincing than Elliott's feeble attempts to remind listeners that "Mother" uses a certain product or that "the Roosevelts" would be glad to tell them more about an advertised brand of soup.[5] Mary Margaret pronounced herself totally nonplussed about her new competition when interviewed by *Time*: "I think she's the greatest woman in the world. I love her to death." Stella took it more territorially: "Mary Margaret's audience is Mary Margaret's audience."[6] She was right, and the Roosevelt show folded soon after.

Eleanor Roosevelt formed many deep friendships with a variety of people during her years in public life, and she counted Mary Margaret as one of those friends. During the war years she began to appear frequently on the show, usually talking about issues related to democracy at home or abroad; after the war, she tirelessly promoted her work at the United Nations and the cause of human rights. Roosevelt always made a special point of giving Mary Margaret her first appearance whenever she published a new book.[7] The First Lady also defended her friend to critics. When someone from Long Island criticized Mrs. Roosevelt for appearing on a program hosted by "a woman who has grown rich by advertising products" and who is "wholly interested in promoting Mary Margaret McBride, with no social conscience whatever," Eleanor Roosevelt defended the radio host as "a fine, human person" and she dismissed as completely out of hand the incongruous assertion that the radio host was a fascist.[8]

In turn Mary Margaret worshiped Eleanor Roosevelt, gushing to her at regular intervals that she was the finest woman in the world and that there was nothing that she wouldn't do for her. In 1939, after they had worked together on a program about infantile paralysis (polio), she gave Roosevelt the highest compliment she could muster: "I have always thought you the finest woman I know, next to my mother."[9] Near the end of her life, the radio host confessed that she had a recurring dream about Eleanor Roosevelt, one no doubt shared by many others who were privileged to be part of the First Lady's circle of friends: "We were hurrying across fields and I was trying, not very successfully, to keep up with her."[10]

Eleanor Roosevelt meant more to Mary Margaret than just an example of compassionate womanhood: she helped give the radio host a social conscience. While wartime priorities certainly helped push Mary Margaret into taking a more political and committed stance on her daily radio show, the example of Eleanor Roosevelt also helped show the way. Grateful for the First Lady's friendship and many kindnesses, Mary Margaret stretched her own social conscience to embrace the issues that Roosevelt held dear, especially civil rights and wider roles for women.[11]

Mary Margaret McBride realized the incongruity of fighting totalitarianism and fascism abroad while still treating African Americans as second-class citizens at home, and in advance of much of the general population, she made civil rights and tolerance important parts of her broadcast arsenal. One of the main ways she did this was by regularly welcoming African Americans on her show and booking guests and selecting topics truly without reference to race or creed. NAACP head Walter White was often a guest, and poet Langston Hughes appeared on the program several times. Dancer Pearl Primus shared stories of her pilgrimage to Africa, and Zora Neale Hurston talked about prejudice and literature. Other guests included diplomat and Nobel Peace Prize winner Ralph Bunche and performers Ethel Waters, William Warfield, and Cab Calloway.[12] Because her program was independently produced and had solid ratings and supportive sponsors, Mary Margaret had much more leeway than did most media personalities at the time to take a liberal stand on race. In this case, as in her designation of tolerance as the theme of her fifteenth anniversary program at Yankee Stadium in 1949, she used her stature in the radio industry for cultural and political results.[13]

When Mary Margaret embraced civil rights, however, she was not talking about political actions like sit-ins or marches. Hers was a more philosophical embrace of the concept of universal brotherhood (in the phrase of the time), of accepting that people were different but not letting those differences be the cause of prejudice and intolerance. "People feeling superior because they were born a certain color, or into a certain religion. I just can't understand it," she said in 1954. "In fact, I am intolerant about intolerance."[14] As early as 1946, she was championing what she referred to as the cause of the Negro. "Why shouldn't I? Aren't they people, just as we are? Who are we to start a superiority complex?" Like other liberals trying to build a consensus on race at the time, however, she rarely talked about the actual mechanics of how such a change would be made.[15]

Paralleling the early warnings that her audience received on the Holocaust, it seems likely that Mary Margaret's regular listeners would have been more aware, and earlier, of the issues of race and civil rights than was the population at large. Because of radio's unique ability to bring voices and ideas to the airwaves in a "color-blind" manner (you can listen to the voice without knowing the race), her program could introduce topics related to race in a low-key, evenhanded manner. Remember that Mary Margaret's guests were never announced in advance, so her listeners were accustomed to absorbing whoever or whatever was being discussed on that day. Even if a listener was not totally sympathetic to African Americans as social equals, she or he probably would have stayed tuned out of curiosity rather than turning off the show in protest. Once that initial barrier had been breached, with Mary Margaret's gentle but firm help, the ideas and examples could begin to speak for themselves, including the obvious point that the African Americans had just as much a right to appear on the show as whites did. At a time when the political discourse on race in the media was still quite rare, this challenge to stereotypes was a limited but important step forward.[16]

Mcbride's outspoken and early support for civil rights makes her uneven position during the McCarthy era more difficult to understand. Although she was critical of the Soviet Union in the years immediately following the war, she was never a rabid cold warrior or especially concerned about Communists as a threat to domestic security. In fact, she initially spoke out against the witch hunts that began in government and the labor unions in the aftermath of the war, giving an editorial on one show in 1949 against "the evils of name calling and Communistbranding."[17] When the right-wing anti-Communist broadside *Counter-attack* claimed that she advertised Polish hams and, by extension, supported the Communist-led Polish regime, she indignantly went on the air to deny the charge as a piece of blatant misinformation.[18]

The nonexistent Polish ham account was the closest that the anti-Communist crusaders ever came to linking Mary Margaret personally with questions about disloyalty and subversive behavior, but many of her guests and friends came under greater suspicion. One day Stella received a call from a sponsor who had just received a delegation of women brandishing a list of some two dozen names of individuals considered suspect or soft on Communism. Who was at the top of the list? Eleanor Roosevelt, followed by Pearl Buck, Carl Van Doren, Fannie Hurst, and many of her best friends—"people whose political opinions I absolutely knew were above reproach" and frequent guests on her program.[19]

McBride decided on the following approach to unsubstantiated charges of this sort:

> I resolved I was not going to condemn them unheard just because a small group of women said they were guilty of having served, perhaps innocently enough, on some committee that later was said to have leanings toward the Reds. That was my contention throughout this time—that nobody has a right to be accuser and judge all in one operation.

This open-mindedness only went so far, however. Writer Howard Fast had been a "great favorite" on the program until it was revealed he was a Communist, a charge he had previously denied to her face on the air. He was never invited back. Mary Margaret drew a clear line: "Except in cases where I was sure from long knowledge what a person's convictions were, I finally yielded to pressure and turned down several who were on the committee lists." These included a famous folk singer and a distinguished actor, neither named in her autobiography. Stella had engaged a lawyer who told them that "it was that or go off the air." They lost only one sponsor (the slot was quickly filled), but at a cost of "lots of spiritual agony."[20]

Stella's fears about being forced off the air seem overblown. After all, the same reputation that had allowed Mary Margaret to speak out on race—her role as an independent producer, her loyal sponsors and audience, and her own track record as a fair-minded host—should have given her similar immunity to invite whatever guests she wanted to appear on her show, despite a hostile political climate. McBride later tried to spread the blame: "If radio as an organization had backed me and others who believed in fair play, there would have been fewer acts of injustice, heartache, and even illness and death as a result of hasty accusation treated as proof." In the end she justified her decision as a necessary compromise to keep her show on the air, reasoning that that was more important in the long run than taking a principled stand over a single guest.[21]

Even though Mary Margaret regretted her lack of backbone for the rest of her life, her actions seem fairly typical of the liberal response at the time, which involved caution when dealing with suspected Communists, making certain adjustments and concessions out of expediency to avoid the impression of condoning subversives, but avoiding the hysteria of the witch hunt. Certainly her behavior was far less blameworthy that those who "named names" and cooperated with various government investigating committees during the McCarthy era. Fears of internal subversion and espionage were quite real to Americans caught up in the cold war struggle against Communism, and, as the blacklisted Hollywood Ten found out, the entertainment industry was an easy target for those who claimed that Communists had infiltrated its very core. Unlike radio personalities such as Walter Winchell, whose anti-Communism was central to his broadcasting persona in these years and who was known as a close friend of FBI director J. Edgar Hoover, McBride never unnecessarily raised her voice in targeting subversives, choosing instead to promote her agenda of general tolerance and goodwill in a political climate that encouraged caution, not strong stands.[22]

Never as deeply involved in matters of political principle and conscience as her idol Eleanor Roosevelt was, Mary Margaret was able to rationalize her behavior and move on—literally. When she discussed this period in her autobiography, it was in a chapter with the improbable title of "A Witch Hunt and a Coronation." After describing what she considered as her cowardly behavior during the black-list period, she barely paused for breath before it was off to England for the coronation of Queen Elizabeth II.[23]

One of the most important bonds between Mary Margaret and Eleanor Roosevelt was a shared commitment to women's advancement. In 1935 Roosevelt supplied an all-purpose definition of feminism to which McBride would have heartily subscribed: "Fundamentally, the purpose of Feminism is that a woman should have an equal opportunity and Equal Rights with any other citizen of the country."[24] Instead of demanding major changes in the prevailing gender system, this position presumed that women's collective success would break down discrimination and male resistance. But coupled with this commitment to equality was a continued belief in women's difference. As Eleanor Roosevelt wrote, "When all is said and done, women *are* different from men. They are equals in many ways, but they cannot refuse to acknowledge their differences. Not to acknowledge them weakens the case."[25]

Mary Margaret had been part of the public debate over the "woman question" since her journalism days in the 1920s. Her ideas strengthened as she grew older but never really changed all that much from her initial stabs at making sense of the complexities of modern women's lives. She was proud of women's accomplishments and felt that no artificial barriers should be placed in an individual woman's way. As she wrote in 1941, "I'm certainly not going to repeat any of the old foolishness about women's place being in the home. An American woman's place is anywhere."[26]

But McBride never held herself up directly as a role model for women, always affirming that the correct choice for most women was family life coupled with involvement in their communities. This "do as I say, not as I do" attitude was quite prevalent among successful career women at the time, who managed to relish their exciting careers without necessarily assuming that their choices were right for the majority of American women. Presenting their choices as individual and highly exceptional (sort of a "three-sex theory"—there's women, there's men, and there's me) deflected society's attention away from the thorny question of what would actually happen if vast numbers of women did indeed follow such paths. Accordingly, the choices made by exceptional women did not necessarily appear as an outright assault on traditional gender roles, which had the effect of making them somewhat less threatening to society as a whole.[27]

Even as McBride regarded her choices as hers alone and praised the women in her radio audience who made home and community their focus, it is quite possible that many of those same women were drawn to Mary Margaret precisely because she symbolized the expanding opportunities for women in modern life that her listeners aspired to in their own lives. Even if those opportunities had passed them by because of their age, they could still hold out hope for their daughters' futures. When *Time* magazine put journalist Dorothy Thompson on the cover in 1939, the magazine explained her appeal to ordinary women by noting that she represented the "typical modern American woman they think they would like to be: emancipated, articulate and successful, living in the thick of one of the most exciting periods of history and interpreting it to millions." Almost the exact words could have been written about Mary Margaret McBride.[28]

Mary Margaret was more than willing to call herself a feminist (she called for Susan B. Anthony's birthday to be made a national holiday and supported the equal rights amendment),[29] but probably the best way to think of her stance on women is to talk about her gender consciousness. She always spoke of women as "we," rather than "they," and if she sometimes held contradictory ideas about women's place in modern society, she was not alone. What is important is that she rarely missed the chance to draw attention to what women were doing and contributing to the modern world and saw her radio show as a way of connecting homebound women with the important questions of the day. She didn't go to the barricades for women as a sex, but she never forgot them. Such a position was in fact quite typical of women at mid-century who were trying to win recognition for women's contributions and activism in a time without an active feminist movement.[30]

One area in which McBride exhibited her gender consciousness was over issues of war and peace, the great challenges of the 1940s. Like many other citizens, male as well as female, she was dismayed at the horror of war. She did not doubt the need to defeat Germany and Japan, but as a woman, she reached out to other women to see whether together they could find a will to peace in order to avoid wars in the future.[31] Of course, such a global stance was increasingly difficult to maintain in the polarized dichotomies of cold war America, when any gesture that looked like a softening of the United States' tough stand against the Soviets was taken almost as treason. But through her guests and interactions with her listeners, as well as her own editorializing on her show, Mary Margaret tried to find a way to mobilize women as women to act as a positive force for world harmony. She once even proposed turning over the running of the planet to its womenfolk for a day or, better yet, a year, "for the sole purpose of testing out a theory I have that going to war in all its forms, the masculine way of settling disagreements, is completely foreign to women."[32] While such a statement strikes modern ears as an essentialist view of women's nature (surely plenty of women are just as warlike as men), it was quite common at the time, providing a convincing pitch to mobilize women worldwide.

McBride pursued a similar agenda in promoting women's community activism in the 1950s. This decade is normally portrayed as a time when women (and men) gladly returned to their suburban homes, filled their kitchens with new appliances, and parked their new cars in the garage, with multitudes of baby-boom children providing the main focus of their existence.[33] Mary Margaret knew from her listeners, though, that their lives encompassed more than diapers and car pools, and in 1952 she established a nationwide program to recognize women's contributions to their communities. The Mary Margaret McBride Project for Community Betterment was launched on her radio show with the cooperation of three major religious groups: the United Church Women, the National Council of Catholic Women, and the National Council of Jewish Women. The project was a response to listeners concerned about preserving peace and democracy who wondered what they could do as individuals or groups to work toward that end. Mary Margaret saw the undertaking as a way of publicizing and sharing successful strategies already under way with women throughout the country who felt similar impulses but needed ideas about where to start.[34]

More than four hundred women were nominated, and the six winners were announced on a special edition of her radio program in 1953. Those honored represented a wide range of activism on the local level: Lulu Fairbank of Seattle for her activities on behalf of civic betterment in Washington State and Alaska; Lilian Bishop of Kansas for an organization aiding mental patients making the transition to life outside institutions; Kate Carter of Salt Lake City for her work preserving the documents and relics of pioneer history; Mother Mary Alice for her charitable work at St. Clare's Hospital in New York; New York City councilwoman Bertha Schwartz for her work with teenage narcotics addicts; and Ruth Suddeth for work in improving Atlanta's jails, neighborhoods, and juvenile delinquent treatment.[35] The program continued for a second year but was discontinued when Mary Margaret retired from her daily network show.[36]

The range of activism uncovered by this contest belies Betty Friedan's contention in *The Feminine Mystique* that in the 1950s, American women were totally consumed by affairs of home and hearth. For one thing, many families (including many of Mary Margaret's listeners, no doubt) could not afford to live the child-centered suburban lifestyle glorified in the pages of *Good Housekeeping* or *McCall's*. More to the point, even if women were raising families and not working outside the home, they still could be vitally interested in politics, especially on the community level. Just because Mary Margaret's listeners were at home each day at one o'clock to listen to her show did not mean that their lives were totally bounded by the four walls of their homes or apartments. Their activism and desire for engagement in the wider world suggest a far more complex view of the 1950s than Friedan assumed.[37]

By the 1950s Mary Margaret was more comfortable with the idea of women combining work and marriage than she had been in the 1920s, although she still felt that this was a highly individual choice that not all women (or men) wanted to make. But she also recognized "that any woman who WANTS TO ENOUGH can handle both a home and a job. In the final analysis, it all depends on the individual."[38] Thirty years earlier, when she started out, the question had been largely hypothetical, but now with between one-fourth and one-third of the nation's married women employed outside the home, Mary Margaret for the first time let herself dream a bit: "Is this hope for the wildly ambitious young girl that she may, if she's lucky, eat her cake and have it too?"[39] Barring that, she pointed her readers to Anne Morrow Lindbergh's *Gift from the Sea* for its lyrical and compassionate treatment of the need for balance in modern women's lives.[40]

Throughout her life Mary Margaret McBride adopted a no-nonsense, practical approach to the question of women's rights. Women should be allowed to do what they wanted and what they did best. There should be no artificial barriers to either sex. Women should recognize rather than gloss over their differences from men. Mary Margaret's feminist consciousness was really quite similar to what made her such a success on the radio: she took women seriously at a time when many of her peers in popular culture and public life did not. Not shy about using the "bully pulpit" of her radio show to draw attention to women's unusual accomplishments, she enthusiastically showcased interesting women alongside men and proudly highlighted women's contributions to public life. Furthermore, she managed to do this without denigrating women's contributions to their homes and families. To her mind, both were equally valid. Mary Margaret McBride may not have ever felt the urge to march for women's rights, but she did prove herself a good friend of many of the ideals of modern feminism.

Mary Margaret tries television, this time filming a commercial for Conti shampoo. *Reprinted by permission of Library of Congress, Prints and Photographs Division.*

17

Television

ON THE FACE OF IT, the reasons why Mary Margaret Mcbride, a middle-aged, almost two-hundred-pound radio talk show host did not make a successful transition to television seem obvious: age, weight, and gender. The camera privileges the young, svelte, and attractive, especially when women are concerned. Older men at least have the option of being distinguished and acting as elder statesmen. There is no equivalent role for women.

Mary Margaret McBride did not become a television star—this much is not in dispute. In fact, most radio stars did not thrive on television. But she actually was much better in the medium than might be expected. Or to put it another way, the things that might have worked against her didn't in the early, experimental days of television. There is no denying, however, that radio was a much better match for her talents than television, as she herself realized. "Since I started out in radio I'll always lean towards it," she told an interviewer in 1958. "Besides being more informal and easier radio tends to bring out more of the person's real character. With television lights and cameras trained on an inexperienced person he is bound to become more tense and self-conscious, whereas on radio he has little to distract him."[1] Or as she put it more forcefully a decade later, "I hated television. People pointing fingers at you, straightening your hair, dabbing at you under those hot lights."[2]

While early radio went through somewhat of a golden age when women's contributions were welcomed and necessary on the air and behind the scenes, television never experienced a similar openness to women's talents.[3] The shift in dominance from radio to television was so quick that television never went through an extended period of experimentation, growth, and then consolidation. Instead, the networks that dominated radio quickly and irrevocably translated that control

197

(along with much of the content) into television. That dominance, epitomized by the classic network system built around NBC, CBS, and ABC, lasted until the 1980s.[4]

To be sure, women like Faye Emerson, Arlene Francis, and Pauline Frederick found opportunities in the new medium, but in many ways the areas in which they could compete in television were significantly narrower than those available in radio. Frederick, who won renown as the United Nations correspondent for a network, pinpointed the phenomenon of "lookism"—women were judged as much for how they looked as for what they said—as significantly holding back women on camera. Almost as pernicious was the line between female-dominated soft news and male-dominated hard news, which Frederick referred to as "the iron curtain."[5] Even Francis's *Home* show, which ran from 1954 to 1957 on NBC, represented a much smaller range of topics and interests defined as feminine than did comparable radio shows like Mary Margaret McBride's. Some of the largest roles open to women, as Lucille Ball and Eve Arden found in *I Love Lucy* and *Our Miss Brooks*, respectively, were in the new prime-time situation comedies.[6]

Media historian Erik Barnouw called the years 1948 to 1952, precisely the period during which McBride was trying to break in to the new medium, " a strange television period—a laboratory period."[7] In September 1948 the Federal Communications Commission (FCC) instituted what became a four-year freeze on new television licenses, which gave a huge advantage to the approximately one hundred stations already on the air or about to start broadcasting. Most of these stations were controlled by the dominant radio stations in those same markets, a concentration of media power that was endorsed by the FCC. Certain cities like New York and Los Angeles had full television operation, with seven stations each, but most cities had only one and some, like Portland, Oregon, or Little Rock, Arkansas, had none at all. This made it difficult for advertisers to get the kind of national coverage or exposure that they could expect from radio programs, which were at a postwar peak of earnings power. Nonetheless, the power of television was already being felt. For example, cities with a television presence experienced a 20 to 40 percent drop in movie attendance in 1951 alone. The time that an average family listened to radio dropped 50 percent from 1948 to 1952, down to just 2.2 hours a day.[8]

It is easy to see how Mary Margaret, based in a major television market with an abundance of stations, would have been swept along in these developments. Starting in 1944, she had done radio broadcasts from both political conventions each election year, and when the networks decided to televise selected coverage of the proceedings in 1948, she went along with the experiment. For the Republican National Convention, she dressed in her trademark dark dress with white collar inserts at the neck and cuffs, topped off by a distinctive hat. Television and radio critic (and friend) Ben Gross told readers of his column that despite her plans to lose twenty pounds before her television debut, she had actually gained three pounds but promised to be slimmer by the time of the Democratic National Convention later that summer. Her fans, both radio and television, enjoyed the chance to see, rather than just hear, Mary Margaret interview major political figures from both parties, although the technology was so intrusive that she remained suspicious she had actually been on the air until she heard confirmation from viewers who had actually seen the show.[9]

In June 1948, just before the political conventions, the major trade publication *Variety* carried the news that McBride (whom they referred to as daytime's "femme gabber") had been signed by the Newell-Emmett agency for a weekly, fifty-minute, prime-time television show. She was to earn $2,500 for each show, and the agency was obligated to line up five sponsors, all of whom (as was true on her radio show) were subject to her acceptance.[10] It was Stella who had gotten excited about television, and as usual Mary Margaret went along, although with markedly less enthusiasm. "I suppose TV has to come," she told an interviewer. "Women write to me all the time wanting to know when I'm going on TV. But I don't want to be on display. I want to make faces and grotesque gestures when I feel like it. I just want to be myself."[11] As she told another television columnist, "The only concession I'll make is a little make-up. They're not going to make me anything I'm not."[12]

It was exciting enough for Mary Margaret's loyal fans that she was going to be on television, but the fact that the show would be on in the evenings was an added bonus. This prime-time slot fulfilled a dream of many of Mary Margaret's loyal female daytime listeners: now their husbands could get to know Mary Margaret as well. The show premiered at 9 P.M. on Tuesday, September 21, 1948, on NBC, just after the enormously popular *Texaco Star Theater* with Milton Berle. Unfortunately "Uncle Miltie," television's first superstar, proved a hard act to follow. As one television critic noted privately, "In my opinion, you were the victim of inexcusably bad 'booking.' The odds of a 'conversation piece' following a hilarious comedy turn are simply prohibitive."[13] In the end, *The Mary Margaret McBride Show* was not renewed after its fall season. "Before I began I wanted to do it and then I didn't want to, and after I got going I knew I really didn't want to—but I had to finish out the thirteen weeks" was how she glumly summed up the experience.[14]

Mary Margaret had always prided herself on never rehearsing her radio programs, and she continued this practice on television, even though it drove the production crews crazy. "If you plan to stand up and walk from here to there, we must know the exact time," the director would say, and she would look at him blankly. "They drew chalk lines to establish positions, they poked cameras at me, they set up prompting boards which I couldn't see without my glasses; and in the end, after the rehearsal, we ad-libbed while the control room went mad." Stella, however, was totally unfazed, calmly calling out the camera shots with this explanation to the harried crew: "Mary Margaret never followed a script in her life—just take it easy, and shoot her the way you would a baseball game!"[15]

The content of the first show is not known, although an assistant production manager at NBC reported the following conversation about it. The family had watched the *Texaco Star Theater* and had decided to keep the set on when they saw the announcement for Mary Margaret McBride. "Are you bored, Jim?" the NBC executive asked his son-in-law. "Good Lord, no, I wonder what she's going to say next." When it was over, his wife (who was not a regular listener of the radio show) bubbled, "This program certainly deserves the extra ten minutes."[16]

The second show revolved around two naturalists with an array of animals, including a praying mantis, a marmoset who almost ate the praying mantis, a mud turtle who was put up at the Waldorf-Astoria (an example of Stella's flair for showmanship), and a toucan who nearly pecked out the television host's eye. Television critic Harriet Van Horne thought that Mary Margaret handled herself with remarkable poise in the midst of such chaos, but she was an old hand at these show-and-tell animal programs from radio. Van Horne also was impressed by how the "motherly" Miss McBride handled the commercials for the five sponsors, oohing and aahing over each product "as if it were a new baby." Indeed, Van Horne pronounced Mary Margaret's commercial pitches even more effective on television when viewers could see the products. Yet the columnist raised a criticism that recurred in many of the reviews: a fifty-minute show needed more than one host and a single theme to sustain interest over such a long period of time. Two guests and a menagerie of animals would have been plenty of material to sustain a radio show of that length, but were not enough for TV's shorter attention span. Perhaps McBride would have done better with a half-hour slot.[17]

Two of the shows survive, offering a glimpse into the early days of television and clues to what McBride was up against. (Each is a kinescope—that is, a film of the program as it appeared on a television screen, the only way of preserving television shows until the introduction of videotape in the 1960s.) The show that aired on November 16, 1948, was styled as a theatrical show in honor of her forty-ninth birthday. Mary Margaret was dressed in an evening gown, complete with corsage, lacquered hair, and pearls. The program featured Pearl Buck and a program of performances inspired by her work with the East/West Association, including a Chinese modern dancer studying with Martha Graham, an Indian dancer, and a traditional Japanese performer. Vincent Connolly appears in a role similar to that of his radio persona, keeping things on track and helping with the products, but hasn't quite gotten the knack of looking at the camera when he speaks. (Nor has Mary Margaret.) And Connolly seems to have forgotten that on camera he can't just get up and leave in the middle of a discussion between two people in the way he could do on radio. It is, however, amusing to see Vincent, Mary Margaret, and her eleven-year-old nephew Tommy do commercials for such products as Sunshine Crackers and Kemtone roller paint (Tommy demonstrates). Even though the interview with Pearl Buck was ad-libbed, it felt more stilted than it would have on the radio.[18]

A show from mid-December, the last one to air, was more lively. By now Mary Margaret was much better at looking at the camera and looks quite attractive in a dark dress with white collar and bow. Her guests were a young couple, Harmon (Bud) and Constance (Connie) Herlmerick, who describe living entirely on their own for a year in Alaska's Brooks Range. They were an engaging and photogenic couple, but what made the program work were the home movies that they showed of their cabin, their daily activities, and their interaction with the local Inuits. It was like watching a travelogue today on public television or cable, only such footage would have been quite fresh and new to viewers in 1948. At some point, the ubiquitous Tommy hands around plates of Sunshine Cookies (a sponsor), and Vincent helps do commercials for a

Squibb angled toothbrush, a Sylvania electronic repair service, Kemtone paint, and Holmes and Edward silver.[19]

Other shows were similar to the kinds of programs that McBride might have aired on radio. She did one on humor with Bennett Cerf, Ilka Chase, and Ogden Nash, their first time before the cameras and years before *What's My Line?* Another program featured foreign correspondents talking about the world situation, including the deepening cold war with the Soviet Union. A show dedicated to the Caribbean featuring dancers like Pearl Primus drew a fan letter from Walter White, who praised the dignity and gaiety of the program, adding, "I have never seen any program where Negroes were treated as human beings so admirably and successfully as you did."[20] A staged dinner party at which distinguished guests like Burl Ives, gourmet Crosby Gaige, and artist James Montgomery Flagg cooked the food had its predictable share of culinary successes and disasters, among the latter being Flagg's custard dessert, which turned to soup. The on-air diners ate it anyway.[21]

Television was still fairly novel in 1948, and viewers were grateful for anything interesting and entertaining to watch. Reviewers were generally kind, too, but Jack Gould of the *New York Times* gave McBride a bad review, which in typical fashion she took personally. Calling her "the usually self-assured matriarch of Radio City," he observed that she had "a howling case of the jitters before the cameras" and "managed to present perhaps television's most distracting offering to date." He then continued with devastating candor:

> And perhaps the ladies in the daytime can survive Miss McBride's effusive and interminable commercials, but for the men at home in the evening they are hard to take after a day at the office. To watch Miss McBride shift—without pause or loss of breath—from eulogy of Kemtone paint to an analysis of Russia is an ordeal not quickly forgotten. If nighttime television is to be daytime radio, away, video, away!

When Mary Margaret took the unusual step of answering his criticisms on a later show, she drew a rebuke from NBC's brass.[22]

She and Gould continued the debate by letter, in which he offered an even more candid (and convincing) analysis of the problems of the show. Gould's main point was that a visual program could not be a mere replication of an aural one:

The leisurely informality of your radio show is ideally suited to the ear. But when the same program is watched intently by the eye, different values do prevail automatically. The eye becomes more restless. It wants movement, more action. The eye, in short, is a much more demanding "critic" than the ear.[23]

As a related point, Gould felt that McBride was imposing too much of a burden on herself as the host to sustain the show visually, noting that even for someone with extensive background in theater or film, this would have been hard to sustain for almost an hour. Reminding her that she was in fact a newspaperwoman, he offered this bit of advice: "If you could think of your program, as you apparently do on the radio, as a sort of capsule newspaper with the variety and timeliness that a newspaper must have, I believe you would have licked what strikes me as many of your problems." Here, in 1948, Jack Gould was anticipating the format of shows like *Today* and *The Home* which still influence the television talk format today.[24]

When Mary Margaret looked back on the programs from the perspective of a decade later, she recognized the validity of some of the criticisms that Gould and others had raised, but she still felt that many of her early shows were actually better than what was being shown on television circa 1960.[25] She was right, up to a point. Her shows were interesting and stimulating in a manner similar to her radio programs, but they still lacked the visual sparkle and faster tempo that were needed to succeed in the cooler medium of television. McBride also was a victim of bad timing, and not just in drawing the time slot after the immensely watchable Milton Berle. In 1948 not enough families owned television sets to create a steady and loyal market for her show in the way her radio program had done. "I plan to wait until a lot more television sets are sold into private homes," she told an interviewer in 1949. "Mine is *not* a bar and grill audience. Then I'm going right back into television. I'll show those old meanies!"[26]

Mary Margaret McBride never had another regular television series, but she did not disappear completely from the television screen, much to the delight of her fans, especially after she gave up her regular radio program in 1954. She was a regular guest on Fridays for Tex McCrary and Jinx Falkenburg's talk show, appeared on Sunday morning programs such as *Frontiers of Faith* (sponsored by the National Council of Churches of Christ), and did occasional commercials for Swansdown Cake Mix and Conti shampoo. "Oh, happy day!" wrote a fan from Santa Maria, California. "That was yesterday when I was dozing away on the couch. I heard your dear voice on T.V. and there you were. . . . I shall go at once and get the Swansdown Instant Cake Mixes for I can always count on the products you recommend."[27] Another viewer from Los Angeles was even more rhapsodic:

> I was sitting here before my television set. . . . And then—oh, Mary Margaret—you came! Why, you came right into my living room here in the little cottage on the side of a quiet street—bringing with you such a delicious cake to share with me as we sat and visited. . . . I could almost taste the delicacy of its flavor for your hands served it to me![28]

Such fan letters suggest that Mary Margaret could have continued to tap a loyal audience who would have responded to her mix of talk and doing the products. Stella and Cynthia Lowry in fact pitched such a show to Pat Weaver at NBC in 1953, but nothing came of it.[29]

One of the most dominant personalities of early television was Edward R. Murrow of CBS, and Mary Margaret appeared both on his news show *See It Now* and its more celebrity-oriented *Person to Person*. A *See It Now* show from May 1953, en route to England for the coronation of Queen Elizabeth, started at Idlewild airport where a Pan Am Stratoclipper prepared to carry sixty people across the ocean on a night flight. Mary Margaret was on a busman's holiday because even though she worked for ABC, she did a quick interview with the flight attendants about the food preparation for the long flight, including ascertaining that they could make a decent cup of tea. The cameras then showed the flight attendants making up sleeping berths for the night and walking up and down the aisle with flashlights tucking in passengers. As the plane approached London's Gatwick Airport, the pilots checked in with air traffic control using what looked like an old-fashioned rotary telephone.[30]

In December 1954, six months after she had retired from her regular radio show, Mary Margaret was a guest on Murrow's *Person to Person*, the invitation confirming her prominent stature as a popular cultural figure in the early 1950s. The show opened with Murrow interviewing Bing Crosby, who took television viewers on a tour of his Beverly Hills mansion, talking about his family, shooting some bil-

liards, and singing and humming as he went. His scenes were intercut
to Murrow, smoking like a chimney, asking questions live from a studio
in New York. Meanwhile Mary Margaret sat nervously in her Central
Park South apartment waiting for her turn. As she shared with readers
of her syndicated column a few days later,

> At 10:30 EST, Mr. Murrow went to call on Bing Crosby in Hollywood.
> Hours passed, or so it seemed to me. I sat in a stiff-backed chair in my
> upstairs living room in a coma. Suddenly out of a little black box I
> heard Ed Murrow's voice asking me a question. I was being gestured
> at by people in the room and somehow I plunged into action.[31]

The show unfolded in a seemingly spontaneous and informal manner, but a surviving script shows how thoroughly planned in advance
the patter was. Murrow introduced Mary Margaret, who was dressed
in a colorfully embroidered Chinese silk jacket and lounging pajamas,
with a short synopsis of her career and then asked her about her two
main passions: books and food. She didn't eat on this broadcast the way
she often did on radio, but her passion for books was very much in evidence as she gave Murrow, and the national television audience, a tour
of her duplex apartment, every single available bit of wall space
crammed to the ceiling with books. Along the way, Mary Margaret
talked about her semiretirement and the column she was writing for the
Associated Press. She showed off her collection of dolls sent in by listeners and also her screen with greetings from all her guests, which she
said she looked at when she was blue. When Murrow asked in a rather
patronizing way about women's faculty for never being on time, it was
Mary Margaret's cue to tell the story of being late to the broadcast with
Eleanor Roosevelt. (This time she embellished it just a bit, saying they
ran hand in hand to the studio.) She also told the zipper story and of
being locked out of a Hollywood hotel room in her flimsy nightgown.
Then it was time to stop. The fifteen minutes passed quickly; everyone
seemed generally at ease with the light banter; the camera cut to a commercial for Permalude Oil; and Murrow signed off with his trademark
"Good night and good luck."[32]

An appearance on NBC's *Home* show in June 1957 showed Mary
Margaret at her most animated and her most nervous. Talking with
hostess Arlene Francis, who was reading from cue cards while "Beautiful Lady" (McBride's radio theme song) played in the background,

Mary Margaret, dressed as usual in a dark dress with white collar and cuffs and pearls, seemed just a little bit out of sorts to be the center of attention but not in control. Francis, who was highly complimentary about her career and her importance for women, then introduced Fannie Hurst, who shared her impressions of why Mary Margaret was so good at what she did, which, according to Hurst, was "raising the cultural level" of American women. Then Mary Margaret and Arlene Francis talked about why she was such a good interviewer and cared so much about her guests. The conversation is a bit stilted but not hard to watch, and yet it is quite clear that Mary Margaret is squirming in the unusual position of being the interviewee rather than the interviewer. Next charming home movies of Mary Margaret's farm in the Catskills are shown, including a tea party that she gave for her West Shokan neighbors, who were no doubt excited about being on national television.[33]

Then Arlene Francis's assistant Hugh Downs joins the conversation, and Mary Margaret tries out her interview technique on him. This section is spontaneous and unscripted, and McBride immediately catches Downs with a leading question: "What is the secret of your management of women?" referring to his success at working alongside talented women. Downs blushes and replies in an amused manner, and they continue talking. Instantly Mary Margaret comes alive, her face animated and her hands gesturing, totally focused on drawing Hugh Downs out and practically oblivious to being on camera. After a minute or so, the camera cuts away to Arlene Francis doing the wrap-up, all the while the McBride-Downs interview is continuing animatedly in the background. The conclusion is clear: Mary Margaret's problems with television have less to do with her appearance or gender and everything to do with her being uncomfortable as the center of attention.[34]

Further confirmation of this comes from her successful stints as a guest host on a variety of shows. "I didn't enjoy being the main thing," she said reflecting on her earlier series, "but lately I have enjoyed being on other people's programs."[35] In addition to her regular slot with Tex and Jinx, she often filled in for Jack Paar. Once when she was a guest, she turned the tables and started interviewing him. Before she was done, he had admitted that he had been married once before and that he wore a hairpiece.[36] Another time she learned about the importance of the visual on television when she told the story of her first, lonely Christmas away from home and everybody laughed. Comedian Dody

Goodman explained why: "No, you told it all right. I think the trouble is, you told it in a mink stole. You'll never get sympathy in a mink stole."[37]

McBride remained bemused at the amount of attention she got through these appearances. "After working my head off in radio for so many years, I found that I was better known for the ten or twelve appearances on the Paar show than for my twenty years in radio. Naturally I'm intrigued," adding, "I must be an awful ham." But network executives looked the other way when she put out feelers about her own show. "Oh, yes, NBC and CBS knew of my desire to return. They've also been aware of my ambitions for a television show. Still, they're not tearing down my door."[38]

In addition to Jack Paar, Mary Margaret bumped up against another emerging television personality in the 1950s: Mike Wallace. In 1956 she appeared on his *Night Beat* show, where she greeted Wallace's question about why she wanted to be famous with, "Don't you understand that? Any ham understands that." When Wallace realized that she had not only confessed to being a ham but had called him one, too, she said, "We're both hams, honey, we're both hams."[39]

The next year the tables were turned, and Mary Margaret was one of three panelists (along with author Al Morgan and sports columnist Jimmy Cannon) who interviewed Wallace on *Entertainment Press Conference*. Even though McBride tried to follow the grand inquisitor style that was already Wallace's trademark, her questions about his religious convictions and his insecurities must have seemed like soft balls lobbed in his direction.[40] An astute reviewer noted that whereas the other two panelists used a direct method of questioning in which the personality of the interviewer plays a major part and the questions are asked in an almost third-degree atmosphere (a stance epitomized by Wallace himself, whom the columnist called "the terrible Torquemada of the TV Inquisition"), Mary Margaret's style was much more self-effacing. "Her questions are invariably well-founded and shrewdly aimed, but they are so quietly spoken, so brief, so worded without color, that all the viewer's consciousness is concentrated on the subject, not upon her."[41] The *Variety* reviewer made a similar point: "As a veteran broadcaster, she handles herself with unquestioned finesse. But it's a kid-glove kind of treatment, hardly in the realm of exploration or controversy."[42]

Those assessments of Mary Margaret's television style, much more than her age or appearance, also suggest why she never became a major star, despite her name's being bandied about as a possible host of shows along the lines of *Night Beat*. Television, at least prime-time talk shows, seemed to prefer a more aggressive and confrontational style of interviewing, one that would have been totally false to her persona. The shows' creators were after a hard-hitting story, whereas her style was to bring out the general personality of her subject.[43]

Much closer to the old Mary Margaret McBride radio shows was the magazine concept of the *Today* show, credited to Pat Weaver at NBC but clearly drawing on the radio roots of shows like McBride's, Arthur Godfrey's, and a host of others.[44] With their combination of light news, short features, and ad-libbed interviews, punctuated by commercials from multiple individual sponsors, these magazine-type shows transferred formats to television that were already well established on radio. Nonetheless, their radio precedents are often absent or overlooked in broadcast history.[45]

Why didn't Mary Margaret end up hosting *Today* or having her own late night chat show? Or why didn't she have a daytime show for housewives, the staple of her audience? Talking about both radio and television in 1957, she noted, "I don't suppose I'll ever get a rating to satisfy the networks. Conversation requires too much concentration and effort on the part of the listeners. I'm sure the housewives prefer a soap opera to my interviews."[46] Something had clearly shifted, since housewives, or at least a sizable minority of the daytime audience, had preferred interviews to soap operas back in the days before radio felt so threatened. Squeezed off radio by the soaps, she found no room on television, where it was easier to make money with situation comedies and reruns of *Gunsmoke*, *I Love Lucy*, or old feature films. Increasingly there was no place for a literate, nonconfrontational interviewer like McBride when ratings increasingly drove the network profit engine.[47]

That television was increasingly inhospitable to Mary Margaret's talents is clear, but there is another side of the equation: she made her name in radio, and her heart would always be there. Her style truly was better suited to the intimacies of radio, where she could use her warm and enfolding voice to draw listeners into an imagined community. As one of her fans noted, "The ability to permeate one's personality through the medium of radio by the discussion of simple everyday topics, without benefit of sound effects, or radio stage trimmings, is a difficult thing to do, and especially to do so day after day. You have succeeded in doing just that."[48] Such a relationship would have been much more difficult in the faster-paced, more gimmicky world of television.

For Mary Margaret McBride to have conquered television in her fifties, after an exhausting twenty-year career in radio, would have called for a measure of commitment and personal reinvention that would have been almost superhuman in its effort. If she had fallen in love with television, perhaps the old drive and ambition would have kicked in, but she seemed to know that she was better off watching television than appearing on it, content to be an occasional host or guest rather than the prime mover behind a show. It is hard to escape the conclusion that television history is bleaker for its inability to find a niche for a talented interviewer like her.

The clock says it all. *Reprinted by permission of Library of Congress, Prints and Photographs Division.*

18

The Last Show: May 14, 1954

COULD MARY MARGARET McBRIDE HAVE SUSTAINED her radio show at its height indefinitely? Probably not, but she certainly could have kept it going for a few years longer. After all, the show was fully subscribed with sponsors, and her listeners remained loyal. After twenty years on the air, she was reaching the daughters of her original listeners, women who had been children at home in the 1930s but were now grown up with young children of their own. Perhaps she wanted to go for three generations before she stopped.

Over the course of her radio career, Mary Margaret McBride claimed to have broadcast nearly fifteen thousand shows and conducted almost thirty thousand interviews.[1] There were no repeats or reruns; each show was unique. The strain of pulling off almost an hour of interesting, fresh, scintillating conversation or discussion five times a week, year after year, was beginning to take its toll. The show—choosing the guests, preparing for the interviews, answering the mail, planning for the next show—consumed her whole life. Her forays into television, while moderately successful, gave her none of the gratification that she received from her daily radio show. The more television she did, the more she realized how much she preferred radio.

Even though she later said she had always wanted to go out on top and leave the show on her own terms rather than have it canceled because of a dwindling audience or declining support from sponsors, that statement rings a bit false given her love of the limelight and her oft-repeated statement that she hoped she would die in front of a microphone. In 1954, she was financially secure, at the height of her powers, and only in her mid-fifties. On the face of it, her decision to give up the show seemed to make no sense at all.

There was a good reason, however, and a poignant one: Stella was dying of cancer. When Mary Margaret had returned from a trip to Norway in the summer of 1953 accompanied by Cynthia Lowry, she realized that the reason Stella had begged off was that she was not feeling well. In February 1954, she was operated on for cancer. The doctors said that the operation had gone well, but they could not make any guarantees for the future. Stella was weak and far from her usual feisty self. She demanded to know the full extent of her condition, and Mary Margaret complied.[2]

It was Stella who decided that they should give up the program. "I'd thought of it but hadn't dared to suggest if for fear of hurting her pride," McBride recalled. "She didn't admit even then that she was too sick to go on. Rather she said I needed a rest after twenty years of broadcasting, that she was sick of fighting with an executive at ABC who annoyed her."[3] They agreed that the last show would be that May, the twentieth anniversary of McBride's debut as Martha Deane back in 1934. For the tenth anniversary, they had taken over Madison Square Garden, and for the fifteenth, she had almost filled Yankee Stadium. For this one, however, they chose not to have a huge public extravaganza, deciding instead to broadcast from Mary Margaret's duplex apartment, where she had done most of her ABC broadcasts.[4]

If Stella had been well, she would have attacked the planning for the last show with gusto, but "this time she let others plan." An extended guest list of the radio family and all the important people in Mary Margaret's and Stella's lives gathered upstairs for the live broadcast and then were called downstairs individually to make their final on-air good-byes. Mary Margaret wore one of her colorful, flowing Chinese silk jackets over a comfortably loose dress, clutching a pair of reading glasses in her hand. Their good friend Gene Leone, the restaurateur, provided a sumptuous spread of squab, lobsters, shrimp, fruit, cheese, and desserts, but the mood was not exactly festive. "We knew it was the end of something we'd greatly cared about," the radio host recalled, and the feelings of loss, even without the Stella's illness, were all around them. As all the tributes poured in, Mary Margaret felt like she was attending her own funeral.[5]

From a distance of fifty years, the last radio broadcast sounds much more like a regular Mary Margaret McBride hour than the teary, sentimental, and heart-wrenching good-bye that might have been expected. Nobody was gloomy or depressed, at least on the air, since they all, Mary Margaret included, seemed to believe that this wasn't really a final good-bye and that she soon would be back on the air in another format. At one point the radio host invoked the great actress Sarah

Bernhardt, who was known for announcing her retirement and then coming back for one more farewell tour, by saying that she would probably be making last appearances for the next forty years. At another point, she confessed, "If I can keep away from radio for three months it will be a surprise to me." Various friends with books in press, like the writer John Kieran, made her promise to come back because nobody could do a book interview better than she could. McBride cheerfully agreed.[6]

On the whole, the show unfolded like a regular program, although listeners were told that because of the special interest, it would be rebroadcast the next day, Saturday, for those who had not been able to catch it on Friday or for listeners who wanted to hear it again. It opened with her trademark music, "Beautiful Lady," and her longtime announcer Vincent Connolly telling listeners, "It's one o'clock and here is Mary Margaret McBride." He and Stella and Mary Margaret reminisced about his joining the show right out of Princeton—Stella had chosen him because, she said, "he's a gentleman." And they all liked his curly hair. Mary Margaret paid tribute to Stella, without whom she was certain that she would never have lasted more than a few weeks on radio, who piped up that Mary Margaret's success was due to "your ability and my bad disposition." True to form, they admitted that they had had quite a big fight that morning about something related to the show. For most of this last broadcast, Stella sat at Mary Margaret's right, decked out in a fancy dress and a show-stopping hat, leaving the technical duties to others.

A variety of guests had been lined up, and it was clear that there would not be enough time for them all. "Speed up, kids," Mary Margaret said at one point, noting that she wished that ABC had given her two or three hours instead of just one. She made sure to recognize members of her radio family, like her secretary Hilda Deichler and leg woman Janice Devine, as well as old favorites like Madame Nikki and Hattie Silverman. Fannie Hurst, Wes Gallagher of the Associated Press, publisher John Farrar, and the president of ABC all paid tribute in words, poem, or, in the case of John Golden, song. Radio critic Ben Gross recalled how he had been critical of her when she first went on the air but had soon converted when he realized that she genuinely believed that women were intelligent beings who were interested in issues and ideas from the world at large. No one turned maudlin or overly sentimental, and the show moved forward briskly.

Then, amazingly, right in the middle of this final broadcast, Mary Margaret devoted at least fifteen minutes to doing the products. Or to put it another way, she wanted to say good-bye to her faithful sponsors in the same way she was saying good-bye to all her friends who had supported her over the years. So one more time, listeners heard her praise H. C. Bohack's supermarkets, which had been on the air with her for thirteen years, and her other long-running sponsor, Dolly Madison ice cream, "the only ice cream I'll spend my calories on." The folks at Dromedary sent a cake and a poem. On her last day on the air, Mary Margaret was just as enthusiastic and convincing about products such as Puss 'n Boots cat food, Fairmount frozen strawberries, Breath of Pine deodorizer, Spirit of Norway sardines, and Devonshire melba toast as if this were an ordinary Friday. All in all, she did twenty products, one for each year.

Who would be the final guest on the final show? Eleanor Roosevelt was a likely candidate, but she had appeared the day before. Instead, Mary Margaret asked the Reverend Norman Vincent Peale, an icon of 1950s religion and popular culture, to do the honors. He was a friend as well as a frequent guest and felt honored at being chosen. He shared his feelings about her with the audience, saying unabashedly that he loved her and comparing her to an institution like the Empire State Building (which brought a few giggles, since they both are very large). Like so many of the other guests, Peale maintained that it was all right if she wanted to have a rest from the show but that he expected her to be back on the air soon. Then, at Mary Margaret's request, he led them all in a short prayer, a benediction as it were, for this great woman and her show. After this final blessing, she managed to say, "Thank you, Norman Vincent Peale," and then, weakly and faintly, her final words "and good-bye."

A candid photograph captured this scene. Mary Margaret sits at the table from which she has broadcast, her head bowed and her hands covering a tear running down her face. Stella sits at her side, a bemused and somewhat distant look on her face, and a friend looks on with concern. The clock behind them shows the time: one minute before two.

19

Cookbooks, Columns, and Commentary

FOR MONTHS AFTER she gave up her regular radio show, Mary Margaret McBride had a recurring nightmare. It is one o'clock, and Vincent is announcing her, "but although I did my best to speak, nothing came out of my paralyzed lips and I could not get on the air." She knew it was the right thing to give up the show because of Stella's illness, but she missed it terribly. It was weeks before she could turn on the radio or television. "I couldn't bear to hear or see others doing what I wanted so much to be doing too."[1]

For someone whose whole life was literally her work, and who came alive most when she was on the air, the end of her program forced a dramatic adjustment in Mary Margaret's daily routine. Even though she now could do things she hadn't been able to do for years, like sit through an entire play without worrying about having to go home and prepare for the next day's show, she missed the structure in her life. Mainly she missed the contact with her fans, whose support and devotion to her personally had helped her through the vicissitudes of her fragile emotional life. As she later told journalist Heywood Hale Broun, "Once you get it, you never want to give it up."[2]

Not surprisingly, she didn't stay off the air for long. When she and Stella returned from a several-month summer stay at their West Shokan farm in September 1954, McBride launched a five-minute, six-day-a-week radio show at 3 o'clock on NBC called *Thought for the Day*. This show, which was mainly commentary devoted to books and current events, had a single sponsor each day, such as Q-Tips, General Foods, or Calgon. As before, McBride retained sole power to veto any advertiser unacceptable to her. NBC promoted it as primarily of interest to a female audience who would enjoy "interesting vignettes, stories, thoughts on current events, wherever her bright fancy and imagination takes her."[3] In a typical week, she might discuss Clinton Rossiter's new book on the presidency or Samuel Lubbell's *Revolt of the Moderates*,

Still in demand as a speaker, Mary Margaret McBride addresses a gathering in
1957. *Reprinted by permission of Library of Congress, Prints and Photographs Division.*

famous women like Clara Barton and Nellie Bly, or a favorite McBride author like P. G. Wodehouse.[4] Stella especially liked the pretaped format of the show because it permitted Mary Margaret "to get off the treadmill" and "at least have a good part of her time without stress and strain."[5]

Devoted fans who were in withdrawal from the cancellation of her regular program probably welcomed the chance to hear her familiar voice, even if for only five minutes a day, but McBride tried to pack so much into these short programs that they had a rushed, almost breathless quality, rather than the leisurely, neighborly pace of her old show. They also sounded more scripted and artificial, each one starting and ending with a mention of that day's sponsor that seemed disconnected from the rest of the show, rather than an integral part of it. And yet sponsors lined up to be on the show.[6]

When the program was canceled in early 1957, *Newsweek* called it "a triumph of accounting over sentiment." The show was still 80 percent sponsored and receiving one thousand letters from listeners each week, but network affiliates were demanding more soap operas to compete with CBS. As the national schedule became increasingly dominated by longer, routinized time slots, there was no room for a five-minute show. Orchestra leader Fred Waring was dropped at the same time as well.[7]

Around the time she decided to give up her forty-five-minute program, Mary Margaret launched another project: building a country home. Having fallen in love with the view from Stella's farm, at some point she bought an acre or so of land from her partner, with vague plans of someday building a house of her own. "And there the matter stood until a spring weekend when I was frantically busy and Stella's house was full of more than usually active guests, including indulgent parents with a spoiled child who had one screaming tantrum after another. Out in Stella's front yard, waving relieved farewells to the departing guests, I announced firmly that I was going to build my house—right away."[8] Like home owners before and since, she had no idea what she was getting into. She entitled this chapter in her autobiography "Barn Yesterday."[9]

"I was never a logical candidate for barn remodeling," Mary Margaret herself admitted, adding that "it would never have occurred to me under ordinary circumstances to convert a two-hundred-year-old barn into a house." Obviously "ordinary circumstances" did not include turning over the whole project to her indomitable partner. Stella quickly lined up a builder, and they went off to inspect the site that Mary Margaret had selected above the apple orchard. By the time they came back several hours later, they had decided that what she really wanted to do was to remodel the old barn, with its original chestnut beams, about fifty yards from the farmhouse. Mary Margaret was not consulted about this decision, nor most of those to follow.[10]

In negotiating radio contracts, Stella was used to getting her own way, and she negotiated with contractors and stone masons in the same fashion. She also was oblivious to money, hers or Mary Margaret's. Whenever Mary Margaret asked how much this barn renovation would cost, Stella reassured her that it would probably cost less than her original dream house because the structure was already standing on the site, no matter that its previous inhabitants had been swallows. As the bills piled up ("I was writing checks at a rate to give me finger cramps")[11] and the plans kept expanding, that prediction proved to be one of several casualties of the process. Stella's original assertion that the barn's original foundation was perfectly sound did not hold up either. One day Mary Margaret went over to observe the work and discovered "a bastion of concrete, thick enough surely to hold up the Empire State Building, running down the south side of the barn. 'Had to do it,' said the workman. 'One of those beams was pretty weak at the base. But it's like Gibraltar now.'"[12]

Then there was the matter of the bedrooms. McBride was constitutionally unable to conceptualize from blueprints what something would look like, so this story is not as far-fetched as it may sound. Fairly far along in the renovation, Mary Margaret took a tour of the work in progress as all of the workers proudly showed off the magnificent upstairs room with its chestnut beams and panoramic views. Where will the bedrooms be, she asked Stella innocently. Blank looks all around. Two days later the bulldozers were back and a concrete foundation was laid for a large addition to house the living quarters. "It's just as well," concluded Stella. "It was too small anyway."[13]

McBride's decision to build the house was clearly linked to the twin factors of having a lot more time on her hands and Stella's recent diagnosis of cancer. Now that they were off the air, the barn restoration offered the two women a chance to collaborate—or, more likely, bicker—on a joint project. "Stella was panting to get the project started," Mary Margaret noted. "She looked and seemed to feel better than she had for months. . . . As only she and I were aware at the time, she desperately needed something to occupy her thoughts."[14]

Finally, at three times what she had budgeted, Mary Margaret had her dream house. From the outside the converted barn looked a bit like a Swiss chalet, albeit one with a California touch owing to the redwood siding that Stella had insisted on. The living room measured a grand forty-by-forty feet, with its cathedral ceiling framing a huge stone fireplace and the massive chestnut beams that had prompted the renovation in the first place. There were bookcases everywhere for Mary Margaret's collection of more than five thousand books. A screened porch off the upper level looked out over the Ashokan reservoir and the mountains beyond. The lower level, which originally had been planned as the kitchen, became a huge guest room, and later, when Mary Margaret started broadcasting on the local Kingston station WGHQ, a space big enough to hold a studio audience. The addition contained bedrooms and baths, as well as the kitchen, which was outfitted with the latest in General Electric appliances, all pink and all obtained at half price, no doubt as part of some deal that Stella struck with the company. All in all, it was a comfortable, if slightly quirky, house, one befitting the spirit of Stella Karn and Mary Margaret McBride.[15]

Another joint project had to do with food. Friends and colleagues had long wondered whether Mary Margaret would ever try her hand at writing a cookbook, and like the barn restoration, that moment came in conjunction with her retirement. The instigator, as usual, was Stella Karn, who always had wanted her partner to write a cookbook and finally overcame Mary Margaret's insistence that she would rather eat food rather than write about it. Actually, McBride didn't need much prodding: after all, with her culinary adventures on the radio, she had been doing informal research for such a book for decades. She also was always willing to try anything once, even write a cookbook. As she explained her decision to columnist Alice Hughes, "I'm not a topnotch cook, nor am I a gourmet. I'm just an enthusiastic appreciater of food, and as I've eaten my way across America collecting recipes (and pounds of weight, alas!) I decided to get them off my mind and hips and into a book."[16]

Plans for the book were already in the works when Mary Margaret gave up her daily radio show, and she and Stella turned their attention to it in part to fill the void of not being on the air and in part to take their minds off Stella's illness. Stella had negotiated a $7,000 advance from G. P. Putnam's Sons, which she promptly spent on hiring researchers and test kitchens to try out recipes, which numbered close to seven thousand. In 1956 Putnam's offered an additional $1,500 to pay the expenses and salary of a home economist to assist in the preparation of the book.[17]

What Mary Margaret and Stella had in mind was not the usual cookbook but a book that would explain the role of food in American history, enhanced by local and regional recipes that revealed the diversity of American cuisine. They consulted with federal and state departments of agriculture across the country, as well as countless libraries, but as Mary Margaret admitted, "If Stella had had her way we'd have traveled to the most remote towns and hamlets of every state and borrowed yellowed recipes out of treasured family books, listened to oldest inhabitants telling food stories from the earliest days." After working on the project for more than four years, Mary Margaret reluctantly concluded that "to do justice to the subject would consume not alone my lifetime but the lifetimes of a staff of researchers as well."[18]

The book, entitled *Mary Margaret McBride's Harvest of American Cooking*, was published in 1957, after having been extensively excerpted in a five-part series in the *Woman's Home Companion* the year before. The final product has a hybrid, almost schizophrenic character to it. The first half of the book, almost 225 pages, crosses the country from east to west, visiting its major regions state by state as part of McBride's attempt to write the history of America through its foods. An odd potpourri of travelogue, human-interest stories, local color, frontier mythology, and antiquarian history, the chapters on each state and territory (Alaska and Hawaii and even American Samoa are included) look at the country's past through the lens of food customs and recipes. McBride's view of American history was often a simplistic one, but there is no doubt that she felt a passion to bring readers not just recipes for roast pork and chocolate cake but also an appreciation of the nation's cultural and historical heritage.[19]

The chapters on two states with special meaning for Mary Margaret—Missouri and her adopted state of Florida—show how she interwove strands of personal material throughout the narrative. She opens the Missouri chapter with a description of the summer when she was six years old, complete with memories of her mother's cooking and the foods that were part of her childhood. She ends that chapter with a collection of family recipes (called "receipts") with names like "Mother Blanton's Corn Dodgers," "Grandma's Way of Cooking Corn," and "Mama's Southern Corn Bread (And no sugar in it, you may be sure)." Why weren't they in the second half of the book along with the other recipes? Because they were "refugees from the test-kitchens," unable to pass the exacting domestic science standards that insisted on level teaspoons and controlled oven temperatures, rather than "butter the size of a walnut" or "cut a young chicken through the back."[20]

Her chapter on Florida is almost as evocative, with memories of her beloved mother alongside those of sleeping surrounded by the fragrance of flowering orange trees, cooking freshly caught fish and potatoes over a fire near the Indian River at a campsite, and exploring the Florida Keys. She also tells the story of how a blackbird pie almost put her and guest Marjorie Kinnan Rawlings in jail. Rawlings had come from her farm, Cross Creek, to be interviewed by McBride, who was doing a remote broadcast from the state. "Suddenly she launched into a rhapsody on the subject of the blackbirds she shot in her orange grove and converted into a deep-dish pie." Soon the sheriff was on the phone, warning that shooting blackbirds was a violation of state game laws. "So I never got to eat blackbird pie, but settled happily for a much more toothsome one made with Florida syrup and pecans." Not every state had a personal connection or funny anecdote, but she did manage to come up with something interesting to say about almost every one of them.[21]

The second half of the book contains one thousand recipes, organized not by state but by type of food: appetizers, sandwiches, poultry, desserts, and so forth. While the narrative section is interesting and fun to read, the recipes are bland, no different from what one would have found in most of the cookbooks of the 1950s. The cuisine relies heavily on meat and potatoes, gravy, and macaroni and cheese. The section on vegetables includes both fresh and newly available convenience—such as frozen—foods. (The recipe for broccoli Parmesan calls for cooking a package of frozen chopped broccoli, pouring garlic sautéed in butter over it, and then sprinkling it with Parmesan cheese. That's it.) One astute reviewer called the recipes "colorless and run-of-the-mill," especially compared with the history section of the book, which contained directions to cooks like "beat like thunder" or "add a dozen squirrels for every hundred gallons of burgoo." The reviewer added, "One suspects that home economists who convert 'two double handsful of light bread crumbs' into '1 1/2 cups crumbs' often sacrifice taste as well as poetry."[22]

It is clear that Mary Margaret's heart was in the narrative history, not the recipes. The cookbook was the culmination of a passion that dated back at least as far as her early days as Martha Deane when she campaigned for the cause of better food in America. With her wide-ranging approach to food as a cultural marker, her attention to the diversity of regional cuisines in an increasingly nationalized society, and her appreciation of the social rituals surrounding food preparation and consumption, McBride anticipated by several decades the scholarly field of culinary history.[23]

While Mary Margaret was working on her cookbook and doing her five-minute radio commentary, she also was writing a daily newspaper column called "Mary Margaret McBride Says" which was distributed by the Associated Press. She had actually started this column in late 1953 before she and Stella decided to terminate the radio program. "It makes a wider network in my life than just radio," she told columnist Sidney Fields in 1953. "It's a lovely thought I can write in the city, the country, any place."[24] Like her radio commentary, these columns were aimed at a female audience and usually ran in the women's pages of daily newspapers, prominently featured in some papers but tucked in the back with the comics and horoscopes in others. Editors liked them because they were short and simple to grasp. "Excellent human interest copy with good homely philosophy running through," said the managing editor of the *Kansas City Star*. "What I like is its universal appeal and down-to-earthiness that lifts rather than pricks or prods," said the women's editor of the *Los Angeles Times*.[25] At its peak the column was carried in ninety-six papers and was available in most major markets. In addition to the *Los Angeles Times*, it ran in the *Chicago Sun Times*, *Detroit Free Press*, *St. Louis Post Dispatch*, *Washington Star*, and in the important New York market, the *New York Mirror*, as well as smaller papers throughout the country.[26]

For an old newspaper reporter like Mary Margaret, it must have been fun to get back into print on a regular basis and with a prestigious nationally syndicated column. She especially enjoyed getting letters from readers, which she specifically asked newspapers to forward to her for her personal attention, even if they had their own procedures for answering such mail. As the AP staff explained to subscribing editors,

"She believes it makes for a stronger bond between herself and her audience, and it is helpful to her to know what people are thinking about and how they react to various columns."[27]

Obviously the column capitalized on McBride's radio popularity, promising the same bond through the written word that she maintained over the air, but like so much else concerning the radio star, when Mary Margaret left the airwaves, she lost something in translation. The columns were easy to read, to be sure—light fluff and general interest, with only occasional forays into serious topics like peace, feminism, or the threat of nuclear contamination. As she did on her radio shows, she talked about what she was doing and reading, but the three hundred to four hundred words often felt trite and forced. One column might talk about junk mail, the next about the noise of a defective refrigerator next door, followed by a story about a skunk under the front porch on her farm. She talked about her own struggles with dieting and her weight and offered humorous insights into building her dream house. Very often she harked back to her Missouri girlhood, drawing parallels between the world in which she was raised and the challenges of the postwar world.[28]

Surprisingly, Stella is rarely mentioned in the columns, unlike the radio shows, in which she was very much part of the picture. Probably Mary Margaret realized she was writing for a larger, more impersonal audience than the intimate rapport she established with her radio listeners. Or maybe the news about Stella was just too grim for the light tone she adopted in this column.[29]

Mary Margaret's last column ran on February 3, 1956, and she addressed it as a personal letter to her readers, with whom she hoped she had established a bond. "I'm a sentimental woman and so I'm not ashamed to record that my heart is heavy and there are tears in my eyes as I put down these final words." Whenever she had read a good book, had an interesting conversation, or eaten an especially delicious meal, "I could hardly wait to share the experience with you." Now that would end. She would especially miss letters from her readers, whom she felt she knew as well as a next-door neighbor. Confessing that she would probably miss writing the column more than they would miss reading it (an interesting admission of how much she depended on the love of her unseen, invisible audiences, either on radio or as newspaper readers), she divulged her true reason for giving it up:

It is because I have come to one of the crossroads all of us reach, and for a while, at least, a daily column is out for me. But I wish you would please hold me in your memory. After all, I am only saying au revoir which means "until we meet again."[30]

This leave taking clearly is about Stella. Nearly everything that had happened since she gave up the show—restoring the barn, writing the cookbook, staying on the air in a less demanding format—was filtered through Stella's last illness. Most of their friends did not realize how seriously ill she was, fooled by Stella's sturdy strength and refusal to act like a sick person. After all, she was barely sixty when the cancer was discovered. "I have a deep sureness," wrote one of their friends in 1955, "that she wouldn't tolerate any such nonsense."[31] Stella and Mary Margaret knew better. When Mary Margaret initially tried to keep the cancer diagnosis from her after the first operation, Stella lit into her. "I want the truth. I have to know what's the matter and I have to face it. You must never lie to me again or let anyone else—promise." For the next three years, as Stella's body grew weaker from the cancer and from the massive doses of radiation that she underwent to keep it at bay, Mary Margaret kept that promise.[32]

Even in illness, Stella was a trooper. She continued to act as Mary Margaret's business manager, but increasingly she was only a shadow of her old self. One day on the bus going home after her radiation treatments, an elderly woman got up and gave Stella her seat. "I must really look sick when a gray-haired old lady gets up to let me sit down," she joked to Janice Devine.[33] Mary Margaret could barely believe that she was dying because it was so contrary to her usual modus operandi: "She never faced the worst until she had to and like Mr. Micawber always felt sure something would turn up."[34]

In January 1957, Mary Margaret closed up the farm and came back to the city for what turned into a death watch. Stella was living at the Waldorf-Astoria at that point, and Mary Margaret would call several times a day and then often come over in the evening just to sit with her and watch television each night until midnight. They rarely spoke— they didn't have to—and Mary Margaret was miserable when they were apart. When Stella insisted that her friend attend a performance of *My Fair Lady*, Mary Margaret cried throughout the play because Stella couldn't be there, too. Even though she had grown weaker, Stella still was able to see the cookbook in galleys, with its prominent and well-deserved dedication: "To Stella whose book this is, with love."[35] Never giving in, she talked about regaining enough strength to go back up to the farm in May. With her dearest friend at her bedside, she died on March 13, 1957.[36]

The memorial service was pure Stella. Mary Margaret had absorbed enough about the publicity racket from her friend to engage not the largest room at the funeral home but a medium-size one. "No vacant seats, baby," Stella had admonished, and sure enough, it was standing room only. The crowd was a mixture of celebrities like Fannie Hurst and the Pickens sisters, old circus folks, and radio friends, who were joined by staff members from the Waldorf-Astoria and the hospital who had been touched by Stella's spirit during her final illness. They all shared favorite stories about this unforgettable character, and everybody agreed that Stella would have loved it.[37]

"Tell her about Stella—my life torn up" Mary Margaret scribbled on the bottom of a letter from a friend a month later.[38] Her friends rallied around her. Travel and food writer Poppy Cannon invited her to go on a gourmet tour of Europe that summer, a trip that Mary Margaret found restorative and fun. She found her way back into the media as a regular Friday guest on the television show hosted by her dear friends Jinx Falkenburg and Tex McCrary. Finally, she put the finishing touches on the cookbook which came out that fall.[39]

The reviews of *Mary Margaret McBride's Harvest of American Cooking*, especially its quirky but entertaining first part, were quite favorable. M. E. Davis noted: "Each state's food preferences are lauded in such succulent adjectives, it becomes obvious why Americans are the best fed (and most overweight) nation in the world."[40] (The review panned the recipes, however.) The cookbook received generally positive treatments in local papers, over the wire services, and in venues like the *New York Herald-Tribune Book Review* which did not usually review cookbooks. (Reviewer Ernestine Evans called it "a fat book and a fattening book.")[41] Nationally syndicated news and gossip columns were more than glad to put in a plug for the book. G. P. Putnam's scheduled the publication day in November, counting on the legions of Mary Margaret's still loyal fans to flock to buy the book for Christmas. That brand-name loyalty, combined with the emphasis on regional cooking and colorful local stories, made for a marketable combination.[42]

In many ways the publication of *Harvest of American Cooking* should have been a triumphant moment for Mary Margaret, but because of

Stella's recent death it was more bittersweet. Stella was certainly there in spirit, however, at the lunch that Putnam's held to celebrate its publication. Speaking of this day, Mary Margaret later recalled, "I kept seeing Stella, full of zest and energy, welcoming her friends, tackling with gusto her favorite squab à la Leone, and making the occasion so much more exciting because she was there."[43] Stella Karn had always been of the "show must go on" persuasion, and this meal certainly did: it was held at a favorite New York restaurant and lasted from noon until 4 P.M. The guest list was vintage Mary Margaret, a reunion of her legendary anniversary shows of the past and all "selected from among those friends for whom I have a genuine kissing affection, not merely-peck-on-the-cheek acquaintances." Eleanor Roosevelt was the featured guest, supplying a nice plug for the cookbook several days later in "My Day."[44]

Mary Margaret no doubt savored the favorable publicity of the event, helped by a toast from guest Ogden Nash which was widely reprinted: "I've concluded as I wander through this Widershin's world and wide, that there are many McBridesmaids but only one McBride."[45] But probably the piece about the cookbook that meant the most to her was one written by fellow journalist Irene Corbally Kuhn, which paid tribute to the book's dedication to Stella by opening, "A marble shaft is a fine memorial. But a good cookbook is a better one."[46] Whenever Mary Margaret picked up the cookbook, she would have seen Stella's influence on every page, the culmination of a life journey—indeed, a love affair—that began with the two young women enthusiastically eating their way through twenty-eight languages in Greenwich Village more than thirty years earlier.

20

"Good-bye, Y'all"

AFTER STELLA'S DEATH, a news service report ran over the wires that Mary Margaret Mcbride was considering marrying her old flame, Richard Dorris, who had recently been widowed.[1] The idea was probably not as wild as it might have seemed at first glance. Mcbride had left a highly successful national career and was comfortable financially. Even though she had never fulfilled her goal to become a great writer, she had proved that a girl from Missouri could make good. And she was devastated by Stella's death. Nothing ever came of the idea, but perhaps it gave her a chance to consider one more time whether marriage was right for her. It hadn't been in 1927, and it wasn't in 1957. Radio, not marriage, was what Mary Margaret needed to fill the huge void left by Stella's death.

One year later Mary Margaret was back on the radio in New York, at least temporarily. "My life lacks flavor when I'm off the air," she told a radio and television columnist in May 1958 as she promoted her new show. The program aired for an hour at 1 P.M. on WNTA, the so-called fourth network, a comparatively small radio station based in New York and Newark, New Jersey. Why that station? Because the major networks weren't interested. It all came down to ratings and sponsors: it was easier to make money from soap operas or music than from a talk show offering literate conversation to housewives in the middle of the day. Columnist Jack Gould, who had panned her initial foray into television, heartily endorsed this new venture: "Daytime radio needs its few islands of literate conversations for the benefit of those housewives who yearn for momentary surcease from children, marketing, dusting, soap operas, and disk jockeys of measured charm."[2]

A Mary Margaret Mcbride show had basically only one format, which this one followed as well. She generally limited herself to one guest per day; Ogden Nash, Lena Horne, and Fannie Hurst appeared early on the show. When a reporter asked Mcbride in 1958 whom she

Mary Margaret McBride on a day when she was not wearing a corset.
Reprinted by permission of Library of Congress, Prints and Photographs Division.

regarded as her most interesting guests, she showed that she retained her enthusiasm for her craft by quickly replying, "The last one is always the most exciting."[3] She started out with several sponsors, but they seem to have evaporated by the end of the year, when WNTA dropped the show because they were unable to make it an economic success.[4]

By 1958, it must have been clear to Mary Margaret that she would never again have the national radio popularity that she had enjoyed when she gave up her flagship program in 1954. Television would never offer more than occasional guest spots either, although Mary Margaret thought that if Stella hadn't become sick, they would have tried it again.[5] More fundamentally, radio was changing. No longer able to compete with television for a national audience, radio increasingly targeted specific demographic groups. The biggest change was the emergence of the Top 40 music format symbolized by the disk jockey. As the 1950s progressed, rock 'n' roll began to dominate the airwaves, symbolic of the newer, younger audience that sponsors desired. The popularity of car radios and transistors (invented in 1947) also changed how and where people listened to the radio. The idea of a housewife sitting by a radio in her kitchen for a quiet hour at midday was becoming a thing of the past.[6]

At this point the balance of Mary Margaret's life began to shift decisively away from the excitement and bustle of New York City, where she had lived for almost forty years, to a more rustic and peaceful life in her converted barn in the Catskills. Over the next two years she wrote the final two volumes of her autobiographical memoirs. *A Long Way from Missouri*, published in 1959, covered her schooling and early days as a reporter and writer and ended with the stock market crash's devastating blow to her finances and self-esteem. *Out of the Air*, her longest and most detailed book, came out the following year and told the story of her radio career in great and almost self-indulgent detail. Recycling stories and even chunks of text from earlier books like *Here's Martha Deane* and her radio broadcasts, *Out of the Air* tries to recreate the ephemeral world of her radio broadcasts in print form. "It's difficult to put down in cold print the enchanting quality of these talented creatures talking frankly about themselves," she admitted candidly, and many reviewers agreed.[7]

Of more historical than literary importance, the book is a scrapbook of Mary Margaret's favorite moments on the show. Like nearly everything she wrote, it is backward rather than forward looking, discussing a radio show that then had been off the air for almost six years. The reviews, which still were generally positive, treated her career as a relic of the radio age, fast receding because of the cultural dominance of television. But at least the books brought McBride back into the public eye, and the W. Colston Leigh speaking agency had no trouble booking lectures for her across the country in 1959 and 1960. As she approached her sixtieth birthday, she gave up her apartment in New York, one of her last links to her earlier life, and contemplated retirement.[8]

"I was at loose ends," she later told an interviewer of the moment when she sent off the manuscript of *Out of the Air*. "I've worked since I was 16 and I guess it gets to be a habit."[9] Eleanor Roosevelt sensed her unhappiness and actively encouraged her to find a new challenge. "Dear Mrs. Roosevelt," Mary Margaret wrote excitedly, "You told me to go to work, so I am!" Just when she was at her lowest, she landed a radio gig that lasted from 1960 until just a few months before her death. She remained forever grateful to the former First Lady for pushing her out of the doldrums, yet another instance of Roosevelt's friendship and kindness over the years. "And if I never did it properly, I want to thank you for advising me to do this radio program here. It has helped such a lot to make my life here serene and contented."[10]

Mary Margaret's saviors were Martin Stone, president of the Herald-Tribune Radio Network, and Harry M. Thayer, general manager of station WGHQ of Kingston, New York. They persuaded her to do a local program called *Your Hudson Valley Neighbor*, which was broadcast three times a week (Monday, Wednesday, Friday) from 11 to 12 noon. Kingston was only twenty-six miles from West Shokan, but just as she had broadcast from her Central Park South apartment, Mary Margaret decided to tape her show in her converted barn, whose ground level with a separate entrance proved perfect for all the necessary radio equipment and a local audience of up to fifty listeners. A major advantage was the informality of the setting. "I won't have to wear a corset," she announced triumphantly.[11]

Because of her contacts, plus West Shokan's proximity to New York City, Mary Margaret could count on more than a local radio show's usual share of famous guests, at least at first. Eleanor Roosevelt, who was, after all, a Hudson Valley neighbor from nearby Hyde Park, remained her favorite guest, driving over for the late morning show and then staying for a picnic lunch to enjoy the spectacular view from the porch. When Roosevelt first visited McBride's converted barn, she insisted on having a full tour, even demanding to look inside a closet where Mary Margaret had hastily dumped all the stuff that she couldn't find another place for. Her sheepish explanation that the closet contained nothing but moths failed to deter the inquisitive visitor, who had learned early on to leave nothing unseen. Another time Roosevelt arrived with some jars of jelly and this explanation: "My housekeeper sent these, but she didn't want to because she thinks you are an authority on food. I talked her out of that, though."[12]

Mary Margaret's final act of devotion to the former First Lady came when Eleanor Roosevelt died on November 7, 1962. The Roosevelt family had invited her to the graveside service at Hyde Park, but, she told Fannie Hurst, she "just couldn't do it. . . . Nothing has been so hard for me since Stella." Instead she and Lorena Hickok taped a moving tribute that aired on the radio the following Sunday.[13]

Even though McBride had dropped from nationally syndicated shows with listeners in the millions to a radio station whose range covered only the Catskills, and from Broadway stars and Pulitzer Prize–winning authors to interviewing local participants at an air show or a neighbor who grew gourds, to Mary Margaret it was all the same. "I love talking to people, that's all," she said in 1975. "It doesn't matter whether the guest is famous or unknown. I'm doing the same show now that I did all those years on the networks, and it's every bit as interesting, even without so-called 'names.'" She attributed this to her ability to draw out people and her unshaken conviction that "famous or obscure, I believe *everybody* has a story to tell."[14] Her thirtieth anniversary on the air in 1964 drew a mention in *Time* magazine and celebratory telegrams from Jack Paar, Bennett Cerf, Mike Wallace, and Lowell Thomas.[15]

Even at a small station with a limited range, Mary Margaret proved able to pull in the sponsors: in 1968 she had between eight and ten for each day of the show, mainly local pharmacies, supermarkets, and bakeries that probably could not afford to advertise on television. For this she was paid $50 a week, plus $10 for expenses (which covered coffee and tea for her guests). Out of her salary she needed to pay for an assistant to help with correspondence as well as to oversee the mechanics of the program, jobs that previously Stella would have handled. "I'm in complete control here," she boasted.[16]

Although she remained grateful to station manager Harry Thayer for offering her the time slot in the first place, she found him an intrusive presence. Perhaps if Stella had been running interference, Thayer wouldn't have been so free with his advice and suggestions. He must quickly have learned how prickly she was about criticism, however, because he prefaced one letter complaining that she had given a certain sponsor short shrift: "I know you're going to hate me but believe that it is said in the very best spirit."[17] Another time he had the opposite task of informing her that she was violating a FCC rule that there could not be more than twenty minutes of commercials per hour: he had clocked her recently at twenty-six. "God bless you, I approve but the FCC does not." This commercial excess came at the expense of listeners, such as one unhappy man who called to complain about five commercials in a row. "Please, my dear, split them up for me, please, a little more than that."[18]

Strained relationships with Harry Thayer spilled over to his wife, who once dared to suggest that Mary Margaret had bad broadcasts as well as good ones. Showing that the years had not mellowed the thin-skinned radio host, McBride offered a detailed rebuttal: "I do not feel that I have ever done up here a wholly bad broadcast. Good guests are a hundred times more difficult to get than they are in New York." Reminding her that the host was more than aware when a program has not gone "swimmingly," she continued, "Suggesting that some programs have been bad is about as helpful as informing an overweight person that he should go on a strict diet." This may have been local radio, but tempers and egos were just as big as at any New York network.[19]

Tempers aside, Mary Margaret continued to broadcast *Your Hudson Valley Neighbor* until 1976. When she ran out of guests, she recycled old AP columns or articles that she had written back in the 1930s, editing them in pencil so that she could read them as if they were fresh copy on the air. When she broke her hip in 1970,[20] which necessitated a seven-month stay in a local hospital, she continued to do her broadcast from her hospital bed, despite being in great pain. One guest recalled the experience: "She would ask me a question and as I was answering I could see her grimacing with pain. But she came right in with the next question and when you heard it on the air, it sounded like a perfectly normal show." He hit on a fundamental truth: "The minute she broadcasts, she comes alive and she knows it. Her life is over off the air."[21]

Another guest who appeared on the show was cookbook writer Bert Greene, who had been a loyal listener as a child and was now fulfilling a lifelong ambition to have written a book that brought an invitation to appear on Mary Margaret McBride's radio program. Bonding over their shared infatuation with chocolate, cured ham, fried chicken, and piccalilli, they instantly began talking like old friends. "Amazingly, she seemed to have memorized our book," said Greene of his host, who was then in her seventies. "Picking the plum anecdotes from the dud avocados," she deftly maneuvered him and his coauthor into telling only the best stories on the air. The next Christmas he received a box of fancy chocolates from her and a card that showed her standing by a maple tree in full fall foliage: "Item of cheer. This gallant old tree has said good-bye to summer but is confidently awaiting spring. Mary Margaret."[22]

Once she exchanged her urban existence for the rhythms of country living, Mary Margaret found a measure of comfort that might have surprised many. "I have no ambition any more," she said in 1960. "It's wonderful."[23] She loved to garden and swapped hints with listeners about the best way to grow petunias. (She sang to hers.) She enjoyed having visitors from the city as long as they didn't stay too long. When she was there by herself, she often ate her meals right out of the pan in which she had cooked her food so she didn't have dishes to wash. She even learned to drive, although it took several learning permits before she felt confident enough to take the test. In a guest column she wrote for *Variety* in January 1962, she wrote, "I haven't been to New York for months and hope I'll not be going soon. Only a dire crisis could send me there."[24]

Even though Mary Margaret found appearing on television difficult, she loved the company that it gave her living alone in an isolated rural area. In 1962 she kept a tally and realized that she was watching television for about forty hours a week. "Night after night, alone on my mountain top, I sit in on some very fine entertainment. By way of my color set, I travel to far places of earth and space in Technicolor. I hear news as it happens and sometimes see it, too."[25] Her favorite shows were *The Defenders* and *That Was The Week That Was*, and she was devastated when they were canceled. In a somewhat ironic twist, since her radio program had competed with radio serials, she became an avid watcher of soap operas, identifying with "the sorely beset characters in the four daytime serials that have become part of my life." Now she pronounced the soaps "a substitute for the big, neighborly way of life in another, more leisurely age."[26]

Starting in the 1960s, journalist Cynthia Lowry began to play an increasingly important role in Mary Margaret McBride's life, eventually moving in with her. Lowry was a longtime employee of the Associated Press, starting out as a general news reporter and later becoming AP's television editor. She had known Mary Margaret since the early 1950s, when the two women traveled to England to cover the coronation of Queen Elizabeth II. Later she worked closely with McBride and her longtime secretary Hilda Deichler on the last volume of McBride's radio memoirs. Lowry had never married and for a while had lived in nearby Chappaqua before permanently settling in with McBride.[27]

Once she retired from the AP in the early 1970s, Cynthia Lowry became more involved in *Your Hudson Valley Neighbor*. At first Lowry had been uncomfortable appearing on talk shows, Mary Margaret noted in 1974, but "since she's come to live here, I can hardly keep her away from the microphones. She'd come on my show every day if I let her."[28] Even though their relationship bore a superficial resemblance to that between Mary Margaret and Stella, Cynthia Lowry never occupied so central a place in McBride's heart as Stella had. Lowry had a somewhat abrasive personality and also was a heavy drinker (ironic given McBride's long-standing temperance) who alienated many of the radio host's old friends.[29]

Nonetheless, Lowry provided companionship and help to a lonely and increasingly infirm woman. The hip that McBride broke in 1970 never fully mended, and she had great difficulty getting around. She tired easily, and sometimes her thoughts wandered, even when she was on the air. In addition, she became so obese that she could barely navigate the aisles of the local supermarket or get in and out of a car. Mary Margaret also suffered from severe arthritis and high blood pressure. "I'm always drained after a broadcast," she admitted in 1971, "but a cup of tea often picks me up and a walk through my garden relaxes me."[30] She still got letters from old fans, and just as she had done since 1934, she answered them all. In the last years of her life she became housebound, unable to go up or down stairs and reduced to sleeping in a recliner in her living room. She also took to wearing a hood over her hair because she had trouble fixing it to her liking. "People must think I'm bald," she admitted, "but I'm old enough to be a character now and so I'll wear my hood."[31]

It probably was Cynthia Lowry who in 1975 suggested to an AP colleague, Kay Bartlett, that McBride would make a good "Where Is She Now?" story. When the story ran in newspapers throughout the country, complete with a photograph of Mary Margaret in her hood, she experienced a gratifying if brief return to the limelight.[32] And when in March 1975 the late-night talk show host Tom Snyder devoted an entire hour of his *Tomorrow* show to McBride, letting her recap her career and many of the famous people that she had interviewed on radio and television, she received fan letters from listeners who remembered how much she had meant to them years earlier. Some of them even complimented her on her appearance "and I like that—I'm vain!" It was her last television appearance.[33]

At the end of her life, Mary Margaret had come home: "I was country to begin with, and now I've come full circle."[34] She spent her old age surrounded by her books, her garden, her mountains, her barn—and her radio audience. "After almost forty years of broadcasting, I still can't stop. It is my whole life," she told a reporter in April 1974. "I think it would be wonderful to die at the microphone."[35] She didn't get that wish, though, dying at home on April 7, 1976, at the age of seventy-six.[36] But if she had been able to sign off from this world, loyal fans knew exactly what she would have said: "Thanks for being fond of me. Good-bye, y'all."

"America's First Lady of Radio." *Reprinted by permission of Library of Congress, Prints and Photographs Division.*

Epilogue

Talk Shows, Then and Now

MARY MARGARET McBRIDE died at an interesting moment in broadcast history, with three major developments that would shape the rest of the twentieth century either incubating or just born: the creation of National Public Radio (NPR), the rise of call-in talk radio, and the dramatic expansion of the daytime television talk show. In each case her radio career contained elements that prefigured or foreshadowed the developments to come, notably her commitment to literate, intelligent commentary; her ability to interact with her listeners over the radio; and her role as a distinctive personality able to deliver a show and its products to an audience primarily composed of women. But several decades separate the height of Mary Margaret McBride's program in the late 1940s and early 1950s from the dominance of television personalities like Oprah Winfrey and Phil Donahue in the 1980s and 1990s. The ongoing information revolution, the blurring of the line between information and entertainment and a general tabloidization of the news, the rise of identity politics, and the drive for media profits all were equally significant factors in shaping the developments that followed as McBride's legacy.

It is hard to imagine that Mary Margaret McBride would not have been a fan of public radio, that is, if her converted barn in the Catskills had been close enough to a station to pick up the signal. Her philosophy of serving the needs of her listeners with information and discussion and creating a community of shared interests over the airwaves was quite similar to the original mandate of National Public Radio. Created as something of an afterthought to the Public Broadcasting System, public radio emerged as a highly decentralized, chronically underfunded group of stations committed to serving the public interest in new and diverse ways. *All Things Considered*, which began in 1971, challenged the top-down, Washington- and New York–driven presentation of the news by going out into the streets and talking to ordinary folks, not just in major cities but in towns and communities across the country. It made the listeners part of the show and encouraged active listening. Especially in its early years, it displayed a playful and innovative use of sound that harked back to the old programs of the 1930s.[1]

One of the most distinctive things about public radio is its enormous range of locally produced programming. Another is that both its programming and its staff include many more women than do the traditional media. From the start, *All Things Considered*, had female and male cohosts, and prominent network correspondents such as Susan Stamberg, Cokie Roberts, Nina Totenberg, and Linda Werthheimer all got their start in the experimental early days of NPR. Today some of public radio's most successful syndicated shows, notably Terry Gross's Philadelphia-based *Fresh Air*, a literate and hard-hitting discussion of books, entertainment, and current affairs, and Washington's *The Diane Rehm Show*, which probes news, politics, and culture, feature women hosts.

With their shared commitment to serious discussion, respectful discourse, and diversity of opinion, these women radio personalities have much in common with Mary Margaret McBride. As Rehm says about her approach, "You get what you give in this business. If you treat guests, listeners, and colleagues with respect, they will, almost without exception, treat you in the same way."[2] These women always keep their cool. One thing that is hard to imagine, however, is Terry Gross or Diane Rehm plugging E-Z Cut-Rite wax paper or Dolly Madison ice cream. Even though public radio has increasingly had to rely on underwriting and corporate sponsorship to stay on the air, there still is a significant difference between its ability to broadcast in the public interest and broadcasting in Mary Margaret's day, when except for a few educational radio stations connected with universities, commercial radio was the only game in town.[3]

Although Mary Margaret would certainly have contributed to her local public radio station each pledge period, it is harder to imagine what she might have thought about the rise of radio call-in shows, first on AM and then later on FM as well. True, those shows fostered active, engaged listening, and they brought new voices and new issues to the airwaves. They also encouraged listeners to think of themselves as part of a community.[4] As Boston radio personality David Brudnoy once remarked, "Talk radio is the last neighborhood in town. People know their talk hosts better than they know the person who lives next to them."[5] But talk shows often lacked the commitment to civil discourse and measured discussion of ideas that had been Mary Margaret's hallmark as a talk show host. Instead, these shows often seemed to go the exact opposite direction, reveling, as media critic Howard Kurtz put it, "in their one-sided pugnacity, spreading wild theories, delicious gossip, and angry denunciations with gleeful abandon."[6]

Mary Margaret McBride foreshadowed some of the interactive aspects of call-in talk radio with her practice of reading listeners' letters on the air, but the telephone played no regular role in her show. Boston's Jerry Williams starting putting callers on the air in 1957, but the practice didn't really catch on until the 1960s and 1970s. The main drawback was the high cost of such formats, which demanded a large production team to screen the calls and exercise the time-delay so that objectionable language could be beeped out. Also, until the introduction of car phones and, later, cell phones, such shows lacked the ability to connect with drive-time commuters. Finally, until the expansion of satellite technology it was difficult for popular shows to reach more than a local audience.[7]

By the time that radio talk show hosts like Don Imus, Howard Stern, and Rush Limbaugh appeared on the national scene in the 1980s, all those drawbacks had been overcome and talk radio was booming. With three hundred shows on the air in the late 1980s and more than one thousand by the mid-1990s, talk shows had become the most popular format after country music. They also had revolutionized how millions of Americans obtained information and formed their opinions about public issues. These shows, whose callers were mainly men, as were their generally conservative hosts, had very little to do with journalism, however, serving more as outlets for hosts and listeners to vent their opinions—the more outrageous the better—and complain about all the changes in American society since the 1960s.[8]

In a rush to deliver more profits for sponsors, radio stations realized that goading people into saying outrageous things on the air drew big audiences. Television executives reached the same conclusion, embracing daytime talk shows for their huge audiences and huge profits. Like almost everything in broadcast history, there are strong antecedents for the daytime talk show. Radio hosts like Mary Margaret McBride and Arthur Godfrey pioneered the magazine-concept show, with multiple guests, multiple sponsors, and ad-libbed dialogue, which was then picked up (without credit) by Pat Weaver as inspiration for the *Today* show. Other forerunners on television included the *Tonight* show, which started in 1954, and daytime celebrity-hosted shows featuring stars such as Mike Douglas, Merv Griffin, and Dinah Shore. More upscale intellectually were the topic-driven shows of David Susskind and Dick Cavett. Arlene Francis's *The Home*, which ran from 1954 to 1957, and Virginia Graham's *Girl Talk*, an early 1960s show modeled on women's magazines, addressed female audiences during the daytime hours.[9]

Phil Donahue is generally credited as the pioneer of the daytime television talk show. He started locally in Dayton, Ohio, in 1967, moved to the Chicago market in 1974, and into national syndication in 1979. His shows tackled issues that at the time were considered shocking and controversial: cross-dressing, incest, lesbian mothers, breast implants, and a whole range of topics subsumed under the feminist slogan "The personal is political." Openly liberal in his political sentiments, he also drew leading political figures to his show, allowing the discussion of more conventional political topics like the equal rights amendment and welfare rights.[10]

Phil Donahue begat Oprah Winfrey, as Winfrey herself realized: "There never would have been an Oprah without a Phil. Phil was the first to understand that the woman at home was an intelligent, sensitive, knowledgeable person who wanted to know more than how to bake Toll House cookies."[11] (Mary Margaret McBride, of course, had come to the same realization on radio fifty years earlier.) Like Donahue, Winfrey started out on local television before moving to Chicago in 1984 to host *A.M. Chicago*, a morning talk show. Renamed *The Oprah Winfrey Show*, it went into national syndication in 1986. With her combination of empathy and charisma, Winfrey quickly rocketed to the top of ratings, surpassing Donahue and her two other competitors: Sally Jesse Raphael and Geraldo Rivera. Listeners especially responded to Winfrey's own compelling personal history—a rags-to-riches saga of a black woman who survived poverty, racism, and sexual abuse to become one of the richest and most successful entertainers in America—as part of the program's narrative structure.[12]

There are striking parallels between Oprah Winfrey and Mary Margaret McBride, starting with the most superficial one: they both were large women who talked candidly about their struggles with their weight. In terms of career trajectory, each started locally and then set up her own production company and sold the show in syndication. Each stamped her own personality, as well as her name, on the final product.

Each broadcast to a predominantly female audience of middle- to lower-income women from their late twenties through their early fifties, offering each day a mix of interviews, products, and advice. Ties between host and listeners were tight, although Winfrey played off a live audience much more than Mary Margaret McBride did.

Most important, both media personalities blurred the line between public and private, repeatedly talking about episodes from their own lives for their national audiences. Just as Mary Margaret shared details about her mother's death or a fight she had had the night before with Stella, so Oprah Winfrey talks about episodes of childhood sexual abuse, cocaine use (conveniently during a "sweeps" period for ratings), and her relationship with her long-term boyfriend. Each host used her own life—or a version of her life—as a way of bonding with her audience and breaking down the barriers between host and listener.[13]

But this seemingly similar practice of sharing personal details and revelations masks important differences in the eras in which each show was broadcast, especially the shifting boundaries between what topics and issues were considered appropriate for public discussion. For example, McBride, too, had a brush with sexual abuse as a child, but she would never have talked directly about it on the air. More to the point, it would have never occurred to her to build a show around the issue of sexual abuse of children. Similarly, although McBride struggled with depression all her life, her references to it on her show were fairly general; her main message was just to pick yourself up and get on with it. On Oprah Winfrey's talk show, a problem like depression would have a cast of victims or sufferers ready to share their pain, an expert or two to help them find the way, and a sympathetic host (who might chime in with her own experiences with depression) ready to facilitate the process.

What had changed so much in just thirty or forty years to mask the line between public and private? Partly it was a more aggressive and less deferential press, the difference between not reporting on Franklin Roosevelt's paralysis from polio or John F. Kennedy's romantic liaisons and MTV's asking President Bill Clinton whether he wore boxers or briefs. Now Americans are able to know everything they want to (and then some) about public figures, right down to their underwear. Also important was the rise of a therapeutic, self-help culture in the 1970s that encouraged citizens, male and female, to talk about their feelings and problems and seek help from the variety of experts and gurus whose books, tapes, and talk show appearances flooded popular culture.[14]

Probably the greatest force for change was the struggle for equality that reshaped American society in the 1960s and beyond, widening the political power and visibility of previously marginalized groups. Indeed, the whole definition of what was political was stretched to include the concerns of women, people of color, gay people, and a range of groups who, thanks to the emergence of identity politics, now felt they had a right to speak. These groups brought their issues and concerns, both personal and political, forcefully into the public sphere and onto the nation's airwaves.[15]

Mary Margaret's talk show operated in more discreet and restrained times. The late twentieth-century confessional style of getting in touch with your feelings was not for her, nor would it have been for most members of her audience.[16] When she shared details of her life, these stories were not confessions or revelations but, more likely, interesting tidbits that she thought would interest her listeners. Guests on her show chatted about their work and their lives but touched on more private matters only with considerable reserve. More to the point, her vision of a talk show had a fundamentally different agenda than that of its later radio and television incarnations, which depended on controversy and confrontation to win high ratings. Mary Margaret always remained more a facilitator and a conduit for ideas and information than a provocateur or therapist. There was no debate or confrontation on her show, just one-on-one conversations in which she and her guests sat down at the microphone and kept talking until their time was up.

To understand Mary Margaret Mcbride and to understand her relevance to broadcast history and twentieth-century popular culture, it is necessary to return to where this book started: sitting by the radio. Mary Margaret McBride's career demonstrates the importance of women to radio and the importance of radio to women. The key to her success and remarkable longevity was her ability to use the intimacy of radio to draw her audience into an imagined community of listeners who actively participated in making the show meaningful to their lives. The radio host did her part from the studio, and then it was up to the listeners to meet her halfway. Unlike television, there were no images or visuals to distract their attention,[17] only McBride's warm, friendly voice bringing information, stories, and products into the home over the airwaves. Proud purveyor of a program that elevated rather than pandered to the tastes of her predominantly female audience, Mary Margaret McBride provides a model of how popular culture can act as a positive force in women's lives.

But it wasn't just a question of mastering the craft of radio. Mary Margaret McBride drew such a loyal audience because she met so many of her listeners' needs. Just as she served as an intermediary between an agrarian, small-town past and the more urbane, cosmopolitan values linked to modern times, she also straddled traditional and more egalitarian gender roles. Through the literate but never overly erudite conversation on her program, she provided her audience with a model of what modern womanhood could be—confident, personable, and well informed. She validated women's contributions to their homes and families but also stretched their minds to confront issues beyond the domestic realm, including some of the most vexing social issues of contemporary life: racial politics, anti-Semitism, consumerism, and global politics. What the media dismissed as "goo" turned out to be an honest and heartfelt attempt by host and listeners alike to deal with the complexities and anxieties of modern life.

An aging listener recently confided that he still liked to say to people at the appropriate point in the afternoon, "It's one o'clock and here is Mary Margaret McBride," even though "no one knows what the hell I'm talking about."[18] Now perhaps they will.

Notes

NOTES TO PREFACE

1. "Mary Margaret Mcbride Zips to New High with Listeners," *Life*, April 5, 1948, 40.
2. A guide to the radio programs can be accessed through SONIC (Sound Online Inventory and Catalogue) at the Library of Congress Web site: http://www.loc.gov.
3. Susan Ware, *Still Missing: Amelia Earhart and the Search for Modern Feminism* (New York: Norton, 1993).

NOTES TO PROLOGUE

1. Eleanor Roosevelt quoted in Enid A. Haupt, "Recruiting Women for Vital National Service," *Philadelphia Inquirer*, July 2, 1944, clipping found in Mary Margaret McBride papers, Manuscript Division, Library of Congress (hereafter cited as Manuscript Division, LC). The quotation also appears in Mary Margaret McBride, *Out of the Air* (Garden City, N.Y.: Doubleday, 1960), 119.
2. Mary Margaret McBride broadcast, May 31, 1944 (LWO 12747-36A2), Motion Picture, Broadcasting, and Recorded Sound Division, Library of Congress (hereafter cited as Recorded Sound, LC). See also the brochure found in the Manuscript Division, LC, "A Great Station and a Great Program Combine in a Great Radio Promotion" (1944), put together by station WEAF, which contains clippings and pictures. Details of the event in the text are drawn from notes from the broadcast and the brochure.
3. Eleanor Roosevelt, "My Day," June 1, 1944, clipping in Manuscript Division, LC.
4. Jo Pearson, "Here's Mary Margaret," *Radio Television Mirror*, August 1951, 89, clipping in the Mary Margaret McBride Papers, Motion Picture, Broadcasting, and Recorded Sound Division, Library of Congress (hereafter cited as Recorded Sound, LC).
5. Mary Margaret McBride, *A Long Way from Missouri* (New York: Putnam, 1959), 171.
6. Niles Trammell to Mary Margaret McBride, June 22, 1944, Recorded Sound, LC.
7. The figures became more and more inflated over the years: up to 54,000 in *Out of the Air* (p. 144) and even 100,000 in an interview toward the end of her life. See Barbara Bedell, "She Only Wanted to Be a Famous Writer," *Sunday Record*, July 29, 1973, clipping in Recorded Sound, LC.
8. McBride, *A Long Way from Missouri*, 171; "The McBride Phenomenon," *Newsweek*, May 30, 1949, 50.
9. Story by Ed Wall for the *World-Telegram*, May 31, 1949, clipping in Recorded Sound, LC.
10. Frank Farrell column (June 1, 1949), clipping in Recorded Sound, LC.
11. Mary Margaret McBride roses are still being grown, as in, for instance, the front yard of my father, Dr. Charles K. Wolfe, and stepmother, Jacqueline Willrich, in Kenilworth, Illinois.

12. Tribute by H. V. Kaltenborn, May 31, 1949, found in Recorded Sound, LC.

13. McBride quotation from notes of tape of broadcast, May 31, 1949 (RWA 1443), Recorded Sound, LC. My general description of the event draws on details gleaned from listening to this recording.

14. Ibid. See also Walter White, "Party for Mary Margaret McBride," *New York Herald-Tribune*, June 1, 1949, clipping found in Recorded Sound, LC.

15. The chronology of her show has been reconstructed from John Dunning, *On the Air: The Encyclopedia of Old-Time Radio* (New York: Oxford University Press, 1998); and reference and cataloging material compiled by Janet McKee at Recorded Sound, LC.

16. Jinx Falkenberg and Tex McCrary, "New York Close Up," *New York Herald-Tribune*, April 5, 1950, clipping in Recorded Sound, LC. NBC claimed that McBride's appeal was too local to New York.

17. The WGN broadcast from April 9, 1951 (RWC 7045-LWO 26484, Recorded Sound, LC), described the new arrangement. From this point on, McBride broadcast mainly from her New York apartment.

18. Dunning, *On the Air*, 440–41; and Erik Barnouw, *The Golden Web: A History of Broadcasting in the United States: Volume II, 1933 to 1953* (New York: Oxford University Press, 1968), 92–94.

19. *Current Biography*, 1954, 420.

20. For McBride's importance to radio and television history, see chapter 3.

21. See Barbara Heggie, "The Forty-five-Minute Tempo," *New Yorker*, December 19, 1942, 33.

22. Michele Hilmes, *Radio Voices: American Broadcasting, 1922–1952* (Minneapolis: University of Minnesota Press, 1997), 277. These tapes were donated to the Library of Congress in 1977.

23. "The McBride Phenomenon," *Newsweek*, May 30, 1949, 50.

24. "Goo," *Time*, November 25, 1940, 56–57; and "Busy Air," *Time*, May 31, 1948, 61.

25. "Gossip of the Kilocycles: Miss McBride (also Miss Deane) Gets Annual Gift Shower," *Newsweek*, November 21, 1938, 22–23.

26. Collie Small, "The Private Life of a Pied Piper," *Collier's*, December 11, 1948, 28.

27. In addition to numerous magazine and newspaper articles, McBride tells her story in three autobiographical volumes: *How Dear to My Heart* (New York: Macmillan, 1940); *A Long Way from Missouri* (New York: Putnam, 1959); and *Out of the Air* (Garden City, N.Y.: Doubleday, 1960).

28. Pearson, "Here's Mary Margaret," 88.

29. McBride, *Out of the Air*, 55.

30. Charles Preston and Edward A. Hamilton, eds., *Mike Wallace Asks: Highlights from 46 Controversial Interviews* (New York: Simon & Schuster, 1958), 75.

31. Mary Margaret McBride, "I Don't Want to Preach," *Woman's Day*, October 1939, 5.

32. Benedict Anderson's *Imagined Communities: Reflections on the Origin and Spread of Nationalism* (London: Verso, 1983) talks about nations as imagined political communities, most of whose members will never know or meet other members, "yet in the minds of each lives the image of their communion" (p. 6). This framing, which has been widely cited to explain a variety of political and cultural contexts, fits radio especially well.

33. Michele Hilmes explores the day*time*/night*time* gender dichotomy in *Radio Voices*. Hilmes is one of the few radio historians to focus on McBride, using her career as the very effective conclusion to her book. Jacqueline St. John also early on realized McBride's significance, prodded by her mother (a former listener) to research the topic and interview McBride: see her "Sex Role Stereotyping in Early Broadcast History: The Career of Mary Margaret McBride," *Frontiers* 3 (1978): 31–38. Professor Beverly Merrick of the Depart-

ment of Journalism and Mass Communications at New Mexico State University has also presented conference papers and published articles on McBride, which were very helpful to my research.

34. These connections are explored in the epilogue.

35. Mary Margaret McBride, *America for Me* (New York: Macmillan, 1941), 62–63.

36. For an exploration of the link between the personal and the political, plus a discussion of the importance of women's partnerships to American history, see Susan Ware, *Partner and I: Molly Dewson, Feminism, and New Deal Politics* (New Haven, Conn.: Yale University Press, 1987).

37. See Joan Shelley Rubin, *The Making of Middlebrow Culture* (Chapel Hill: University of North Carolina Press, 1992); the quotation is from p. xii. Comparing the master index of guests who appeared on Mary Margaret's shows with the names sprinkled throughout Rubin's book confirms this connection vividly. See chapter 2 for a fuller discussion.

38. In "Rethinking Radio," Michele Hilmes suggests that this neglect may be changing. See Michele Hilmes and Jason Loviglio, eds., *Radio Reader: Essays in the Cultural History of Radio* (New York: Routledge, 2002), 1–20. That certainly is one of my goals for this radio biography.

39. Gerald Nachman, *Raised on Radio* (New York: Pantheon Books, 1998), 9.

NOTES TO CHAPTER 1

1. Quotation from Curtis Mitchell, "Mary Margaret's Magic," *Coronet*, January 1954, clipping found in Mary Margaret McBride papers, Motion Picture, Broadcasting, and Recorded Sound Division, Library of Congress (hereafter cited as Recorded Sound, LC). The following day in the radio life of Mary Margaret McBride, set in the late 1940s or early 1950s, is reconstructed from the following sources: Barbara Heggie, "The Forty-five-Minute Tempo," *New Yorker*, December 19, 1942; Barbara Heggie, "Mary Margaret's Miracle," *Woman's Home Companion*, April 1949; Jo Pearson, "Here's Mary Margaret," *Radio Television Mirror*, August 1951; Allen Churchill, " Mary Margaret McBride," *American Mercury*, January 1949; Philip Hamburger, "Mary Margaret McBride: A Supersaleswoman Shares Adventures of Mind and Stomach with a Host of Radio Listeners," *Life*, December 4, 1944; and Collie Small, "The Private Life of a Pied Piper," *Collier's*, December 11, 1948.

2. "Mary Margaret McBride Says—She's a Horrible Example as a Time Waster," AP column, December 20 (1953–56), Recorded Sound, LC.

3. Dick Willard was another announcer associated with the show at various points in the 1930s and 1940s, but judging by the lack of mention to him in McBride's various autobiographical writings and interviews, he seems not to have been considered part of the radio family in the way that Vincent was. He did, however, have an excellent voice and on occasion would sing musical selections, accompanied by a studio organ, for the audience. In addition, Kenneth Roberts was a third announcer who appeared off and on over the years, often on McBride's shorter programs. By focusing almost exclusively on Vincent Connolly in my retelling of the radio years, I may have inadvertently consigned Dick Willard and Kenneth Roberts to radio and historical oblivion, for which I apologize.

4. Mary Margaret McBride, *Here's Martha Deane* (Garden City, N.Y.: Garden City Publishing, 1936), 30.

5. Walter White, "A Party for Mary Margaret McBride" (1949), clipping in Recorded Sound, LC.

6. "The McBride Phenomenon," *Newsweek*, May 30, 1949, 50.

7. Churchill, "Mary Margaret McBride," 10.

8. Barbara Donelson to McBride, December 6, 1948, Recorded Sound, LC.

9. Bennett Cerf, "Here Comes Mcbride," *Saturday Review of Literature*, March 1, 1947, 4–6, reprint in Mary Margaret McBride papers, Manuscript Division, Library of Congress (hereafter cited as Manuscript Division, LC). The title of the article, which was often repeated, suggested the title for this chapter.

10. ABC advertising brochure, "This Is Radio's Best Co-op Buy" (1951), found in Recorded Sound, LC.

11. WGN ad for Mary Margaret McBride program in *Variety*, January 25, 1950, found in Recorded Sound, LC. This aspect of the program is explored more fully in chapter 5.

12. Sid Weiss, "Words and Music," *Radio Daily*, August 28, 1941, clipping in Manuscript Division, LC.

13. Mary Margaret McBride, *Out of the Air* (Garden City, N.Y.: Doubleday, 1960), 210.

14. See, for example, this ending to a 1938 article: "All I can say is that she's a brilliant woman in an unusually fresh, youthful way; inconsistent in a delightfully human fashion and rock-bound when it comes to a principle or conviction. When I first knew her maybe I was jealous because she had a metropolitan byline while I had only young hopes. I didn't like her, too well. That's what time does, because now I'm like her fans. I want to know whether the new hat has a veil. I think it would emphasize the wise, wide, kindly, understanding brown eyes of Mary Margaret McBride." Julia Shawell, "She Has a Million Friends," *Woman's World*, September 1938, 16.

15. McBride, *Out of the Air*, 210.

16. "Goodness," *Time*, December 2, 1946, 81.

17. "Mary Margaret McBride Says—Star Makers Are a Funny Bunch," AP column, May 19 (1953–56), Recorded Sound, LC.

18. "Mary Margaret McBride Tells How to Make Friends," *Christian Herald*, December 1957, 29; and "Mary Margaret McBride Says—Here's How to Make People Talk," AP column, January 10, 1955, Recorded Sound, LC.

19. "Mary Margaret McBride Says—Save Her from Leisure Time," AP column, July 25, 1955, Recorded Sound, LC.

20. McBride, *Out of the Air*, 32; Mary Margaret McBride, *A Long Way from Missouri* (New York: Putnam, 1959), 109.

21. Mary Margaret McBride, *Tune in for Elizabeth: Career Story of a Radio Interviewer* (New York: Dodd, Mead, 1945). This book for young adults shamelessly recycles material from McBride's career to tell the story of a young woman working for a famous and successful radio personality.

22. Cynthia Lowry and Mary Margaret McBride, "'I've Learned to Love': A Talk with Mary Margaret McBride," *Woman's Home Companion*, May 1954, 66.

23. "Looking and Listening, with Ben Gross," clipping (no date) in Manuscript Division, LC.

24. Ibid. See also a letter from a fan named Natalie to Mary Margaret (1962) about Stella: "She was a rare individual, with one consuming passion in her life—Mary Margaret McBride. On one of the occasions when we had the pleasure of talking to her, she went on at great length about you." Manuscript Division, LC.

25. Hamburger, "Mary Margaret McBride," 48.

26. Pearson, "Here's Mary Margaret," 89. Stella used exactly the same words to describe her contribution to the McBride phenomenon on their last network show. Mary Margaret McBride broadcast, May 14, 1954 (RWC 7043 B1), Recorded Sound, LC.

27. Stephen C. Riddleberger to Susan Ware, June 9, 1999.

28. Mercer MacPherson to James Gaines, October 17, 1947; Gaines to McBride, October 28, 1947; Gaines to Stella Karn, October 28, 1947, Recorded Sound, LC.

29. McBride, *Out of the Air*, 33.

30. "Looking and Listening, with Ben Gross," Recorded Sound, LC.

31. McBride, *Out of the Air*, 34.

32. Mary Margaret McBride, "My Most Unforgettable Character," *Reader's Digest*, January 1960, 101. In the tape of the February 22, 1951, broadcast (LWO 15577 R114; Recorded Sound, LC), the banging is quite noticeable.

33. Ruth Pierpont Stephens to McBride, March 22, 1937, Manuscript Division, LC.

34. Heggie, "The Forty-five-Minute Tempo," 28.

35. McBride, *Out of the Air*, 188.

36. Heggie, "Mary Margaret's Miracle," 82.

37. *Princeton Alumni Weekly*, April 6, 1988, 52. Further information on Connolly was provided in a letter to me dated June 16, 1999, from his brother Richard (Dick), in Fort Lauderdale, Florida; a letter dated June 22, 1999, from a nephew, Michael Reynolds, of Boulder, Colorado; and phone conversations with Hanson Reynolds, a lawyer in Boston, Massachusetts. See also the letter dated July 7, 1999, from Mrs. F. C. Jones to Susan Ware, which mentions her friendship with Vincent and his friend George Makepeace.

38. McBride, *Here's Martha Deane*, 80. The quotation is McBride's approximation of the original column.

39. For the presence of gays and a "swish" style on network radio and how common this was, see Matthew Murray, "'The Tendency to Deprave and Corrupt Morals': Regulation and Irregular Sexuality in Golden Age Radio Comedy," in *Radio Reader: Essays in the Cultural History of Radio*, edited by Michele Hilmes and Jason Loviglio (New York: Routledge, 2002). See also George Chauncey, *Gay New York: Gender, Urban Culture, and the Makings of the Gay Male World, 1890–1940* (New York: Basic Books, 1994). Vincent Connolly is not, however, an example of this "swish" style.

40. Hamburger, "Mary Margaret McBride," 50.

41. McBride, *Out of the Air*, 32.

42. Janice Devine notes, August 11, 1939, found in Manuscript Division, LC. See also McBride, *Out of the Air*, 32–33.

43. McBride, *Out of the Air*, 33.

44. Ibid., 32.

45. For an excellent introduction to the Jack Benny radio family, see Margaret T. McFadden, "'America's Boy Friend Who Can't Get a Date': Gender, Race, and the Cultural Work of the Jack Benny Program, 1932–1946," *Journal of American History* 80 (June 1993): 113–34.

46. Ben Gross, *I Looked and I Listened: Informal Recollections of Radio and Television* (New York: Random House, 1954), quoted in Beverly G. Merrick, "Mary Margaret McBride, Talk Show Host: The Perfect Proxy for Radio Listeners," paper presented at the Association for Education in Journalism and Mass Communication convention, Atlanta, August 1994. Merrick speculates that it was Stella Karn who convinced Gross to listen again.

NOTES TO CHAPTER 2

1. Cynthia Lowry and Mary Margaret McBride, "'I've Learned to Love': A Talk with Mary Margaret McBride," *Woman's Home Companion*, May 1954, 67.

2. Mary Margaret McBride, *Out of the Air* (Garden City, N.Y.: Doubleday, 1960), 266.

3. "Mary Margaret McBride Reviews Her Career on Radio," *Publishers Weekly*, December 12, 1960, clipping in the Mary Margaret McBride papers, Manuscript Division, Library of Congress (hereafter cited as Manuscript Division, LC).

4. Alexander Kropotkin, "To the Ladies," *Liberty*, October 3, 1936, 58, clipping found

in the Mary Margaret Mcbride papers, Motion Picture, Broadcasting, and Recorded Sound Division, Library of Congress (hereafter cited as Recorded Sound, LC).

5. Allen Churchill, "Mary Margaret Mcbride," *American Mercury*, January 1949, 10.

6. Lucy Greenbaum, "All about M. M. McB.," *New York Times*, May 28, 1944.

7. Mcbride, *Out of the Air*, 29.

8. Mary Margaret Mcbride, "Secrets," *Good Housekeeping*, March, 1950, 194.

9. Barbara Heggie, "Mary Margaret's Miracle," *Woman's Home Companion*, April 1949, 36.

10. Mcbride, *Out of the Air*, 44.

11. Heywood Hale Broun, telephone interview with me, August 10, 1999.

12. Sylvia Wright, "Commentators: Female of the Species," *Magazine Digest*, February 1954, 60, clipping found in Recorded Sound, LC. A good example of Mcbride following this practice is the tape of a broadcast interview with journalist Marguerite Higgins, March 19, 1951 (LWO 15577 R147A), Recorded Sound, LC.

13. Lorraine Mount (State College, Pa.) to Susan Ware, June 23, 1999.

14. Sid Weiss, "Words and Music," *Radio Daily*, August 28, 1941, clipping in Manuscript Division, LC.

15. Mary Margaret Mcbride, *Here's Martha Deane* (Garden City, N.Y.: Garden City Publishing, 1936), 85.

16. Jo Pearson, "Here's Mary Margaret," *Radio Television Mirror*, August 1951, clipping in Recorded Sound, LC.

17. Heggie, "Mary Margaret's Miracle," 36.

18. Mcbride, *Here's Martha Deane*, 87.

19. Mcbride, *Out of the Air*, 203.

20. Ibid., 29.

21. Bennett Cerf, "Here Comes Mcbride," *Saturday Review of Literature*, March 1, 1947, 4–6.

22. "Mary Margaret Mcbride Tells How to Make Friends," *Christian Herald*, December 1957, 55.

23. For more on gossip columnists, see Neil Gabler, *Winchell: Gossip, Power and the Culture of Celebrity* (New York: Knopf, 1994); and Donna Halper, *Invisible Stars: A Social History of Women in American Broadcasting* (Armonk, N.Y.: Sharpe, 2001). The Louella Parsons broadcast aired on February 7, 1944. LWO 12747 36B2, Recorded Sound, LC.

24. Fred Gipson to Mcbride, October 14, 1946, Recorded Sound, LC.

25. Bentz Plagemann to Mcbride, September 27, 1949, found in Mcbride papers, Recorded Sound, LC.

26. Jane Engel to Mcbride, October 21, 1949, found in Mcbride papers, Manuscript Division, LC.

27. Mcbride, *Out of the Air*, 56, 203, 252, and 61. For an example of a good theater interview, see the appearance of Lillian and Dorothy Gish on the program on May 30, 1947 (RWA 1437 LWO 17105), Recorded Sound, LC.

28. Mcbride, *Out of the Air*, 322, 12.

29. John K. Hutchins, "On Books and Authors," *New York Herald-Tribune Book Review*, June 20, 1954, 2. He was lamenting the loss to the publishing industry when she gave up her daily show.

30. See Joan Shelley Rubin's superb discussion of this cultural moment in *The Making of Middlebrow Culture* (Chapel Hill: University of North Carolina Press, 1992). For nineteenth-century scribbling women, see Ann Douglas, *The Feminization of American Culture* (New York: Knopf, 1977); and Mary Kelley, *Private Woman, Public Stage: Literary Domesticity in Nineteenth-Century America* (New York: Oxford University Press, 1984).

31. Rubin, *The Making of Middlebrow Culture*, 269.

32. For example, Judith Waller's *Radio: The Fifth Estate* (Boston: Mifflin, 1946), 155–56, provides a literal transcription of part of an interview. Even though Waller refers to McBride's style as a "legend" and praises her "completely natural and unself-conscious manner," when the dialogue is reduced to words on a page, it falls flat.

33. McBride broadcast, November 11, 1947 (RWA 6735 B2), Recorded Sound, LC.

34. McBride broadcast, January 12, 1951 (RWA 1468 LWO 17105), Recorded Sound, LC.

35. McBride broadcast, March 2, 1943 (RWO 6944), Recorded Sound, LC.

36. McBride, *Out of the Air*, 56, 327–28.

37. Barbara Heggie, "The Forty-five-Minute Tempo," *New Yorker*, December 19, 1942, 27.

38. Churchill, "Mary Margaret McBride," 14. Diane Rehm cites similar examples in *Finding My Voice* (New York: Knopf, 1999), 163–65.

39. McBride, *Out of the Air*, 61.

40. This hilarious interchange is found in one of my favorite shows: McBride broadcast, September 29, 1952 (LWO 12747), Recorded Sound, LC. McBride also discusses this incident in *Out of the Air*, 294.

41. McBride, *Out of the Air*, 62. The incident provoked this letter from C. L. Menser, a vice president of NBC, who reviewed the production report of the Laurette Taylor program. After noting that the following words and phrases had been uttered ("nigger," "damn," "oh, God," and "mad as hell"), he said: "I don't think I need to tell you what's wrong with this picture. In spite of the fact that I come from Indiana where four-letter words are pretty generally accepted, even I feel that most of these expressions have no place on the air." He then reminded McBride that she was responsible for her guests and that "it would be awfully nice if you would also be responsible for having them sweep the mud off their feet before they come into our nice quarters." Menser to McBride, April 10, 1945, Recorded Sound, LC.

42. Heggie, "Mary Margaret's Miracle," 36, 82.

43. "The McBride Phenomenon," *Newsweek*, May 30, 1949, 50.

44. Elliot Graham to McBride, October 17, 1948, Manuscript Division, LC.

45. McBride broadcast, April 9, 1951 (RWC 7045 LWO 26484), Recorded Sound, LC.

46. Transcribed list of autographs and tributes (probably done in preparation for the last volume of her autobiography), found in Recorded Sound, LC. See also McBride, *Out of the Air*, 194–95. It is not clear what happened to the screen. It was not among the mementos donated to the Library of Congress. Perhaps it is sitting in someone's attic somewhere.

47. Johnson O'Connor to McBride, March 12, 1942, Recorded Sound, LC.

48. Buel W. Patch to McBride, June 28, 1943, Recorded Sound, LC.

49. Harris Wofford to McBride, February 19, 1946, Recorded Sound, LC.

50. McBride, *Out of the Air*, 270–71.

51. Lowry and McBride, "'I've Learned to Love,'" 67.

52. Mary Margaret McBride, "This Is My Faith," *True Confessions*, April, 1944, 19.

53. Elsie Robinson, "Listen World" (1951), clipping found in McBride papers, Manuscript Division, LC.

54. Karen Hanson, "'It's One O'Clock and Here Is Mary Margaret McBride': Radio Holdings in the Collection of the Library of Congress," in *Performing Arts Broadcasting*, edited by Iris Newsom (Washington, D.C.: Library of Congress, 2002), 19. The show aired on February 6, 1939 (LWO 15577).

55. Typed credo, no date, found in Recorded Sound, LC.

56. McBride to Dr. Flanders Dunbar, January 10, 1949; Dunbar to McBride, February

18, 1949; Mcbride to Dunbar, February 24, 1949, all in Recorded Sound, LC. She ended the last letter, "I really am horrified and I still can hardly believe that you, yourself, signed that letter."

57. "Mary Margaret McBride Says—She's a Poor Sport, So What?" AP column, September 2 (1953–56), Recorded Sound, LC.

58. Ben Gross to McBride, December 15, 1950, which sounds fairly similar to his letter to McBride on December 8, 1949, both in Recorded Sound, LC. See also a letter from Richard Laurence Vinick to Susan Ware, June 8, 1999, which draws a similar conclusion about her "need to give and to receive affection."

59. "Mary Margaret McBride Says—What Does Happiness Mean to You?" AP column, October 5 (1953–56), Recorded Sound, LC.

60. McBride to Jan Weyr, April, 1953, Manuscript Division, LC.

61. McBride, *Out of the Air*, 55.

NOTES TO CHAPTER 3

1. Mary Margaret McBride, *Out of the Air* (Garden City, N.Y.: Doubleday), 27–28. The chapter title comes from Michele Hilmes, *Radio Voices: American Broadcasting, 1922–1952* (Minneapolis: University of Minnesota Press, 1997), 154. See the discussion at the end of the chapter of the wide-ranging implications of daytime programming for women's lives and women's history, which is greatly indebted to Hilmes's interpretation.

2. Harry Field and Paul F. Lazarsfeld, *The People Look at Radio* (Chapel Hill: University of North Carolina Press, 1946), 5. For a lively general introduction to the history of radio that emphasizes the experience of listening, see Susan J. Douglas, *Listening In: Radio and the American Imagination* (New York: Times Books, 1999). A more theoretical overview is Daniel J. Czitrom's *Media and the American Mind: From Morse to McLuhan* (Chapel Hill: University of North Carolina Press, 1982). See also Tracy F. Tyler, ed., *Radio as a Cultural Agency: Proceedings of a National Conference on the Use of Radio as a Cultural Agency in a Democracy* (Washington, D.C.: National Committee on Education by Radio, 1934); and Judith C. Waller, *Radio: The Fifth Estate* (Boston: Mifflin, 1946).

3. Field and Lazarsfeld, *The People Look at Radio*, vii.

4. Michele Hilmes, *Only Connect: A Cultural History of Broadcasting in the United States* (Belmont, Calif.: Wadsworth, 2002), 51.

5. Fred Allen, quoted in Michael Kammen, *American Culture, American Tastes: Social Change and the 20th Century* (New York: Knopf, 1999), 87.

6. Gerald Nachman, *Raised on Radio* (New York: Pantheon Books, 1998), 6.

7. Douglas, *Listening In*, 7, 27.

8. Hadley Cantril and Gordon W. Allport, *The Psychology of Radio* (New York: Harper Bros., 1935), 260.

9. See Lizabeth Cohen, *Making a New Deal: Industrial Workers in Chicago, 1919–1939* (Cambridge: Cambridge University Press, 1990), 129–43.

10. Hadley Cantril and Gordon Allport realized this in 1935: "Every city dweller who has suffered that familiar boredom which comes after a few days in a rural community had only to turn on the radio to realize how much stimulation it brings into the cultural wastelands of America." Note, however, the disparaging view of the hinterlands. Cantril and Allport, *The Psychology of Radio*, 21–22.

11. Derek Valliant, "'Your Voice Came in Last Night . . . But I Thought It Sounded a Little Scared': Rural Radio Listening and 'Talking Back' during the Progressive Era in Wisconsin, 1920–1932," in *Radio Reader: Essays in the Cultural History of Radio*, edited by Michele Hilmes and Jason Loviglio (New York: Routledge, 2002), 63–88. See also Evelyn

Birkby, *Neighboring on the Air: Cooking with the KMA Radio Homemakers* (Iowa City: University of Iowa Press, 1991).

12. Robert S. Lynd and Helen Merrell Lynd, *Middletown: A Study in Contemporary American Culture* (New York: Harcourt, Brace, 1929), 269.

13. Robert S. Lynd and Helen Merrell Lynd, *Middletown in Transition: A Study in Cultural Conflicts* (New York: Harcourt, Brace, 1937), 264.

14. For general discussion of radio in the 1930s and 1940s, see Erik Barnouw, *The Golden Web: A History of Broadcasting in the United States, Volume II, 1933 to 1953* (New York: Oxford University Press, 1968). An excellent study of the war years is Barbara Dianne Savage's *Broadcasting Freedom: Radio, War, and the Politics of Race, 1938–1948* (Chapel Hill: University of North Carolina Press, 1999).

15. Paul F. Lazarsfeld and Patricia L. Kendall, *Radio Listening in America: The People Look at Radio—Again* (New York: Prentice-Hall, 1948), 109.

16. Cantril and Allport, *The Psychology of Radio*, 23–24.

17. Hilmes, *Only Connect*, 78. This period also is discussed extensively in Susan J. Douglas, *Inventing American Broadcasting, 1899–1922* (Baltimore: Johns Hopkins University Press, 1987); Susan Smulyan, *Selling Radio: The Commercialization of American Broadcasting, 1920–1934* (Washington, D.C.: Smithsonian Institution Press, 1994); and Erik Barnouw, *A Tower in Babel: A History of Broadcasting in the United States: Volume I, – to 1933* (New York: Oxford University Press, 1966).

18. The fullest discussion of the events leading up to the Communications Act of 1934 is found in Robert W. McChesney, *Telecommunications, Mass Media, and Democracy: The Battle for the Control of U.S. Broadcasting, 1928–1935* (New York: Oxford University Press, 1994). See also Hilmes, *Radio Voices*.

19. See McChesney, *Telecommunications, Mass Media, and Democracy*; and Hilmes, *Only Connect*, chap. 4.

20. For an overview of women's roles, see Donna L. Halper, *Invisible Stars: A Social History of Women in American Broadcasting* (Armonk, N.Y.: Sharpe, 2001). See also Catharine Heinz, "Women Radio Pioneers," *Journal of Popular Culture* 112 (fall 1979): 305–13.

21. Ruth Adams Knight, *Stand by for the Ladies! The Distaff Side of Radio* (New York: Coward-McCann, 1939), 44, 147.

22. See Cari Beauchamp, *Without Lying Down: Frances Marion and the Powerful Women of Early Hollywood* (New York: Scribner, 1997); Ally Acker, *Reel Women: Pioneers of the Cinema* (New York: Continuum, 1991); and Susan Ware, *Beyond Suffrage: Women in the New Deal* (Cambridge, Mass.: Harvard University Press, 1981). A similar phenomenon was at work in aviation. See Susan Ware, *Still Missing: Amelia Earhart and the Search for Modern Feminism* (New York: Norton, 1993).

23. Michele Hilmes discusses Brainard's career in both *Radio Voices*, 138–40, and *Only Connect*, 46–49. See also Halper, *Invisible Stars*.

24. For Waller, see Hilmes, *Radio Voices*, 139–140; Halper, *Invisible Stars*; and Cary O'Dell, *Women Pioneers in Television: Biographies of Fifteen Industry Leaders* (Jefferson, N.C.: McFarland, 1997), 195–206.

25. Information about Mack can be found in John Dunning's *On the Air: The Encyclopedia of Old-Time Radio* (New York: Oxford University Press, 1998); and "Women in Radio: Illustrated by Biographical Sketches," *Women's Bureau Bulletin*, May 1947, 6.

26. "Women in Radio," *Women's Bureau Bulletin*, May 1947, vi.

27. Knight, *Stand by for the Ladies*, 55.

28. Quoted in Hilmes, *Radio Voices*, 142. See also Anne McKay, "Speaking Up: Voice Amplification and Women's Struggle for Public Expression," in *Women and Radio: Airing Differences*, edited by Caroline Mitchell (London: Routledge, 2000).

29. Quoted in Hilmes, *Radio Voices*, 143.

30. Cantril and Allport, *The Psychology of Radio*, 127.

31. "Women in Radio," *Women's Bureau Bulletin*, May, 1947, vi.

32. The standard biography of Thompson is Peter Kurth, *American Cassandra: The Life of Dorothy Thompson* (Boston: Little, Brown, 1990). See also Susan Ware, *Letter to the World: Seven Women Who Shaped the American Century* (New York: Norton, 1998).

33. For Cravens, see Halper, *Invisible Stars*, 68, 96, 249, and 260. See also Dunning, *On the Air*, 501–2, which contains the quotation.

34. Hilmes, *Radio Voices*, 143. Jennifer Hyland Wang explores a similar split in the early days of television in "'The Case of the Radio-Active Housewife': Relocating Radio in the Age of Television," in Hilmes and Loviglio, eds., *Radio Reader*, 343–66.

35. For *Amos 'n' Andy*, see Melvin Patrick Ely, *The Adventures of Amos 'n' Andy: A Social History of an American Phenomenon* (New York: Free Press, 1991). For Gertrude Berg's career, see Joyce Antler, *The Journey Home: Jewish Women and the American Century* (New York: Free Press, 1997); and O'Dell, *Women Pioneers in Television*, 41–52.

36. General sources include Nachman, *Raised on Radio*; Leonard Maltin, *The Great American Broadcast: A Celebration of Radio's Golden Age* (New York: Dutton, 1997); and J. Fred MacDonald, *Don't Touch That Dial! Radio Programming in American Life from 1920 to 1960* (Chicago: Nelson-Hall, 1979). For an interpretation of the "War of the Worlds," see Edward D. Miller, *Emergency Broadcasting and 1930s American Radio* (Philadelphia: Temple University Press, 2003).

37. Hilmes, *Radio Voices*, 78–82. For more on the role of advertising, see Jennifer Scanlon, *Inarticulate Longings: The* Ladies' Home Journal, *Gender, and the Promises of Consumer Culture* (New York: Routledge, 1995).

38. Quoted in Hilmes, *Only Connect*, 110. For more on early advertising, see Herman Hettinger, *A Decade of Radio Advertising* (Chicago: University of Chicago Press, 1933).

39. See Michele Hilmes, "Desired and Feared: Women's Voices in Radio History," in *Television, History, and American Culture: Feminist Critical Essays*, edited by Mary Beth Haralovich and Lauren Rabinowitz (Durham, N.C.: Duke University Press, 1999), esp. 19–20. See also Eileen R. Meehan, "Heads of Household and Ladies of the House: Gender, Genre, and Broadcast Ratings, 1929–1990," in *Ruthless Criticism: New Perspectives in U.S. Communication History*, edited by William S. Solomon and Robert W. McChesney (Minneapolis: University of Minnesota Press, 1993).

40. Bertha Brainard quoted in Hilmes, *Only Connect*, 49.

41. In addition to Dunning, *On the Air*, see Arthur J. Singer, *Arthur Godfrey: The Adventures of an American Broadcaster* (Jefferson, N.C.: McFarland, 2000).

42. Wilbur Schramm, ed., *Mass Communications* (Urbana: University of Illinois Press, 1949), 551.

43. For a general introduction to soap operas, see Robert Allen, *Speaking of Soap Operas* (Chapel Hill: University of North Carolina Press, 1985); Hilmes, *Radio Voices*; and Nachman, *Raised on Radio*.

44. Quoted in Allen, *Speaking of Soap Operas*, 11.

45. Anne Hummert quoted in Nachman, *Raised on Radio*, 381. See also Hilmes, *Radio Voices*.

46. Rudolph Arnheim, "The World of the Daytime Serial," in *Radio Research, 1942–1943*, edited by Paul F. Lazarsfeld and Frank N. Stanton (New York: Duel, Sloan and Pearce, 1944), 81.

47. Herta Herzog, "What Do We Really Know about Day-Time Serial Listeners?" in Lazarsfeld and Stanton, eds., *Radio Research, 1942–1943*, 5–6.

48. Ibid., 24–25.

49. Arnheim, "The World of the Daytime Serial," 44.

50. Hilmes, *Radio Voices*, 151–82, *passim*. Janice Radway makes a similar point about the readers of romance novels in *Reading the Romance: Women, Patriarchy, and Popular Literature* (Chapel Hill: University of North Carolina Press, 1984).

NOTES TO CHAPTER 4

1. Quoted in *Current Biography*, 1954, 422. Originally from Isabelle Taves, *Successful Women and How They Attained Success* (New York: Dutton, 1943).

2. Mary Margaret McBride, *Here's Martha Deane* (Garden City, N.Y.: Garden City Publishing, 1936), 68.

3. Mary Margaret McBride, *Out of the Air* (Garden City, N.Y.: Doubleday, 1960), 27.

4. Barbara Hotchkiss Posener (Amagansett, N.Y.) to Susan Ware, June 18, 1999.

5. *New York Daily Worker*, May 1949, 13, quoted in Beverly G. Merrick, "Mary Margaret McBride, Talkshow Host: The Perfect Proxy for Radio Listeners," paper presented to the Association for Education in Journalism and Mass Communication Convention, Atlanta, August 1994.

6. Jo Pearson, "Here's Mary Margaret," *Radio Television Mirror*, August 1951, 89.

7. "Women in Radio: Mary Margaret McBride," *Beauty Fair*, November 1949, 44–45.

8. Cynthia Lowry and Mary Margaret McBride, "'I've Learned to Love': A Talk with Mary Margaret McBride," *Woman's Home Companion*, May 1954, 67.

9. Mary Margaret McBride, *America for Me* (New York: Macmillan, 1941), 95.

10. McBride, *Out of the Air*, 100, 76.

11. McBride, *Here's Martha Deane*, 42.

12. McBride, *Out of the Air*, 72. See also McBride, *Here's Martha Deane*, 45.

13. McBride, *Out of the Air*, 68.

14. Mary Margaret McBride, "I Don't Want to Preach," *Woman's Day*, October 1939, 5.

15. McBride, *Out of the Air*, 68.

16. Farm shows and the religious programs also received large amounts of mail. See Derek Vaillant, "'Your Voice Came in Last Night . . . But I Thought It Sounded a Little Scared': Rural Radio Listening and 'Talking Back' during the Progressive Era in Wisconsin, 1920–1932"; and Tona Hangen, "Man of the Hour: Walter A. Maier and Religion by Radio on the *Lutheran Hour*," both in *Radio Reader: Essays in the Cultural History of Radio*, edited by Michele Hilmes and Jason Loviglio (New York: Routledge, 2002). Further examples come from Evelyn Birkby, *Neighboring on the Air: Cooking with the KMA Radio Homemakers* (Iowa City: University of Iowa Press, 1991): "It is impossible to exaggerate the closeness the listeners felt toward the women who were radio homemakers during the early days of broadcasting" (p. 319). Birkby quoted a letter from a listener in rural Iowa: "I grew up hearing the voices of the radio ladies. They made me feel that they were real friends who cared about my entire family. They were closer to us than some of our own relatives" (ibid.).

17. Birkby, *Neighboring on the Air*, 43.

18. McBride, *Out of the Air*, 68. See also *Current Biography*, 1954, 421.

19. This insight was made by one of the anonymous reviewers of the manuscript for New York University Press, November 2003.

20. McBride, *Here's Martha Deane*, 41.

21. McBride, "I Don't Want to Preach," 5.

22. McBride, *Out of the Air*, 68.

23. Birkby, *Neighboring on the Air*, 321. Mark Williams noticed a similar phenomenon on cooking shows on television in Los Angeles in the 1950s. See "Considering Monty

Margetts's *Cook's Corner*: Oral History and Television History," in *Television, History, and American Culture: Feminist Critical Essays*, edited by Mary Beth Haralovich and Lauren Rabinowitz (Durham, N.C.: Duke University Press, 1999), esp. 44–45.

24. The letter continues: "When we women live within a wall of drudgery, near poverty and dullness, and then someone outside this wall whom we have never seen can find time to send words of praise and friendliness, how could we help but see the world through rose-colored glasses?" See Dick Dorrance, "The Pleasure of Simple Things," clipping (ca. 1940) found in Mary Margaret McBride papers, Manuscript Division, Library of Congress (hereafter cited as Manuscript Division, LC).

25. Bebe Fleiss Orzaz (Hewlett Harbor, N.Y.) to Susan Ware, June 13, 1999.

26. Mcbride, "I Don't Want to Preach," 5.

27. [Name missing] to Martha Dean [*sic*], January 7, 1937, Manuscript Division, LC.

28. John B. Landry (Sarasota, Fla.) to Susan Ware, June 24, 1999.

29. Joan Conroy to Susan Ware, July 6, 1999.

30. Lorraine G. Mount (State College, Pa.) to Susan Ware, June 23, 1999.

31. Mrs. Frank Wus to McBride, December 28, 1961, Manuscript Division, LC.

32. Joan Conroy to Susan Ware, July 6, 1999.

33. Patricia Goldstein (Gaithersburg, Md.) to Susan Ware, June 21, 1999.

34. Dick McBride (Sag Harbor, N.Y.) to Susan Ware, June, 1999. The writer is not a relation of the radio star.

35. Sally Sacks to Susan Ware, June 17, 1999.

36. Allen Churchill, "Mary Margaret McBride," *American Mercury*, January 1949, 12.

37. Bert Greene, *Bert Greene's Kitchen Bouquets: A Cookbook of Favored Aromas and Flavors* (Chicago: Contemporary Books, 1979), 68–69. See chapter 20 for his appearance on the show.

38. Lore Steinitz (Antigonish, Nova Scotia) to Susan Ware, June 8, 1999.

39. Shirley Budhos (New York, N.Y.) to Susan Ware, June 6, 1999.

40. McBride, *Out of the Air*, 68.

41. McBride, "I Don't Want to Preach," 40.

42. This survey was done in November 1954, after McBride had given up her daily show. It was part of a proposal submitted to NBC in 1955, and the survey had probably been commissioned in order to show NBC executives and prospective sponsors what the demographics of an audience for a new fifteen-minute show might be. "Mary Margaret McBride's market is the married woman with children . . . larger families . . . bigger incomes. Mary Margaret's ability to sell this group is a matter of broadcasting history." Found in Recorded Sound, LC.

43. WEAF promo, "A Great Station and a Great Program Combine in a Great Radio Promotion," 1944, Manuscript Division, LC.

44. Susan Douglas, *Listening In: Radio and the American Imagination* (New York: Times Books, 1999), 226.

45. For general background on women's lives in this period, see Susan Ware, *Holding Their Own: American Women in the 1930s* (Boston: Twayne, 1982); Susan M. Hartmann, *The Home Front and Beyond: American Women in the 1940s* (Boston: Twayne, 1982); and Winifred Wandersee, *Women's Work and Family Values, 1920–1940* (Cambridge, Mass.: Harvard University Press, 1981). For women and household technology, see Susan Strasser, *Never Done: A History of American Housework* (New York: Pantheon Books, 1982). For more on material culture, see Harvey Green, *The Uncertainty of Everyday Life, 1915–1945* (New York: HarperCollins, 1992).

46. Contrast the depictions of American culture found in, for example, Robert S. Lynd and Helen Merrell Lynd's *Middletown: A Study in Contemporary American Culture* (New

York: Harcourt, Brace, 1929); and their *Middletown in Transition: A Study in Cultural Conflicts* (New York: Harcourt, Brace, 1937); with Lizabeth Cohen's *A Consumers' Republic: The Politics of Mass Consumption in Postwar America* (New York: Knopf, 2003).

47. For women and work, see Wandersee, *Women's Work and Family Values*; and Alice Kessler-Harris, *Out to Work: A History of Wage-Earning Women in America* (New York: Oxford University Press, 1982). For an overview of the modern women's movement, see Ruth Rosen, *The World Split Open: How the Modern Women's Movement Changed America* (New York: Viking, 2000).

48. For an excellent discussion of race and radio in the 1940s, see Barbara Dianne Savage, *Broadcasting Freedom: Radio, War, and the Politics of Race, 1938–1948* (Chapel Hill: University of North Carolina Press, 1999).

49. For a discussion of the general "whiteness" of radio then, see Judith E. Smith, "Radio's 'Cultural Front,' 1938–1948," in Hilmes and Loviglio, eds., *Radio Reader*, 209–30. For Mary Margaret's attitudes toward race, see chapter 16.

50. See Barbara Miller Solomon, *In the Company of Educated Women: A History of Women and Higher Education in America* (New Haven, Conn.: Yale University Press, 1985). Figures cited in Ware, *Holding Their Own*, 58–59, show that in 1930 only 10.5 percent of women aged eighteen to twenty-one were enrolled in institutions of higher learning. This figure was 12.2 percent in 1940 and 17.9 percent in 1950.

51. McBride, *America for Me*, 41.

52. Gerald Nachman, *Raised on Radio* (New York: Pantheon Books, 1998), 406.

53. Although not without some doubts about whether this was truly appropriate, as one male listener confessed to Martha Deane: "For quite a while I thought I was going 'sissy' because I enjoyed your program" (McBride, *Here's Martha Deane*, 52). Sissy, of course, was often a stand in for homosexual, so clearly there were gender anxieties at work.

54. See the introduction to Blanche Wiesen Cook's *Eleanor Roosevelt: Volume I, 1884–1933* (New York: Viking, 1992).

55. McBride, "I Don't Want to Preach," 40.

NOTES TO CHAPTER 5

1. Mary Margaret McBride, *How Dear to My Heart* (New York: Macmillan, 1940), 47. The chapter title comes from Joan Jacobs Brumberg, *Fasting Girls: The Emergence of Anorexia Nervosa as a Modern Disease* (Cambridge, Mass.: Harvard University Press, 1988), in which it is used to show that Victorian girls used appetite and food as a symbolic language: "The popularity of food restriction or dieting, even among normal girls, suggests that in bourgeois society appetite was (and is) an important voice in the identity of a woman" (p. 188). I am using the phrase in a somewhat different way to draw attention to the link between McBride's overweight (the twin sister of eating disorders like anorexia nervosa) and her public and private identity as a woman.

2. Mary Margaret McBride, *Here's Martha Deane* (Garden City, N.Y.: Garden City Publishing, 1936), 157.

3. Collie Small, "The Private Life of a Pied Piper," *Collier's*, December 11, 1948, 139.

4. Mary Margaret McBride, *Out of the Air* (Garden City, N.Y.: Doubleday, 1960), 40–41; Mary Margaret McBride, *Mary Margaret McBride's Harvest of American Cooking* (New York: Putnam, 1957), xvii. This phrase appears in numerous other places—clearly it was one of Mary Margaret's favorites.

5. Mary Margaret McBride, "Please Pass the Turkey," *Cosmopolitan*, December 1940, 48–49.

6. Barbara Heggie, "The Forty-five-Minute Tempo," *New Yorker*, December 19, 1942, 34.

7. McBride, *Here's Martha Deane*, 159. The range of ethnic and regional cuisines was culled from this book.

8. Alice Hughes, "A Woman's New York," November 8, 1957, clipping found in Mary Margaret McBride papers, Manuscript Division, Library of Congress (hereafter cited as Manuscript Division, LC).

9. Barbara Heggie, "Mary Margaret's Miracle," *Woman's Home Companion*, April 1949, 80.

10. Mary Margaret Mcbride, *America for Me* (New York: Macmillan, 1941), 52.

11. McBride, "Please Pass the Turkey," 48.

12. McBride, *Here's Martha Deane*, 187.

13. M. B. S. Parker, "Mary Margaret McBride: Her Broadcast," *Read*, July 1944, 14.

14. Mildred Mastin, "She Stoops to Conquer," *Radio Stars*, December 1938, 25, clipping found in Manuscript Division, LC.

15 Heggie, "Mary Margaret's Miracle," 81–82.

16. "Mary Margaret McBride Says—Here's Her Favorite Recipe," AP column, February 3 (1953–56), found in Mary Margaret McBride papers, Motion Picture, Broadcasting, and Recorded Sound Division, Library of Congress (hereafter cited as Recorded Sound, LC).

17. Bob and Ray, "Mary McGoon's Recipe for Frozen Ginger Ale Salad," undated clipping found in Recorded Sound, LC. In another sketch, every Thanksgiving McGoon made "mock turkey" out of mashed potatoes shaped to look like a turkey, with hot dogs as drumsticks. Bob and Ray started out on Boston radio in 1946, and their show was picked up by NBC in 1951. Mary McGoon, who had a recipe and menu talk show, was one of their earliest characters. For more on Bob and Ray, see John Dunning, *On the Air: The Encyclopedia of Old-Time Radio* (New York: Oxford University Press, 1998), 99–101.

18. This episode is available on a video of *I Love Lucy* called "The Classics: Volume 6," distributed by CBS Video. My thanks to Joyce Antler for bringing this to my attention.

19. "Mary Margaret McBride Says—Fine Food Is Hard on the Feet," AP column, June 1, 1955, Recorded Sound, LC.

20. McBride, *Here's Martha Deane*, 158.

21. Mary Margaret McBride, *A Long Way from Missouri* (New York: Putnam, 1959), 179.

22. McBride, *Here's Martha Deane*, 157. For a discussion of international cooking in the interwar years, which points out the availability of such cuisines while making the point that they still were seen as inferior to "American" food, see Sherrie A. Inness, *Dinner Roles: American Women and Culinary Culture* (Iowa City: University of Iowa Press, 2001), chap. 5.

23. Mary Margaret McBride, *Out of the Air* (Garden City, N.Y.: Doubleday, 1960), 33. She wore an embroidered silk jacket for her last broadcast in May 1954 and again later that year when she was interviewed on Edward R. Murrow's television program *Person to Person*.

24. Alice Hughes, "A Woman's New York," Manuscript Division, LC.

25. Julia Shawell, "She Has a Million Friends," *Woman's World*, September 1938, 16.

26. "Be Yourself," *True Story*, March, 1945, 153, clipping found in Recorded Sound, LC.

27. The broad outlines of this change are treated in Hillel Schwartz, *Never Satisfied: A Cultural History of Diets, Fantasies, and Fat* (New York: Free Press, 1986); and Peter N. Stearns, *Fat History: Bodies and Beauty in the Modern West* (New York: New York University Press, 1997). See also Brumberg, *Fasting Girls*; and Susan Bordo, *Unbearable Weight: Feminism, Western Culture, and the Body* (Berkeley: University of California Press, 1993). Kim

Chernin, *The Obsession: Reflections on the Tyranny of Slenderness* (New York: Harper & Row, 1981), provides one of the earliest feminist critiques of how women's obsession with thinness was linked to their unequal status in society.

28. Cynthia Lowry and Mary Margaret Mcbride, "'I've Learned to Love': A Talk with Mary Margaret Mcbride," *Woman's Home Companion,* May 1954, 68.

29. Naomi Wolf, *The Beauty Myth: How Images of Women Are Used against Women* (New York: Morrow, 1991), 187.

30. "Mary Margaret Mcbride Says—A Diet Leads to Dreams of Food," AP column, April 9 (1953–56), Recorded Sound, LC.

31. Mcbride, *Out of the Air,* 350.

32. For a contemporary account of how girls and women talk about fatness, especially how they employ self-deprecating language as comedy and as an example of identity politics, see Mimi Nichter, *Fat Talk: What Girls and Their Parents Say about Dieting* (Cambridge, Mass.: Harvard University Press, 2000). See also Marcia Millman, *Such a Pretty Face: Being Fat in America* (New York: Norton, 1980); and Susie Orbach, *Fat Is a Feminist Issue* (New York: Paddington Press, 1978).

33. "Mary Margaret Mcbride Says—Emotions Need Outlets," AP column, June 29 (1953–56), Recorded Sound, LC.

34. "Mary Margaret Mcbride Says—Why Specialize in Red Heads?" AP column, January 13 (1953–56), Recorded Sound, LC.

35. See Dick Mcbride to Susan Ware, June 1999; and Carl Gutman to Susan Ware, June 8, 1999.

36. "Mary Margaret Mcbride Zips to New High with Listeners," *Life,* April 5, 1948, 40.

37. Estella Karn, "The Secret Life of Mary Margaret," *Modern Television and Radio,* December 1948, 74. For other versions of the story, see Jo Pearson, "Here's Mary Margaret," *Radio Television Mirror,* August 1951, 89; and "Mary Margaret Mcbride Says—She's the Original Zipper Girl," AP column, March 5 (1953–56), Recorded Sound, LC.

38. For a discussion of the issues of physique and body image in popular culture in these years, see Susan Ware, *Still Missing: Amelia Earhart and the Search for Modern Feminism* (New York: Norton, 1993), 153–56. See also Stearns, *Fat History;* and Joan Jacobs Brumberg, *The Body Project: An Intimate History of American Girls* (New York: Random House, 1997).

39. See Richard K. Hayes, *Kate Smith: A Biography* (Jefferson, N.C.: McFarland, 1995).

40. Robert King Merton, *Mass Persuasion: The Social Psychology of a War Bond Drive* (New York: Harper Bros., 1946), quoted in George Lipsitz, *Time Passages: Collective Memory and American Popular Culture* (Minneapolis: University of Minnesota Press, 1990), 269.

41. Stella describers her "ice-cream technique" in "The Secret Life of Mary Margaret," 51.

42. Mary Margaret Mcbride, *America for Me* (New York: Macmillan, 1941), 86–87.

43. Carole Counihan and Penny Van Esterik, eds., *Food and Culture: A Reader* (New York: Routledge, 1997). The section on food, body, and culture containing essays by Hortense Powdermaker, Hilde Bruch, Susan Bordo, and others is a good introduction to this literature. The quotation from Bruch is found on p. 221. See also Carole M. Counihan, *The Anthropology of Food and Body: Gender, Meaning, and Power* (New York: Routledge, 1999). Chernin, *The Obsession,* and Ruth Raymond Thone, *Fat—A Fate Worse Than Death? Women, Weight, and Appearance* (New York: Haworth, 1997), describe the demonization of those who fail to live up to these standards in contemporary America.

44. Emily Post, *Etiquette* (New York: Funk & Wagnalls, 1940), quoted in Stearns, *Fat History,* 79. Stearns notes that Post says nothing comparable about overweight men. For more on NAAFA, see Counihan, *The Anthropology of Food and Body.*

NOTES TO CHAPTER 6

1. Quoted in Philip Hamburger, "Mary Margaret Mcbride: A Supersaleswoman Shares Adventures of Mind and Stomach with a Host of Listeners," *Life*, December 4, 1944, 50.

2. Mcbride discusses her approach to commercials and her relationships with advertisers in the chapter entitled "They Paid the Bills," in *Out of the Air* (Garden City, N.Y.: Doubleday, 1960), 79–93; and in "Those Fairy Godfathers," in *Here's Martha Deane* (Garden City, N.Y.: Garden City Publishing, 1936), 15–26. The quotation is from *Out of the Air*, 84. For an example of Mary Margaret and Vincent's having a good time while doing the products, see the broadcast from July 6, 1945 (RWA 1811—LWO 17243), in which they have a riddle for each product. I even solved the one for Sell's liver paté! Tape in Motion Picture, Broadcasting, and Recorded Sound Division, Library of Congress (hereafter cited as Recorded Sound, LC).

3. Mcbride, *Here's Martha Deane*, 16.

4. Susan Strasser, *Satisfaction Guaranteed: The Making of the American Mass Market* (New York: Pantheon Books, 1989), 15. For more on the emerging mass culture, see Michael Kammen, *American Culture, American Tastes* (New York: Knopf, 1999); Lynn Dumenil, *The Modern Temper: American Culture and Society in the 1920s* (New York: Hill & Wang, 1995); and Lizabeth Cohen, "The New Deal and the Making of Citizen Consumers," in *Getting and Spending: European and American Consumer Societies in the Twentieth Century*, edited by Susan Strasser, Charles McGovern, and Matthias Judt (Cambridge: Cambridge University Press, 1998). For the role of advertising in twentieth-century American culture, see Roland Marchand, *Advertising the American Dream: Making Way for Modernity, 1920–1940* (Berkeley: University of California Press, 1985); and Richard Tedlow, *New and Improved: The Story of Mass Marketing in America* (New York: Basic Books, 1990).

5. In addition to Strasser's *Satisfaction Guaranteed*, see her earlier *Never Done: A History of American Housework* (New York: Pantheon Books, 1982). Also of interest is Warren Belasco and Philip Scranton's *Food Nations: Selling Taste in Consumer Societies* (New York: Routledge, 2002).

6. See Tracey Deutsch, "Untangling Alliances: Social Tensions Surrounding Independent Grocery Stores and the Rise of Mass Retailing," in Belasco and Scranton, eds., *Food Nations*, 156–74.

7. For an introduction to the field of food and culinary history, see Barbara Haber, *From Hardtack to Home Fries: An Uncommon History of American Cooks and Meals* (New York: Free Press, 2002); Leslie Howsam, *Food, Cooking and Culture* (Windsor, Ont.: Humanities Research Group, University of Windsor, 1998); and Sherrie Inness, ed., *Kitchen Culture in America: Popular Representations of Food, Gender, and Race* (Philadelphia: University of Pennsylvania Press, 2000). See also chapter 19 in this book.

8. Barbara Heggie, "The Forty-five-Minute Tempo," *New Yorker*, December 19, 1942, 34.

9. Walter White, "A Party for Mary Margaret Mcbride" (1949), clipping found in the Mary Margaret Mcbride papers, Manuscript Division, Library of Congress (hereafter cited as Manuscript Division, LC).

10. Mcbride, *Out of the Air*, 85.

11. See Gerald Nachman, *Raised on Radio* (New York: Pantheon Books, 1998), espescially chapter13.

12. Mcbride, *Here's Martha Deane*, 20.

13. "Mary Margaret Mcbride Zips to New High with Listeners," *Life*, April 5, 1948, 40.

14. Mcbride Broadcasts, December 22, 1943 (actual broadcast on January 1, 1944)

(LWO 15577 R205 A1), and September 19, 1945 (LWO 12747 R38B), Recorded Sound, LC. For radio quiz shows, see Nachman, *Raised on Radio*, chap. 16.

15. Radio critic Jay Nelson Tuck quoted in Beverly G. Merrick, "Mary Margaret McBride, Talkshow Host: The Perfect Proxy for Radio Listeners," paper presented to the Association for Education in Journalism and Mass Communication convention, Atlanta, August 1994.

16. McBride, *Here's Martha Deane*, 21–22.

17. Stella was notorious for giving sponsors a hard time. "I don't know what our ratings are. I don't care anything about them. Ratings don't matter. We don't sell ratings. We sell Mary Margaret McBride. Mary Margaret sells products. You want to sell your products, don't you?" McBride, *Out of the Air*, 36.

18. See the brochure prepared by NBC Spot Sales, May 10–23, 1943, found in Mary Margaret McBride papers, Motion Picture, Broadcasting, and Recorded Sound Division, Library of Congress (hereafter cited as Recorded Sound, LC). See also Mary Margaret McBride to Paul Arnold, April 22, 1952, Mary Margaret McBride papers, Manuscript Division, Library of Congress (hereafter cited as Manuscript Division, LC). The business, Arnold's Bakers of Port Chester, New York, did not take her up on her offer but hoped to be back on the program soon.

19. Nachman, *Raised on Radio*, 261. See also John Dunning, *On the Air: The Encyclopedia of Old-Time Radio* (New York: Oxford University Press, 1998).

20. See the fliers from ABC advertising this arrangement in Recorded Sound, LC.

21. See the conclusion to Michele Hilmes, *Radio Voices: American Broadcasting, 1922– 1952* (Minneapolis: University of Minnesota Press, 1997), 270–90.

22. Material on Dolly Madison and other sponsors can be found in Recorded Sound, LC. Morris Scheck, whose advertising agency handled the Dolly Madison account, wrote to Mary Margaret, October 21, 1953, "When we asked you to take on our Dolly Madison, we thought we would stay with you the customary 13 weeks. Just think of it—these 13 weeks have grown to 19 years." Quoted in WABC program schedule, November 1953, Recorded Sound, LC. For an example of eating ice cream on the air, listen to the broadcast from May 3, 1939 (RWC 6780, Recorded Sound, LC), where its arrival is greeted by gasps of delight from host and guests alike.

23. McBride, *Here's Martha Deane*, 22. The broadcast for her sixth anniversary on June 3, 1940 (LWO 12747, Recorded Sound, LC), mentions Dolly Madison parties. And the broadcast from June 30, 1939 (RWA 1461, Recorded Sound, LC), describes a Martha Deane dinner, at which each course features a product or recipe from the program, including the dog, who is given Red Heart Dog Food, also a sponsor.

24. WABC promotional brochure, November 1953, Manuscript Division, LC.

25. Walter Bruce to Estella Karn, December 17, 1945, Manuscript Division, LC.

26. Curtis Mitchell, "Mary Margaret McBride's Magic," *Coronet*, January 1954, clipping in Manuscript Division, LC.

27. WEAF promotional brochure (ca. 1942), Recorded Sound, LC.

28. Charles Zimmerman to Martha Deane, April 4, 1939, Manuscript Division, LC.

29. Charles Gristede to Martha Deane, March 18, 1938, Manuscript Division, LC.

30. Hamburger, "Mary Margaret McBride," 47. Hamburger is a good example of the disparaging tone that often accompanied articles about the radio host, especially ones written by men. In 1942, describing an offer for noodle soup that drew almost fourteen thousand responses, he noted that they "had become helpless addicts"; on the same page he described listeners "who would plunge headlong into bowls of dehydrated split-pea soup rather than call her by any other name."

31. WEAF promotional brochure, Recorded Sound, LC.

32. Henry B. Sell quoted in *Food Merchants Advocate*, January 1946, 14–15, Recorded Sound, LC.

33. Marguerite Walton to Mary Margaret McBride, November 2, 1945, Manuscript Division, LC.

34. Heggie, "The Forty-five-Minute Tempo," 29. Another variation on this was a letter from M. B. in the Bronx: "This A.M. at breakfast my husband said Mary Margaret has a new brand of coffee and he also said he hopes you never sponsor mink coats or diamond bracelets. But he likes Savarin and from now on that is our coffee." WEAF promotional brochure, Recorded Sound, LC.

35. McBride, *Out of the Air*, 80; Bennett Cerf, "Here Comes McBride," *Saturday Review of Literature*, March 1, 1947, clipping in Manuscript Division, LC. For more examples of Vincent and Mary Margaret doing the products, see the transcription in Judith C. Waller, *Radio: The Fifth Estate* (Boston: Mifflin, 1946), 156. See also a five-page letter, dated August 9, from Mary Margaret to Vincent about the products. It was to be used while she was on vacation and approximates that part of the program but without the spontaneity of a live broadcast. Recorded Sound, LC.

36. Cerf, "Here Comes McBride."

37. McBride, *Out of the Air*, 91.

38. McBride had asked Hughes whether he could deliver her commercial as a poem, and he rose to the challenge: "Dromedary, help me carry, news of chocolate cake. Also, news of gingerbread for all the folks who bake." Quoted in Karen Hansen, "'It's One O'-Clock and Here Is Mary Margaret McBride': Early Radio Holdings in the Collections of the Library of Congress," in *Performing Arts Broadcasting*, edited by Iris Newsom (Washington, D.C.: Library of Congress, 2002), 28.

39. Jo Pearson, "Here's Mary Margaret," *Radio Television Mirror*, August 1951, clipping in Recorded Sound, LC.

40. McBride, *Out of the Air*, 90.

41. McBride broadcast, September 29, 1952 (LWO 12747 60A), Recorded Sound, LC.

42. McBride, *Out of the Air*, 79.

43. Ibid., 79.

44. McBride, *Here's Martha Deane*, 25–26.

45. Ibid., 25.

46. McBride, *Out of the Air*, 81.

47. WEAF promotional brochure, Recorded Sound, LC. The broadcast from June 30, 1942 (RWC 6748, Recorded Sound, LC), features a letter from a listener that wins her a $5 certificate at Bohack's.

48. All quotations found in WEAF promotional brochure, Recorded Sound, LC.

49. Hamburger, "Mary Margaret McBride," 49.

50. McBride, *Out of the Air*, 82. For examples of almost commercial-free Thanksgiving programs, see the broadcasts of November 26, 1942 (LWO 12747 R25B2), and November 25, 1943 (LWO 12747 R35B1), Recorded Sound, LC.

51. McBride, *Out of the Air*, 81.

52. Ibid.

53. Quoted in promotional flyer, February 14, 1950, Manuscript Division, LC.

54. McBride, *Out of the Air*, 91.

55. Harry Field and Paul Lazarsfeld, *The People Look at Radio* (Chapel Hill: University of North Carolina Press, 1946), 18. According to its tabulations, listeners fell into four categories: 23 percent were in favor of commercials, 41 percent did not mind them, 26 percent put up with them, and only 7 percent wanted to get rid of them completely. The survey also found that if people liked radio generally, they generally had the same views of

advertisements. A list of the products that were considered in bad taste or not suitable for radio in the 1940s can be found on p. 34.

56. Mary Margaret's closest competition in this area was Arthur Godfrey, who also had near perfect pitch when it came to hawking products. As Larry King once said, "If Godfrey talked about peanut butter, I had to have that peanut butter." Quoted in Nachman, *Raised on Radio*, 354.

57. Examples of these print advertisements can be found in Recorded Sound, LC.

58. Clara Brown Lyman, "Women's Fight for Truth Now Brings Opportunity to the Advertiser," *Printers' Ink*, January 5, 1939, 65–66.

59. WEAF promotional brochure, Recorded Sound, LC.

60. Michela Mitchell, "Meet Mary Margaret," *Westchester Life*, September 1951, 35.

61. Press releases prepared by Ted Hartman for programs that aired on February 6, 1950, and December 28, 1950, found in Manuscript Division, LC.

NOTES TO CHAPTER 7

1. The information about this episode is drawn from the tape of the January 16, 1940, broadcast (RWC 6688—LWO 25588), Motion Picture, Broadcasting, and Recorded Sound Division, Library of Congress (hereafter cited as Recorded Sound, LC).

2. An example is the broadcast from July 1, 1938 (LWO 15777), Recorded Sound, LC.

3. "Mary Margaret McBride Says—Never Underrate Mama," AP column, May 7, 1954, found in Recorded Sound, LC. Other articles that McBride wrote about her mother include "Are You Listening, Mama?" *True Confessions*, June 1945, 51; "My Mother," *Life Story Magazine*, May 1944, 46–47; "The Hardest Lesson," *Guideposts*, October 1949, 1, 22–24; and "My Mother's Day," *Cosmopolitan*, June 1940, 66–67. Many of these were recycled from Mary Margaret McBride, *How Dear to My Heart* (New York: Macmillan, 1940).

4. McBride broadcast, January 17, 1940 (RWC 6688—LWO 25588), Recorded Sound, LC.

5. McBride broadcast, January 18, 1940 (RWC 6689), Recorded Sound, LC. In her autobiography, she had this to say about the show: "Among the records is the one in which I talk about my mother in a tight, strained voice that is like that of a very little girl. I have heard it only twice, and doubt if I'll ever play it again." Mary Margaret McBride, *A Long Way from Missouri* (New York: Putnam, 1959), 97.

6. McBride broadcast, June 1, 1937 (RWC 6824—LWO 26484), Recorded Sound, LC.

7. McBride, *How Dear to My Heart*, 18.

8. Examples of these jam sessions in which Stella, Mary Margaret, and friends traded old stories are the broadcasts from April 22, 1950 (LWO 15577 R209), and January 26, 1951 (LWO 15577 R94), Recorded Sound, LC.

9. Mary Margaret McBride, *Here's Martha Deane* (Garden City, N.Y.: Garden City Publishing, 1936), 37.

10. Barbara Heggie, "The Forty-five-Minute Tempo," *New Yorker*, December 19, 1942, 30; and Enid Haupt, "Radio's Miss Aladdin," *Movie-Radio Guide*, January 31, 1943, clipping found in the Mary Margaret McBride papers, Recorded Sound, LC.

NOTES TO CHAPTER 8

1. Mary Margaret McBride, *America for Me* (New York: Macmillan, 1941), 1.

2. See the correspondence (1958–60) between McBride and her lecture agent, W. Colston Leigh, found in the Mary Margaret McBride papers, Motion Picture, Broadcasting,

and Recorded Sound Division, Library of Congress (hereafter cited as Recorded Sound, LC).

3. Mary Margaret McBride, *Mary Margaret McBride's Harvest of American Cooking* (New York: Putnam, 1957), 115.

4. Writers' Project of the Works Progress Administration, comp., *Missouri: The WPA Guide to the "Show Me" State* (1941; repr., St. Louis: Missouri Historical Society Press, 1998), xiii, 369.

5. For background on McBride's family, see the chapter entitled "The McBrides versus the Craigs," in Mary Margaret McBride, *How Dear to My Heart* (New York: Macmillan, 1940), 60–72. See also Mary Margaret McBride, "And How Are All Your Folks?" *Cosmopolitan*, March 1940, 54ff. If not otherwise specified, the general material on McBride's childhood is drawn from *How Dear to My Heart* and the set of articles that ran in *Cosmopolitan* from 1939 to 1941, which were adaptations of the book.

6. The final chapter of Mary Margaret McBride's *Here's Martha Deane* (Garden City, N.Y.: Garden City Publishing, 1936) is about her upbringing and is entitled "When I Was Very Young"; the quotation is from p. 288.

7. Of all her siblings, Mary Margaret remained closest to her brother Tommy her entire life. He became a doctor and settled in Florida, where he was known for his old-fashioned medical practice. See "A Country Doctor Slows Down," *Orlando Sentinel Sunday Magazine*, November 12, 1972, clipping found in the Mary Margaret McBride papers, Manuscript Division, Library of Congress (hereafter cited as Manuscript Division, LC.)

8. McBride, *How Dear to My Heart*, 90.

9. Ibid., 2.

10. Mary Margaret McBride, "My Mother's Day," *Cosmopolitan*, June, 1940, 66. See also McBride, *How Dear to My Heart*, 1–4, 133–34.

11. McBride, *How Dear to My Heart*, 4; Cynthia Lowry and Mary Margaret McBride, "'I've Learned to Love': A Talk with Mary Margaret McBride," *Woman's Home Companion*, May 1954, 66.

12. Mary Margaret McBride, *A Long Way from Missouri* (New York: Putnam, 1959), 101. See also McBride, *How Dear to My Heart*, 179–81. As she concluded in her talk with Cynthia Lowry for *Woman's Home Companion*, May 1954, "I seem rather mixed up about him" (p. 66).

13. McBride, *How Dear to My Heart*, 140–41.

14. Mary Margaret McBride, "Please Pass the Turkey," *Cosmopolitan*, December 1940, 48.

15. McBride, *How Dear to My Heart*, 104. See also pp. 37–39.

16. As she told readers of her AP column in the 1950s, "But all through my life I've had two happy backstops: work in which I'm interested and for which there are deadlines, and—perhaps even more important to carry me out of myself—books." "Mary Margaret McBride Says—You Can Outwit Loneliness," AP column, February 9 (1953–56), Recorded Sound, LC.

17. "Mary Margaret McBride Says—Who's Afraid of a Big, Bad Debt? (She Is)," AP column, September 30, 1954, found in Recorded Sound, LC.

18. Lowry and McBride, "'I've Learned to Love,'" 68.

19. McBride, *A Long Way from Missouri*, 239.

20. McBride, *How Dear to My Heart*, 43–45, 83–84. See also Mary Margaret McBride, "Some Like It Cold," *Cosmopolitan*, February 1940, 52ff.

21. She tells this story in *How Dear to My Heart*, 92–94.

22. McBride, *Harvest of American Cooking*, 115–116. See also McBride, *How Dear to My Heart*, 125–37.

23. McBride, *How Dear to My Heart*, 135–37. See also Mary Margaret McBride, "Deep Summer," *Cosmopolitan*, August 1939, 82.

24. Mary Margaret McBride, *The Growing Up of Mary Elizabeth* (New York: Dodd, Mead, 1966), 96–97. She also talked about this incident in her AP column: "Mary Margaret McBride Says—Explain Death to a Child," July 1 (1953–56), Recorded Sound, LC.

25. McBride, *A Long Way from Missouri*, 211.

26. McBride, *How Dear to My Heart*, 185–186; "Mary Margaret McBride Says—Editors Don't Even Let Her Confess," AP column, May 4, 1954, Recorded Sound, LC.

27. McBride, *How Dear to My Heart*, 193.

28. Other episodes involved midnight feasts in the dorms, at which Mary Margaret consumed prodigious quantities of food that arrived in a box sent from some student's home. McBride, *How Dear to My Heart*, 189–91.

29. Mary Margaret McBride, "Mary *Was a* Little Lamb," *Cosmopolitan*, October 1940, 56.

30. Mary Margaret McBride, "I Came, I Saw, and This Is What *I Did!* " *Cosmopolitan*, November 1939, 63.

31. Ibid.

32. *Missouri: The WPA Guide*, 369; Mary Margaret McBride, "A New Year's Resolution Changed My Life," *Cosmopolitan*, February 1941, 56.

33. McBride, *A Long Way from Missouri*, 14.

34. "Radio's First Lady Has That Certain Knack," *Columbian Missourian* (1975), clipping found in the Mary Margaret McBride papers, Manuscript Division, Library of Congress.

35. Some sources list her degree date as 1919, but University of Missouri records confirm the 1918 date. Perhaps she was trying to shorten the years before she managed to get herself to New York so she went along with 1919, which would have made her twenty when she graduated. If she graduated in 1918, however, she would have been only nineteen, which raises questions about her 1899 birth date, but Missouri did not keep birth records that far back. For a discussion of the discrepancy in dates, see Beverly G. Merrick, "Mary Margaret McBride, The College and Cub Reporting Years: An Early Graduate Makes the Most of Missouri's Journalism Schooling," paper presented to the Association for Education in Journalism and Mass Communication convention in Anaheim, Calif., August 1996.

36. McBride, *A Long Way from Missouri*, 12.

37. Ibid., 13.

38. Merrick, "Mary Margaret McBride, The College and Cub Reporting Years," provides well-researched coverage of this period on pp. 8–15.

39. McBride, *A Long Way from Missouri*, 19.

40. Ibid., 20, 21–22.

41. McBride, *A Long Way from Missouri*, 22. See also McBride, "I Came, I Saw, and This is What *I Did!* "

42. McBride, *A Long Way from Missouri*, 23.

NOTES TO CHAPTER 9

1. "Looking and Listening with Ben Gross," (no date), clipping found in the Mary Margaret McBride papers, Manuscript Division, Library of Congress (hereafter cited as Manuscript Division, LC). See also Estella Karn, "The Secret Life of Mary Margaret," *Modern Television and Radio*, December 1948, 50ff.

2. Mary Margaret McBride, *Out of the Air* (Garden City, N.Y.: Doubleday, 1960), 42. For

more on Stella's importance to Mary Margaret's career, see Beverly G. Merrick, "Estella Karn, The Tough-Talking Program Manager behind the Radio Talkshow of Mary Margaret McBride," paper presented to the Association for Education in Journalism and Mass Communication conference, Washington, D.C., August 1995.

3. Mary Margaret McBride, *A Long Way from Missouri* (New York: Putnam, 1959), 30.

4. Mary Margaret McBride, "My Most Unforgettable Character," *Reader's Digest*, February 1962, 99.

5. Linda M. Kahn to Susan Ware, June 25, 1999.

6. Barbara Kahn to Susan Ware, August 15, 2000.

7. Estella Karn, "Winging with the Bluebirds," *American Girl*, April 1934, 5, clipping found in the Mary Margaret McBride papers, Motion Picture, Broadcasting, and Recorded Sound Division, Library of Congress (hereafter cited as Recorded Sound, LC).

8. McBride, *Out of the Air*, 33.

9. McBride, *A Long Way from Missouri*, 45.

10. Karn, "Winging with the Bluebirds," 7.

11. McBride, *A Long Way from Missouri*, 43–44.

12. Ibid., 40–41.

13. "Mary Margaret McBride Says—Departure from Winter Quarters Is Happy Time for Circus Folk," AP Column, March 11, 1955, Recorded Sound, LC. There must have been a certain poignancy to Mary Margaret's memories in 1955, since Stella was very ill with the cancer that killed her two years later. Any thought of winging with the bluebirds would have been more nostalgic than a real possibility at that point.

14. McBride, *A Long Way from Missouri*, 83–84.

15. McBride, *Out of the Air*, 34, 42.

16. Ibid., 34–35.

17. Ibid., 36–38.

18. McBride, "My Most Unforgettable Character," 102; Collie Small, "The Private Life of a Pied Piper," *Collier's*, December 11, 1948, 39.

19. McBride, "My Most Unforgettable Character," 101, 99. See also Mary Margaret McBride, "Never Take 'No' for an Answer," featured on a package of Nucoa Margarine, whose package wrapper is found in the Manuscript Division, LC.

20. McBride, *Out of the Air*, 185.

21. "Looking and Listening with Ben Gross," Manuscript Division, LC.

22. Karn, "The Secret Life of Mary Margaret," 74. For someone who prided herself as a supporter of civil rights, McBride's choice of the word *lynching* seems inappropriate, indeed offensive, but there is no record of complaints from listeners or network executives the way there were after Laurette Taylor's use of the word *nigger* around the same time.

23. The quotation comes from "Your Hudson Valley Neighbor," *Kingston Week*, July 20, 1967, clipping found in Manuscript Division, LC.

24. Newsclipping from the Kingston paper, September 7, 1939, found in Mary Margaret McBride papers, Motion Picture, Broadcasting, and Recorded Sound Division, Library of Congress (hereafter cited as Recorded Sound, LC). It was sent by the former secretary to the mayor, Thomas W. Miller, to McBride on October 9, 1970, when she was recovering from a broken hip. See also McBride, *Out of the Air*, 382.

25. Mary Margaret McBride, *Mary Margaret McBride's Harvest of American Cooking* (New York: Putnam, 1957), 15. She had already changed her tune by 1943, as seen in a letter to her brother Milton, dated September 1, 1943, "I'm feeling pretty good (for an old lady) and this summer have been enjoying Stella's farm in the Catskills. It is perfectly beautiful up there and I keep thinking how Mother and Dad would have enjoyed it." McBride papers, Recorded Sound, LC.

26. For the farm and Stella, see McBride, *Out of the Air*, 372–84. For background on the Ashokan reservoir, which was built in 1913 by damming the Esopus Creek and flooding four hamlets, see Lisa W. Foderaro, "'Watery Graves' Was No Figure of Speech," *New York Times*, May 14, 2002.

27. McBride, *Out of the Air*, 50.

28. Philip Hamburger, "Mary Margaret McBride: A Supersaleswoman Shares Adventures of Mind and Stomach with a Host of Radio Listeners," *Life*, December 4, 1944, 49. For an aural introduction to the farm, see the broadcast from July 14, 1945 (RWA 1810 LWO 17243), where Vincent pays his first visit and is given an on-air tour of the house and grounds by his two hostesses.

29. "Looking and Listening with Ben Gross," clipping (no date) found in Manuscript Division, LC; McBride, "My Most Unforgettable Character," 99.

30. McBride, *Out of the Air*, 39. Beverly Merrick suggests that Mary Margaret's pattern of being "alternately scolded and petted" in relationships actually dates back to her days as a student at William Woods. See Merrick, "Estella Karn, Tough-Talking Program Manager." In many ways McBride found herself in a similar pattern at the end of her life with her housemate Cynthia Lowry. See chapter 20.

31. McBride, *Out of the Air*, 38.

32. Ibid., 39.

33. For general background on the history of sexuality, including same-sex love, see John D'Emilio and Estelle Freedman, *Intimate Matters: A History of Sexuality*, 2nd ed. (Chicago: University of Chicago Press, 1997); Lillian Faderman, *Surpassing the Love of Men: Romantic Friendships and Love between Women from the Renaissance to the Present* (New York: Morrow, 1981); Lillian Faderman, *Odd Girls and Twilight Lovers: A History of Lesbian Life in Twentieth Century America* (New York: Columbia University Press, 1991); and Leila J. Rupp, *A Desired Past: A Short History of Same-Sex Love in America* (Chicago: University of Chicago Press, 1999). For descriptions of New York City's homosocial world in the 1920s and 1930s, see Susan Ware, *Partner and I: Molly Dewson, Feminism, and New Deal Politics* (New Haven, Conn.: Yale University Press, 1987); and Blanche Wiesen Cook, *Eleanor Roosevelt: Volume I, 1884–1933* (New York: Viking, 1992).

34. There are scattered references in the radio correspondence to Stella's possible proclivities, mainly in the material about her problems with the NBC brass, which suggest her bossy temperament was caused by sexual frustration linked to her unmarried state. For example, see Mercer C. Macpherson to James Gaines, October 17, 1947, Recorded Sound, LC: "The only unpleasant note in the proceedings was that caused by our having to work with Estella Karn. She is a most arrogant and unpleasant person. Perhaps caused by frustration."

35. McBride to "Aida," November 29, 1946, Recorded Sound, LC. See chapter 19 for Stella's final illness and death.

NOTES TO CHAPTER 10

1. "Mary Margaret McBride Says—Good-bye Nellie Bly (She Hopes)," AP column, June 3 (1953–56), found in the Mary Margaret McBride papers, Motion Picture, Broadcasting, and Recorded Sound Division, Library of Congress (hereafter cited as Recorded Sound, LC).

2. Mary Margaret McBride, *A Long Way from Missouri* (New York: Putnam, 1959), 70.

3. "Mary Margaret McBride Says—Good-bye Nellie Bly (She Hopes)," Recorded Sound, LC.

4. Ishbel Ross, *Ladies of the Press: The Story of Women in Journalism by an Insider* (New York: Harper, 1936), 254.

5. Draft manuscript entitled "Sob Sister," Recorded Sound, LC.

6. McBride, *A Long Way from Missouri*, 160.

7. *The Matrix*, June 1924, 18, quoted in Wendy Holliday, "The Woman Newspaperman: Gender, Work, and Identity in the 1920s," seminar paper, New York University, 1990.

8. Ross, *Ladies of the Press*, 13.

9. Quoted in Nancy F. Cott, *The Grounding of Modern Feminism* (New Haven, Conn.: Yale University Press, 1987), 238. For a fuller discussion of feminism and individualism in these years, see Susan Ware, *Still Missing: Amelia Earhart and the Search for Modern Feminism* (New York: Norton, 1993), chap. 4.

10. Figures quoted in Susan Ware, *Holding Their Own: American Women in the 1930s* (Boston: Twayne, 1982), 75. For general figures on journalism, see *Historical Statistics of the United State: Colonial Times to 1970* (Washington, D.C.: U.S. Government Printing Office, 1975), 40.

11. As she told them, "I just don't think there ought to be any part of your paper that isn't for everybody." Speech quoted in AP newsletter, ca. 1953–56, Recorded Sound, LC.

12. For overviews, see Maurine H. Beasley and Sheila J. Gibbons, *Taking Their Place: A Documentary History of Women and Journalism*, 2nd ed. (State College, Pa.: Strata Publishers, 2003); and Kathleen A. Cairns, *Front-Page Women Journalists, 1920–1950* (Lincoln: University of Nebraska Press, 2003). Earlier studies include Barbara Belford's *Brilliant Bylines* (New York: Columbia University Press, 1986); Marion Marzolf's *Up from the Footnote* (New York: Hastings House, 1977); and Kay Mills's *A Place in the News* (New York: Dodd, Mead, 1988).

13. "Sob Sister" draft, Recorded Sound, LC.

14. McBride, *A Long Way from Missouri*, 74.

15. "Mary Margaret McBride Says—Women Should Be Proud of Themselves," AP column, March 18, 1954, Recorded Sound, LC.

16. A good collection of McBride's clippings from the *Evening Mail*, especially from 1921 and 1922, can be found in her papers in Recorded Sound, LC. She shared the story of her reaction to finding these clippings thirty years later in "Mary Margaret McBride Says—Only Yesterday Lives Today," AP column, August 13 (1953–56), Recorded Sound, LC.

17. Cott discusses the genesis of the word in *The Grounding of Modern Feminism*.

18. McBride, *A Long Way from Missouri*, 15.

19. Ibid., 188.

20. She later turned her experience of meeting celebrities in New York Harbor into the excuse to write a book about her reactions to America. See Mary Margaret McBride, *America for Me* (New York: Macmillan, 1941).

21. McBride, *A Long Way from Missouri*, 165. The story is also recounted in Jo Pearson, "Here's Mary Margaret," *Radio Television Mirror*, August 1951, 88; as well as in Cynthia Lowry and Mary Margaret McBride, "'I've Learned to Love': A Talk with Mary Margaret McBride," *Woman's Home Companion*, May 1954, 56.

22. For the New York newspaper world in these years, see Holliday, "The Woman Newspaperman." See also Frank Luther Mott, *American Journalism: A History, 1690–1960*, 3rd ed. (New York: Macmillan, 1962).

23. McBride, *A Long Way from Missouri*, 167.

24. Ross, *Ladies of the Press*, 23.

25. Mary Margaret McBride, "My Most Unforgettable Character," *Reader's Digest*, January 1962, 100.

26. Pearson, "Here's Mary Margaret," 88.

27. Ann Douglas, *Terrible Honesty: Mongrel Manhattan in the 1920s* (New York: Farrar, Straus & Giroux, 1995), makes this claim on p. 350.

28. Mcbride's papers at the Library of Congress, both in Recorded Sound and the Manuscript Division, contain copies of many of these articles. *Charm* was published by the Rae D. Henkle Company in New York, with illustrations by her good friend, Elmer S. Hader.

29. Mary Margaret Mcbride, "Ghost Writing," *The Matrix* (no date, probably late 1920s or early 1930s), 3, Manuscript Division, LC.

30. Janice Bates, "Following a Dream to Fame," *The Matrix*, November–December 1959, 3. See also the earlier piece from *The Matrix*, "Ghost Writing."

31. The Paris and London books were published by Coward-McCann; the New York and Germany books by Putnam. Harry Hansen's column, "The First Reader," reviewed the Germany book and noted (as did other reviews) its rather tame chapter about visiting a nudist colony, concluding, "Ho hum—we light a Murad." See also the lukewarm review in the *New York Herald-Tribune Books Section*, May 22, 1932. Both clippings are in Recorded Sound, LC.

32. H. C. Paxton to Mary Margaret Mcbride, July 22, 1931; and Helen Walker to M. D. Blackenhorn (Mcbride's agent), April 16, 1929, both in Recorded Sound, LC.

33. A fragment of the Clarissa Trimble story, and several versions, all equally awful, of "Prudence Studies Harmony" are in Recorded Sound, LC. One fiction piece that was published was Mary Margaret Mcbride, "Sarah Elizabeth Edits the News," *American Girl*, October 1933, 20ff. No surprise: it was about a girl on a small-town country newspaper.

34. Georgina Campbell, "The Wandering Mind: A Column of This and That," *Hobo News* (no date, probably 1940s), Manuscript Division, LC.

35. Mary Margaret Mcbride, *Out of the Air* (Garden City, N.Y.: Doubleday, 1960), 384.

NOTES TO CHAPTER 11

1. Mary Margaret Mcbride, *A Long Way from Missouri* (New York: Putnam, 1959), 22.

2. Mary Margaret Mcbride, "I Come to New York," *Scribner's*, March 1931, 317.

3. Jo Pearson, "Here's Mary Margaret," *Radio Television Mirror*, August 1951, 87, clipping found in the Mary Margaret Mcbride papers, Motion Picture, Broadcasting, and Recorded Sound Division, Library of Congress (hereafter cited as Recorded Sound, LC). Showing once again how Mary Margaret recycled old stories in multiple venues, she told the brandied-peaches story in *A Long Way from Missouri*, 52, and shared it with the readers of her syndicated column in the 1950s ("Mary Margaret Mcbride Says—Dear Reader, Watch Thyself," AP column, January 20 [1953–56], Recorded Sound, LC).

4. Estella Karn, "The Secret Life of Mary Margaret," *Modern Television and Radio*, December 1948, 73.

5. Pearson, "Here's Mary Margaret," 87.

6. Caroline F. Ware, *Greenwich Village, 1920–1930: A Comment on American Civilization in the Post-War Years* (Boston: Houghton Mifflin, 1935), 42–43.

7. Ibid., 93, 5.

8. Mcbride, *A Long Way from Missouri*, 55–56.

9. Mary Margaret Mcbride broadcast, April 22, 1950 (L 15577), Recorded Sound, LC. She also tells the "Chaos" story in Pearson, "Here's Mary Margaret," 87, and in *A Long Way from Missouri*, 54, among other places.

10. Mcbride, *A Long Way from Missouri*, 59.

11. Mcbride, "I Come to New York," 316. See also Mcbride, *A Long Way from Missouri*, 100–104.

12. McBride, "I Come to New York," 318.

13. Ibid., 318, 319.

14. McBride, *A Long Way from Missouri*, 26, 54–55.

15. Pearson, "Here's Mary Margaret," 88.

16. McBride, *A Long Way from Missouri*, 101–2.

17. Burton Bernstein to Susan Ware, June 7, 1999.

18. Mary Margaret McBride, "What Price Career?" *Independent Woman*, September 1928, 389. In "Marriage on a Fifty-Fifty Basis," *Scribner's*, December 1929, 657, McBride refers to an "intimate friend of mine [who] recently had a chance to become such a wife. She went back to her old home town fully resolved to marry a young man there who proposed to her six years ago, provided, of course, he was still in the mood." He was, but she refused, saying that she found his idea that she could continue her career there unrealistic. This certainly sounds a lot like what McBride had just gone through.

19. When Mary Margaret was honored in 1940 in Mexico, Missouri, the only awkward moment occurred when "I momentarily failed to recognize an old beau in the line of greeters and I remember his wife laughed sardonically." The old beau was almost certainly Dick Dorris. This episode is mentioned in an article in the Mexico, Missouri, *Ledger*, November 23, 1953, quoted in Beverly G. Merrick, "Mary Margaret McBride, The Conquering Talk Show Host Wears a Mink: City Editor Broadcasts Her Own Triumphant Return," paper presented to the Association for Education in Journalism and Mass Communication convention, Anaheim, Calif., August 1996.

20. Mary Margaret McBride, *Here's Martha Deane* (Garden City, N.Y.: Garden City Publishing, 1936), 230. In a fiction book written for young adults called *Tune in for Elizabeth: Career Story of a Radio Interviewer* (New York: Dodd, Mead, 1945), McBride describes a very similar situation: "And don't think I didn't love him—as much I think as a woman like me can love any man. But I loved my dream of success more than I did him" (pp. 128–29).

21. McBride, *Here's Martha Deane*, 27.

22. Cleveland Amory column, undated clipping (1950s), found in Mary Margaret McBride papers, Manuscript Division, Library of Congress (hereafter cited as Manuscript Division, LC).

23. Cynthia Lowry and Mary Margaret McBride, "'I've Learned to Love': A Talk with Mary Margaret McBride," *Woman's Home Companion*, May 1954, 68.

24. McBride, "Marriage on a Fifty-Fifty Basis," 661. In 1927 McBride inscribed a copy of *Charm* "To Inez Hayes Irwin and Will Irwin, the only two people I know who have made a really charming venture of matrimony!" Copy found at the Schlesinger Library, Radcliffe Institute for Advanced Study, Harvard University.

25. Mary Margaret McBride, "Husband Hunting: The 1930 Girl Has Her Own Ideas about Woman's Best Career," *Country Gentleman*, October 1930, 24, clipping in Recorded Sound, LC.

26. Pearson, "Here's Mary Margaret," 88.

27. McBride, "Husband Hunting," 83.

28. Mary Margaret McBride, *Out of the Air* (Garden City, N.Y.: Doubleday, 1960), 363.

29. McBride, *A Long Way from Missouri*, 199–200; and clipping from the *Seattle Post-Intelligencer*, January 21, 1960, Recorded Sound, LC.

30. "Mary Margaret McBride Says—Maidens Are Spinsters at 30," AP column, August 3 (1953–56), Recorded Sound, LC.

31. Karn, "The Secret Life of Mary Margaret," 75.

32. Clipping from the *Seattle Post-Intelligencer*, January 21, 1960, Recorded Sound, LC.

NOTES TO CHAPTER 12

1. Mary Margaret McBride, *A Long Way from Missouri* (New York: Putnam, 1959), 147.

2. Ibid., 244.

3. A rare letter from Elizabeth Craig McBride to a relative back in Missouri, postmarked Paris, August 31, 1926, describes the trip in literate and colorful detail. Found in Mary Margaret McBride papers, Manuscript Division, Library of Congress (hereafter cited as Manuscript Division, LC). See also McBride, *A Long Way from Missouri*, 89, 207–11.

4. One exception was a two-month visit in 1935 or 1936, when both her parents stayed with her younger brother, Boone, in the Bronx. Her father died in 1937, and her brother soon afterward, leaving a nephew that she often mentioned on the air. See Mary Margaret McBride, *Here's Martha Deane* (Garden City, N.Y.: Garden City Publishing, 1936), 291, 287.

5. For the change in family circumstances and the move to Florida, see McBride, *A Long Way from Missouri*, 101, 211–13. She talked about her father's inheritance in her AP column in the 1950s in the context of changing attitudes toward money: "And when . . . my father inherited $10,000 from an aunt, it made him seem a rich man. He could pay the debts that had hung over him and still have enough cash on hand to sink in the Florida boom." "Mary Margaret McBride Says—Money Has Changed—And People Too," AP column, September 22 (1953–56), found in the Mary Margaret McBride papers, Motion Picture, Broadcasting, and Recorded Sound Division, Library of Congress (hereafter cited as Recorded Sound, LC).

6. Frederick Lewis Allen devotes a whole chapter, "Home Sweet Florida," to the Florida boom in his classic *Only Yesterday* (New York: Harper Bros., 1931).

7. McBride, *A Long Way from Missouri*, 218–19.

8. Ibid., 216.

9. Ibid., 216–17.

10. For an overview, see William Leuchtenburg, *The Perils of Prosperity, 1914–1932*, 2nd ed. (Chicago: University of Chicago Press, 1993).

11. McBride, *A Long Way from Missouri*, 201.

12. Mary Margaret McBride, "I Came, I Saw, This is What *I Did!*" *Cosmopolitan*, November 1939, 150.

13. McBride, *A Long Way from Missouri*, p. 222. She also talks about the crash in "Mary Margaret McBride Says—Remember the Golden Age," AP column, October 28 (1953–56), Recorded Sound, LC.

14. McBride, *A Long Way from Missouri*, 223–24.

15. Ibid., 228.

16. Ibid., 243–44. She talked about money and the impact of the crash in her AP column in the 1950s: "I remember just after the 1929 crash, broke and worried, saying to a friend, 'If I could only be SURE of $50 a week for the rest of my life, I'd be all right. I could take care of my mother and father in Florida and support myself.'" "Mary Margaret McBride Says—Money Has Changed—and People Too."

17. In 1930, she published several articles in *McCall's*, *Harper's Bazaar*, *Ladies' Home Journal*, and the *Saturday Evening Post*, among others. Clippings can be found in Recorded Sound, LC.

18. See Mary Margaret McBride, *The Story of Dwight W. Morrow* (New York: Farrar and Rinehart, 1930). She also published an article entitled "Dwight W. Morrow" in *Charm*, November 1930, 27ff. (clipping found in Recorded Sound, LC).

19. Mary Margaret McBride, *America for Me* (New York: Macmillan, 1941), 61.

20. McBride, *A Long Way from Missouri*, 249.

21. Star Library Publications published McBride's profiles of Clark Gable, Constance Bennett, Robert Montgomery, and Greta Garbo that were more on the level of a *Photoplay* article than an actual book. See McBride, *A Long Way from Missouri*, 251–53.

22. McBride, *America for Me*, 77–78. For yet another rendition of the nightgown story, see "Mary Margaret McBride Says—'This Ought to Be Censored!'" AP column, January 18, 1954, Recorded Sound, LC.

23. McBride, *A Long Way from Missouri*, 248.

24. Mary Margaret McBride, *Here's Martha Deane* (Garden City, N.Y.: Garden City Publishing, 1936), 5. Further evidence of a breakdown in the winter of 1930/31 is found in a December 22, 1930, letter from a *McCall's* editor to McBride turning down a manuscript on cereals: "I am genuinely sorry to learn that you collapsed soon after leaving my office. Washington seems to be a kind of Jericho for journalists." Found in McBride papers, Recorded Sound, LC. McBride later talked about the experience on her radio show, referring to her "sort of a breakdown" in the broadcast of January 26, 1951 (LWO 15577 R43), Recorded Sound, LC.

25. McBride, *America for Me*, 62. She didn't go directly from a nervous breakdown to radio. For a while she filled in as woman's page editor for the Newspaper Enterprise Association, a job that she continued occasionally even after she started on the radio, probably to hedge her bets in case her new career didn't work out. See clippings in Recorded Sound, LC; and McBride, *A Long Way from Missouri*, 253.

NOTES TO CHAPTER 13

1. Mary Margaret McBride, *Out of the Air* (Garden City, N.Y.: Doubleday, 1960), 19.

2. Ibid., 20, 22.

3. Mary Margaret McBride, "I Don't Want to Preach," *Woman's Day*, October 1939, 5.

4. Mary Margaret McBride, *Here's Martha Deane* (Garden City, N.Y.: Garden City Publishing, 1936), 7–9.

5. "Woman to Woman," *Woman's Day*, May 1938, 30.

6. McBride, *Out of the Air*, 27.

7. McBride, *Here's Martha Deane*, 10–11.

8. Ibid., 19.

9. Dick Dorrance, "The Pleasure of Simple Things" (ca. 1940), features the trained flea version and listeners' enthusiastic response. Clipping found in the Mary Margaret McBride papers, Manuscript Division, Library of Congress (hereafter cited as Manuscript Division, LC). Other versions include Enid Haupt, "Radio's Lady Aladdin," *Movie-Radio Guide*, January 31, 1943; Curtis Mitchell, "Mary Margaret's Magic," *Coronet*, 1954; Jo Pearson, "Here's Mary Margaret," *Radio Television Mirror*, August 1951; Barbara Heggie, "The Forty-five-Minute Tempo," *New Yorker*, December 19, 1942; Allen Churchill, "Mary Margaret McBride," *American Mercury*, January 1949; Philip Hamburger, "Mary Margaret McBride," *Life*, December 4, 1944; and *Current Biography* (1941).

10. As evidence of the power of suggestive thinking, see McBride, "I Don't Want to Preach," October 1939: "This spring on the fifth anniversary of the 'rebellion' broadcast in which I 'killed' Grandmother Deane, more than fifty women came into the studio and told about it word for word! I couldn't remember—but they did" (p. 5). The tape of that May 3, 1939, broadcast can be found in the Motion Picture, Broadcasting, and Recorded Sound Division, Library of Congress (hereafter cited as Recorded Sound, LC). McBride told the story about the grandchildren and the flea circus again on her final show on May 14, 1954 (RWC 7043 B 1, Recorded Sound, LC), but admitted that at that point she didn't know whether it was real or a legend.

11. McBride, *Out of the Air*, 24.
12. WOR promotional flyer, June 1, 1934, found in Recorded Sound, LC. A copy of another WOR promo showing the range of potential listeners can also be found there.
13. McBride, *Here's Martha Deane*, 9–11, and *Out of the Air*, 23–24.
14. McBride, *Here's Martha Deane*, 22.
15. Ibid., 15.
16. Ibid., 27–28.
17. In her *New Yorker* profile, "The Forty-five Minute Tempo," 28, Barbara Heggie called the program a "fair oral counterpart" of "My Day."
18. McBride, *Out of the Air*, 33.
19. McBride, *Here's Martha Deane*, 265.
20. McBride, *Out of the Air*, 32.
21. For a general background on women and the Great Depression, see Susan Ware, *Holding Their Own: American Women in the 1930s* (Boston: Twayne, 1982). Also see chapter 4 of this book.
22. McBride, *Here's Martha Deane*, 19–20.
23. WOR promotional, "Thank you, Martha Deane," *Variety*, April 8, 1936, Recorded Sound, LC. The promo used a photograph of McBride that was often reproduced in the 1930s for publicity purposes, in which her hair is closely cropped (but still a bit wavy on top) in a rather severe, almost "butch" style. It is not entirely clear when she grew out her hair, but it probably was in the early 1940s.
24. McBride, *Out of the Air*, 55.
25. McBride, *Here's Martha Deane*, 286.
26. Mary Margaret McBride, *How Dear to My Heart* (New York: Macmillan, 1940), 196.

NOTES TO CHAPTER 14

1. Mary Margaret McBride, *Out of the Air* (Garden City, N.Y.: Doubleday, 1960), 107, 108.
2. Mary Margaret McBride, *A Long Way from Missouri* (New York: Putnam, 1959), 95; McBride, *Out of the Air*, 382. This is the invitation that led to Stella's finding her farm in nearby West Shokan.
3. Her fans were just as loyal as ever. See the letter from N. W. Cook to McBride, May 22, 1939, on behalf of "Utica's Mary Margaret Club." The club even had its own stationery, complete with the logos of LaFrance and Satina. Found in Mary Margaret McBride papers, Motion Picture, Broadcasting, and Recorded Sound Division, Library of Congress (hereafter cited as Recorded Sound, LC). For an example, see the broadcast of March 13, 1939 (LWO 15577 R4732), which describes visiting a flower show. It is all talk, no guests. Recorded Sound, LC.
4. McBride, *Out of the Air*, 55, 102. The last show aired on June 30, 1939 (RWA 1432, Recorded Sound, LC).
5. McBride, *Out of the Air*, 97–99.
6. Ibid., 103–4. Beatty didn't last long, and the spot was taken over by Marion Young in 1941. Young developed her own successful style as Martha Deane and remained on the air at WOR until 1956. See John Dunning, *On the Air: The Encyclopedia of Old-Time Radio* (New York: Oxford University Press, 1998), 503.
7. Mary Margaret McBride broadcast, September 20, 1940 (LWO 25588), Recorded Sound, LC. See also the broadcast from September 6, 1940 (RWC 6690 LWO 25588), in which she explains her decision to give up the program.

8. McBride, *Out of the Air*, 100–102, also contains a full, almost verbatim description. She likely had listened to the tape before writing that section of the book.

9. McBride, *Out of the Air*, 103, 106–107. See also Mary Margaret McBride, *Mary Margaret McBride's Harvest of American Cooking* (New York: Putnam, 1957), 78–82.

10. McBride, *Out of the Air*, 104.

11. See Beverly G. Merrick, "Mary Margaret McBride, the Conquering Talk Show Host Wears a Mink: City Editor Broadcasts Her Own Triumphant Return to the *Mexico Ledger*," paper presented to the Association for Education in Journalism and Mass Communication convention, Anaheim, Calif., August 1996.

12. McBride, *Out of the Air*, 105–6. On forgetting to mention grapefruit, see Merrick, "Mary Margaret McBride, the Conquering Talk Show Host Wears a Mink." For the broadcast, see RWA 1806, November 22, 1940, Recorded Sound, LC. She talked about preparations for the event on November 21, 1940 (RWG 6699), and was still talking about it the following Monday, November 25, 1940 (RWG 6699).

13. McBride, *Out of the Air*, 106, 107.

14. Merrick, "Mary Margaret McBride, the Conquering Talk Show Host Wears a Mink." The broadcast of the last show (RWC 6834 LWO 26484) is found in Recorded Sound, LC.

15. McBride, *Out of the Air*, 107.

16. Barbara Heggie, "The Forty-five-Minute Tempo," *New Yorker*, December 19, 1942, 32–33.

NOTES TO CHAPTER 15

1. Mary Margaret McBride, *Out of the Air* (Garden City, N.Y.: Doubleday, 1960), 109.

2. Mary Margaret McBride, *America for Me* (New York: Macmillan, 1941), 1.

3. It did, however, inspire a patriotic tune called "America for Me" (1942), copyrighted by McBride, Victor Mizzy, and Irving Taylor. Sheet music found in the Mary Margaret McBride papers, Motion Picture, Broadcasting, and Recorded Sound Division, Library of Congress (hereafter cited as Recorded Sound, LC).

4. General overviews of wartime radio include Michele Hilmes, *Radio Voices: American Broadcasting, 1922–1952* (Minneapolis: University of Minnesota Press, 1997), chap. 8; and Susan J. Douglas, *Listening In: Radio and the American Imagination* (New York: Times Books, 1999). See also Barbara Dianne Savage, *Broadcasting Freedom: Radio, War, and the Politics of Race, 1938–1948* (Chapel Hill: University of North Carolina, 1999).

5. Savage, *Broadcasting Freedom*, 1–2.

6. McBride, *Out of the Air*, 113.

7. She also appeared in a print campaign sponsored by the American Fat Salvage Association, Inc., urging housewives to turn in used fats. Clipping (no date) found in Recorded Sound, LC. For an excellent discussion of wartime rationing, see Amy Bentley, *Eating for Victory: Food Rationing and the Politics of Domesticity* (Urbana: University of Illinois Press, 1998).

8. McBride, *Out of the Air*, 110; Mary Margaret McBride broadcast, March 16, 1942 (LWO 12747-20 B1), Recorded Sound, LC.

9. Examples of war-related guests from McBride's papers at Recorded Sound and the Manuscript Division, LC, include representatives of the War Shipping Administration, the Veterans Administration, the U.S. Naval Training Center, C.A.R.E., the Office of Defense Transportation, and the Greek War Relief Association.

10. Mary Margaret McBride broadcast, February 3, 1943 (RWA 1433 AI), Recorded Sound, LC.

11. Mary Margaret Mcbride broadcasts, November 26, 1942 (LWO 12747-25 B2), and May 5, 1943 (LWO 12747-31 B1), Recorded Sound, LC. See also the interview with exiled writer Emil Ludwig recorded on December 22, 1943, but broadcast on January 1, 1944 (LWO 15577-R205 A1), which makes a similar point.

12. Mcbride, *Out of the Air*, 110–11. One 1943 bond drive in which Mcbride participated raised $500,000 at a theater party. See John W. Clark to Mary Margaret Mcbride, September 23, 1943, found in Mary Margaret Mcbride papers, Manuscript Division, Library of Congress (hereafter cited as Manuscript Division, LC).

13. In addition to Bentley, *Eating for Victory*, additional information on women's wartime roles, including employment, can be found in Susan Hartmann, *The Home Front and Beyond* (Boston: Twayne, 1982); Sherna B. Gluck, *Rosie the Riveter Revisited: Women, the War, and Social Change* (Boston: Twayne, 1987); and Ruth Milkman, *Gender at Work: The Dynamics of Job Segregation by Sex during World War II* (Urbana: University of Illinois Press, 1987).

14. Mary Margaret Mcbride broadcast, March 16, 1942 (LWO 12747-20 B1), Recorded Sound, LC.

15. Mcbride, *Out of the Air*, 111.

16. Mary Margaret Mcbride broadcast, November 25, 1943 (LWO 12747-35 B1), Recorded Sound, LC.

17. Ibid.

18. Mcbride, *America for Me*, 100–101.

19. General sources on the home front during World War II include John Morton Blum, *V Was for Victory: Politics and American Culture during World War II* (New York: Harcourt Brace Jovanovich, 1976); and William L. O'Neill, *A Democracy at War: America's Fight at Home and Abroad in World War II* (New York: Free Press, 1993). See also William M. Tuttle Jr., *"Daddy's Gone to War": The Second World War in the Lives of America's Children* (New York: Oxford University Press, 1993).

20. Most of the refugees were from Europe, which may have promoted a somewhat Eurocentric view of the fighting. Starting with the Guadalcanal campaign in 1942/43, however, events in the Pacific received more coverage. See, for example, the following broadcasts: February 3, 1943 (RWA 1433 A1), and especially May 5, 1943 (LWO 12747-31 B1), in which British nurse Gwen Priestwood talks about escaping from a Japanese prisoner of war camp in Hong Kong.

21. Douglas, *Listening In*, makes a similar point about the broadcast journalism during the war. It is possible to track the various guests and topics in wartime through the online sound recording catalog (SONIC) at the Library of Congress Web site.

22. Mcbride, *Out of the Air*, 113–17. For example, on the November 26, 1942, program (LWO 12747-25 B2), Bella Fromm specifically thanks American citizens for joining the war effort.

23. Mary Margaret Mcbride broadcast, November 26, 1942 (LWO 12747-25 B2), Recorded Sound, LC.

24. See David S. Wyman, *The Abandonment of the Jews: America and the Holocaust, 1941–1945* (New York: Pantheon Books, 1984), for a discussion of when information on the extermination camps became available and the limited response of the Roosevelt administration, which claimed that the best way to save the Jews was to win the war. Wyman disputes this assessment, claiming that much more could have been done.

25. Mcbride tells this story in *Out of the Air*, 119–21.

26. Mcbride strongly opposed the dropping of atomic bombs on Hiroshima and Nagasaki and was quite surprised to find public opinion so evenly divided on the subject. See Mcbride, *Out of the Air*, 122.

27. Winifred Van Duzer, "What Pictures Couldn't Tell," clipping (ca. 1945) found in McBride papers, Manuscript Division, LC. See also McBride, *Out of the Air*, 124.

28. Van Duzer, "What Pictures Couldn't Tell."

29. McBride, *Out of the Air*, 125.

30. Ibid., 126.

31. Van Duzer, "What Pictures Couldn't Tell."

32. Mary Margaret McBride broadcasts, September 18, 1945 (LWO 12747), and September 19, 1945 (LWO 12747), Recorded Sound, LC.

33. "Hurts of Others Subject of Miss McBride Talk," *Kansas State Collegian*, April 23, 1959, clipping found in McBride papers, Manuscript Division, LC.

34. McBride, *Out of the Air*, 124.

NOTES TO CHAPTER 16

1. This story was told many times. See, for example, Bennett Cerf, "Here Comes McBride," *Saturday Review of Literature*, March 1, 1947, 6; and Collie Small, "The Private Life of a Pied Piper," *Collier's*, December 11, 1948, 39. Ehler's Tea was one of her sponsors.

2. Mary Margaret McBride, *Out of the Air* (Garden City, N.Y.: Doubleday, 1960), 323–24.

3. Ibid., 325. The Eleanor Roosevelt papers at the Franklin D. Roosevelt Library, Hyde Park, New York (hereafter cited as ER, FDRL), contain correspondence documenting the visit. See, for example, Eleanor Roosevelt to McBride, January 13, 1941, and McBride's reply (no date), followed by a telegram confirming the invitation on February 1, 1941.

4. McBride, *Out of the Air*, 323.

5. "On the Air," *New Republic*, December 25, 1950, 21. The article was dismissively entitled "Soap and the Roosevelts."

6. "Opposites," *Time*, October 9, 1950, 58.

7. For example, Mary Margaret interviewed Eleanor Roosevelt about her second volume of memoirs, *This I Remember* (New York: Harper, 1949), on November 7, 1949 (LWO 12747 R120, Recorded Sound, LC). So determined was McBride to get Roosevelt first that she did the broadcast from Lake Success, New York, where Roosevelt was fulfilling her duties at the United Nations.

8. Mrs. James J. Kolar to Eleanor Roosevelt, May 28, 1944, and Roosevelt's reply, June 3, 1944, ER, FDRL. This exchange was prompted by Eleanor Roosevelt's appearance at Mary Margaret's tenth anniversary program at Madison Square Garden and by the recent appearance of Mr. and Mrs. Louis Fischer on the program, who had written about developments in the Soviet Union.

9. McBride to Roosevelt, January 28, 1939, ER, FDRL.

10. McBride, *Out of the Air*, 331.

11. McBride, *Out of the Air*, 332. For more on Roosevelt's wartime and postwar activities, see Allida M. Black, *Casting Her Own Shadow: Eleanor Roosevelt and the Shaping of Postwar Liberalism* (New York: Columbia University Press, 1996).

12. Karen Hansen, "'It's One O'Clock and Here Is Mary Margaret McBride': Early Radio Holdings in the Collections of the Library of Congress," in *Performing Arts Broadcasting*, edited by Iris Newson (Washington, D.C.: Library of Congress, 2002), 24. The Pearl Primus show aired on July 11, 1950 (RWC 69973, Recorded Sound, LC).

13. Mary Beth Haralovich and Lauren Rabinowitz make a similar point about stars like Lucille Ball in the 1950s, Sheldon Leonard and Robert Culp in the 1960s, and Oprah Winfrey in the 1980s in their introduction to their *Television, History, and American Culture: Feminist Critical Essays* (Durham, N.C.: Duke University Press, 1999), 9.

14. Cynthia Lowry and Mary Margaret McBride, "'I've Learned to Love': A Talk with Mary Margaret McBride," *Woman's Home Companion*, May 1954, 67.

15. "Broadcaster," *Christian Herald*, April 1946, 26, clipping found in Mary Margaret McBride papers, Motion Picture, Broadcasting, and Recorded Sound Division, Library of Congress (hereafter cited as Recorded Sound, LC).

16. Barbara Savage's *Broadcasting Freedom: Radio, War, and the Politics of Race, 1938–1948* (Chapel Hill: University of North Carolina Press, 1999), is the best discussion of how radio unevenly, but forcefully nonetheless, introduced the topic of race to the airwaves in the 1940s. For another example of Mary Margaret's response to the issue, see the discussion of the Laurette Taylor episode in chapter 2.

17. Diggery Venn to Mary Margaret McBride, June 21, 1949, found in Mary Margaret McBride papers, Manuscript Division, Library of Congress (hereafter cited as Manuscript Division, LC).

18. McBride, *Out of the Air*, 145.

19. Ibid., 145–46.

20. Ibid., 146, 147.

21. Ibid., 146.

22. For general background on the impact of McCarthyism on American cultural and political life, see Ellen Schrecker, *Many Are the Crimes: McCarthyism in America* (Princeton, N.J.: Princeton University Press, 1998). See also Ellen Schrecker's earlier book, *No Ivory Tower: McCarthyism and the Universities* (New York: Oxford University Press, 1986); and Richard Gid Powers, *Not without Honor: The History of American Anti-Communism* (New York: Free Press, 1995). Neal Gabler's biography, *Winchell: Gossip, Power, and the Culture of Celebrity* (New York: Knopf, 1994), describes his role in this period and documents Winchell's ties to Hoover.

23. McBride, *Out of the Air*, 147–56, describes this trip. Her traveling companion to England was journalist Cynthia Lowry, who lived with McBride at the end of her life.

24. Eleanor Roosevelt quoted in Ruby A. Black, "Is Mrs. Roosevelt a Feminist?" *Equal Rights*, July 27, 1935, 163.

25. Eleanor Roosevelt, *It's Up to the Women* (1933), quoted in Allida Black, ed., *What I Hope to Leave Behind: The Essential Essays of Eleanor Roosevelt* (Brooklyn, N.Y.: Carlson, 1995), 238–39.

26. Mary Margaret McBride, *America for Me* (New York: Macmillan, 1941), 41.

27. For a discussion of this stance, see Susan Ware, *Letter to the World: Seven Women Who Shaped the American Century* (New York: Norton, 1998).

28. "Cartwheel Girl," *Time*, June 12, 1939, 47, quoted in Ware, *Letter to the World*, 77–78.

29. For her views on feminism in the 1950s, see "Mary Margaret McBride Says—Prejudice Is Where You Find It," May 16, 1955; "Mary Margaret McBride Says—Remember Susan B. Anthony," February 15, 1955; and "Mary Margaret McBride Says—Rights Are Important," February 3 (1953–56), AP columns found in Recorded Sound, LC. When endorsing the equal rights amendment ("so that I can be a first-class citizen from now on—which I mistakenly thought I was all the time"), she explained her support in this way: "I've never felt an urge to parade for women's rights, but all this is behind me for I've been exposed to Alice Paul." She then explained how the federal government, the nation's largest employer, discriminated against women in the civil service by allowing any hiring officer to ignore their high marks simply on the basis of sex and hire a man instead. That injustice turned Mary Margaret into "an angry female" ready to write letters to her representatives in Congress.

30. At base McBride retained a sense that women were fundamentally different from men, and she embraced those differences: "Women don't want to be prominent. They

want to be loved. I tire of just listening to men; it's fun to chime in. . . . Yes, we could have a woman president. I would like it. Women are more conscientious about details than men, but they are more emotional. Women do have tact. Seems we ought to educate the mothers and the career girls differently—but we don't know who's going to be what" (*Seattle Post Intelligencer*, January 21, 1960, clipping found in Manuscript Division, LC). In that muddled string of ideas lies the dilemma of modern feminism: how to make it as a woman and make it in a man's world. For further discussion, see Nancy Cott, *The Grounding of Modern Feminism* (New Haven, Conn.: Yale University Press, 1987).

31. See "Mary Margaret Bride Says—Women Are Ready to Live for Their Country," July 15 (1953–56); and "Mary Margaret McBride Says—War CAN Be Eliminated," February 14, 1955, AP columns, Recorded Sound, LC.

32. "Mary Margaret McBride Says—Let Joan Do It," AP column, February 17, 1955, Recorded Sound, LC.

33. For traditional views of the 1950s, see Betty Friedan, *The Feminine Mystique* (New York: Norton, 1963); and Elaine Tyler May, *Homeward Bound: American Families in the Cold War Era* (New York: Basic Books, 1988). For views that stress a more nuanced view of the decade, see Joanne Meyerowitz, ed., *Not June Cleaver: Women and Gender in Postwar America, 1945–1960* (Philadelphia: Temple University Press, 1994); and Eugenia Kaledin, *Mothers and More: American Women in the 1950s* (Boston: Twayne, 1984).

34. For background on this project, see ABC press release, June 25, 1953, and Stella Karn press release (ca. 1953), both found in Manuscript Division, LC.

35. Profiles of all these women in the form of press releases prepared by Stella Karn are in Manuscript Division, LC.

36. "Mary Margaret McBride Says—It isn't True, What They Say about Activity Women," AP column, May 25, 1954, Recorded Sound, LC. The second group of winners included Priscilla Shaw, first woman mayor in South Carolina; Frances Morton for slum clearance work in Baltimore; Edith Murphey of California for working with local Indians on food supplies; and Lillian Weser of Huntington, West Virginia, for her advocacy on mental health. The article also mentions eight other women, including Mary McLeod Bethune for her work in education.

37. For more on the community activism of women in the decade, especially through the League of Women Voters, see Susan Ware, "American Women in the 1950s: Nonpartisan Politics and Women's Politicization," in *Women, Politics, and Change*, edited by Louise A. Tilly and Patricia Gurin (New York: Russell Sage, 1990).

38. "Mary Margaret McBride Says—Let's Outlaw Predatory Wives," July 19, 1954, and "Mary Margaret McBride Says—Career and Marriage Do Mix," December 30 (1953–56), AP columns, Recorded Sound, LC.

39. "Mary Margaret McBride Says—Women Can Have Career and Home," February 1 (1953–56), AP column, Recorded Sound, LC.

40. "Mary Margaret McBride Says—For Harmony, Try Solitude," March 16 (1953–56), AP column, Recorded Sound, LC.

NOTES TO CHAPTER 17

1. Jackie Hudgins, "Clubwomen Will Hear Experiment," *Richmond (Va.) New Leader*, October 21, 1958, clipping found in the Mary Margaret McBride papers, Manuscript Division, Library of Congress (hereafter cited as Manuscript Division, LC).

2. Gerry Raker, "Radio Pioneer Didn't Understand Auditions, Disliked Her Sponsors," *Poughkeepsie (N.Y.) Journal*, November 23, 1969, clipping in Manuscript Division, LC.

3. For background on women and television, see Cary O'Dell, *Women Pioneers in Television: Biographies of Fifteen Industry Leaders* (Jefferson, N.C.: McFarland, 1997); Donna L. Halper, *Invisible Stars: A Social History of Women in American Broadcasting* (Armonk, N.Y.: Sharpe, 2002); and Mary Beth Haralovich and Lauren Rabinowitz, eds., *Television, History, and American Culture: Feminist Critical Essays* (Durham, N.C.: Duke University Press, 1999).

4. For general overviews of the early days of television, and how it supplanted radio, see Erik Barnouw, *Tube of Plenty: The Evolution of American Television*, 2nd ed. (New York: Oxford University Press, 1990); Michele Hilmes, *Only Connect: A Cultural History of Broadcasting in the United States* (Belmont, Calif.: Wadsworth, 2002); William Boddy, *Fifties Television: The Industry and Its Critics* (Urbana: University of Illinois Press, 1993); and Lynn Spigel, *Make Room for TV: Television and the Family Ideal in Postwar America* (Chicago: University of Chicago Press, 1992).

5. O'Dell, *Women Pioneers in Television*, 100.

6. Michele Hilmes, *Radio Voices: American Broadcasting, 1922-1952* (Minneapolis: University of Minnesota Press, 1997), 286.

7. Barnouw, *Tube of Plenty*, 113.

8. Ibid., 113–14, and Hilmes, *Only Connect*, 157.

9. Margaret Mara, "Ladies from Brooklyn Are All Dewey-Eyed like Their Menfolk," *Brooklyn Eagle*, June 23, 1948, and "Looking and Listening with Ben Gross," June 25, 1948, clippings found in the Mary Margaret McBride papers, Motion Picture, Broadcasting, and Recorded Sound Division, Library of Congress (hereafter cited as Recorded Sound, LC). For one of the radio programs McBride aired during the conventions, see the July 14, 1948, special broadcast from the Democratic convention (LWO 12747 R78), Recorded Sound, LC.

10. *Variety*, June 9, 1948. See also the *Newell Post*, May–June 1948, 6. Both clippings found in Recorded Sound, LC.

11. Jo Pearson, "Here's Mary Margaret," *Radio Television Mirror*, August 1951, 89, clippin in Recorded Sound, LC.

12. Sidney Fields, "Only Human," *Sunday Mirror*, October 4, 1953, 41, clipping in Recorded Sound, LC.

13. Jack Gould to Mary Margaret McBride, December 1, 1948, Manuscript Division, LC.

14. Mary Margaret McBride, *Out of the Air* (Garden City, N.Y.: Doubleday, 1960), 135. Here is how the *New York Times* covered the cancellation on November 28, 1948: "Mary Margaret McBride is the first major figure indigenous to the medium of radio to prove an early fatality in the field of television. . . . Miss McBride in the main had followed her radio format, which before the cameras proved static and lacking in visual diversity."

15. McBride, *Out of the Air*, 135–36.

16. Edwin Dunham to Mary Margaret McBride, September 22, 1948, Manuscript Division, LC.

17. Harriet Van Horne, "Miss McBride Has Video Zoo, "*New York World Telegram*, September 30, 1948, clipping in Manuscript Division, LC. An example of a similar show in radio format aired on July 6, 1945 (RWA 1811 LWO 17243), Recorded Sound, LC. Mary Margaret is in her element, but Vincent is clearly quite nervous, which adds to the program's enjoyment.

18. Kinescope of *Mary Margaret McBride Time* (FUA 0218), November 16, 1948, Motion Picture Reading Room, LC.

19. Kinescope of *Mary Margaret McBride Time* (FUA 0219), December 14, 1948, Motion Picture Reading Room, LC.

20. Walter White to Mary Margaret McBride, December 10, 1948, Manuscript Division, LC.

21. McBride, *Out of the Air*, 137–38.

22. Jack Gould, "Miss McBride," *New York Times*, September 26, 1948. One of Mary Margaret's friends tried to buck up her spirits afterward: "About the television story, you shouldn't give it another thot [*sic*]. Don't you know that nobody reads the newspapers, anyway? I'm surprised at you, letting one little person's statement make you even pause. Seems to me that only a short time ago the newspapers said that television couldn't last. You look fine! John Gordon thot [*sic*] you were pretty." Frances to "Mary Marg," September 29, 1948, Manuscript Division, LC.

23. Jack Gould to Mary Margaret McBride, December 1, 1948, McBride papers, Manuscript Division, LC. He was extremely gracious in this interchange, assuring her that he bore her no ill will and respected her as a journalist. But he didn't mince words: "I'd be less than honest if I did not say I thought your program was bad. I did, Mary Margaret." He then politely but firmly turned down her offer to continue the conversation as a guest on her radio program.

24. Ibid.

25. Fifteen years later she finally admitted that her debut was a "dismal failure" in a March 1975 interview with *Tomorrow* host Tom Snyder. Quoted in Jacqueline D. St. John, "Sex Role Stereotyping in Early Broadcast History: The Career of Mary Margaret McBride," *Frontiers* 3 (1978): 37.

26. Barbara Heggie, "Mary Margaret's Miracle," *Woman's Home Companion*, April 1949, 83, clipping in Recorded Sound, LC.

27. "Comments on Television Appearances," no date (1950s), Manuscript Division, LC.

28. Ibid.

29. Henry Jaffe to Pat Weaver, November 27, 1953, Recorded Sound, LC. Jaffe seems to have been acting as an agent or go-between. The pitch also included letters from Cynthia Lowry and Stella Karn.

30. Edward R. Murrow, *See It Now*, May 24, 1953, tape (B606) available at the Museum of Television and Radio, New York City .

31. "Mary Margaret McBride Says—Even Now She Gets Stagefright," AP column, December 9, 1954, Recorded Sound, LC. This column shared a humorous description of the upheaval that having a television crew come to one's house can cause. Actually, this being New York City, the biggest hurdle was the threat from McBride's building's management to stop the broadcast of the show because it violated her lease. Luckily an agreement was negotiated to everyone's satisfaction. See Donald R. Bacon to Mary Margaret McBride, October 28, 1954, Recorded Sound, LC.

32. Edward R. Murrow, *Person to Person*, December 3, 1954, tape (B605) available at the Museum of Radio and Television, New York City. See also the script for show, Manuscript Division, LC.

33. Kinescope of *Home*, June 4, 1957, Motion Picture Reading Room, LC.

34. Ibid. The log for the show ("Master Broadcast Report, Home Show no. 844") also has the rough script that Arlene Francis followed, which allows the viewer to follow the supposedly spontaneous chatter.

35. "Osgood Observes," *Detroit Free Press*, February 14, 1954, clipping in Manuscript Division, LC.

36. "Jack O'Brien News," *New York Journal American,* October 10, 1957, clipping in Manuscript Division, LC.

37. Mary Margaret Mcbride, *A Long Way from Missouri* (New York: Putnam, 1959), 22.

38. Marie Torre, "Television Today," May 29, 1958, clipping in Manuscript Division, LC.

39. Charles Preston and Edward A. Hamilton, eds., *Mike Wallace Asks: Highlights from 46 Controversial Interviews* (New York: Simon & Schuster, 1958), 75.

40. A set of notes from her papers (Manuscript Division, LC) is entitled "I'm going to ask Mike Wallace if he's a prude" and includes these topics: "religion—Mike Quill, prude—old-fashioned, crusader? liberal? Young Man in a Hurry, psycho-analysis, insecurity, did you dread this program? what do you do when you aren't working? What would you like to do if you do anything you liked? Does lack of approval bother you? Poison pens? Criticism?"

41. "TV: Tables Are Turned," *New York Times*, April 17, 1957; and Jack Nelson Tuck, "On the Air," *New York Post*, April 17, 1957, clipping in Manuscript Division, LC.

42. *Variety*, April 24, 1957, clipping in Manuscript Division, LC.

43. Clipping of "L. Sobol" column, May 21, 1957, Recorded Sound, LC.

44. Gerald Nachman noted that radio hosts like Arthur Godfrey "invented and personified the informal, often aimless conversational style that would, in TV, become a mammoth industry." Nachman, *Raised on Radio* (New York: Pantheon Books, 1998), 354.

45. Hilmes, *Radio Voices*, develops this point fully in her conclusion. This lack of credit is part of the general historical invisibility of radio as an influential popular culture medium.

46. Marie Torre, "Television Today," May 27, 1958, clipping in Manuscript Division, LC.

47. Jay Nelson Tuck makes this point in an insightful column that begins, "Where are the dames of yesteryear?" In addition to Mary Margaret McBride, he bemoans the absence of Kate Smith, Faye Emerson, Maggi McNellis, Virginia Graham, and others. As he concluded, "It is surely a loss when live local programming gives way to reruns of 'Beulah,' 'My Little Margie,' and 'Amos 'n' Andy.'" See "On the Air, " April 18, 1957, clipping in Manuscript Division, LC.

48. E. C. Morrison to Mary Margaret McBride, December 26, 1938, Manuscript Division, LC. Suggesting that the correspondent was male, the letter continued, "I am sure that you have a large male audience listening to your home-spun philosophy, and it is the sincere wish of another native Missourian that 1939 will bring you a continuance of merited success in your chosen field."

NOTES TO CHAPTER 18

1. Donald G. Godfrey and Frederic A. Leigh, eds., *Historical Dictionary of American Radio* (Westport, Conn.: Greenwood Press, 1998), 253–55.

2. McBride devotes the next-to-last chapter of *Out of the Air* (Garden City, N.Y.: Doubleday, 1960), to this period. Instead of calling the chapter "The Last Show," she entitled it "Tragedy."

3. McBride, *Out of the Air*, 367.

4. Press coverage of the last show is represented in clippings in Mary Margaret McBride's papers in the Manuscript Division and the Motion Picture, Broadcasting, and Recorded Sound Division of the Library of Congress.

5. McBride, *Out of the Air*, 367, 368.

6. Mary Margaret McBride broadcast, May 14, 1954 (RWC 7043 B1), Recorded Sound, LC. Unless otherwise noted, all quotations and information come from that broadcast.

NOTES TO CHAPTER 19

1. Mary Margaret McBride, *Out of the Air* (Garden City, N.Y.: Doubleday, 1960), 369.

2. Heywood Hale Broun phone conversation with me, August 10, 1999.

3. Promotional flyer in *Variety* (no date); contract between Ted Cott (NBC vice president) and Mary Margaret McBride, September 23, 1955; NBC "Time and Program Information" (1954), all found in Mary Margaret McBride papers, Motion Picture, Broadcasting, and Recorded Sound Division, Library of Congress (hereafter cited as Recorded Sound, LC).

4. "Mary Margaret McBride NBC Schedule," May 21, 1956, Recorded Sound, LC. Recorded Sound (RWA 1851 LWO 17243) contains examples of the five-minute broadcasts from 1955.

5. Stella Karn to E. C. Mills, September 30, 1954, found in Mary Margaret McBride papers, Manuscript Division, Library of Congress (hereafter cited as Manuscript Division, LC).

6. For the audience's reaction, see Mr. and Mrs. W. E. Kernahan to the National Broadcasting Company, September 28, 1954, and E. C. Mills to Estella Karns [*sic*], September 28, 1954, Manuscript Division, LC.

7. "Exit Mary Margaret," *Newsweek*, January 14, 1957, 52.

8. McBride, *Out of the Air*, 373–74. This seems to have been either 1953 or 1954, after she started writing her AP column.

9. McBride, *Out of the Air*, 375.

10. Ibid., 373. See also "Mary Margaret Says—Her Dream House Is a Barn," AP column, September 29 (1953–56), Recorded Sound, LC.

11. McBride, *Out of the Air*, 379. See also "Mary Margaret Says—Everybody's an Expert," November 1, and "Mary Margaret McBride Says—A House Is But a Headache," January 17 (1953–56), AP columns, Recorded Sound, LC.

12. McBride, *Out of the Air*, 377.

13. Ibid., 379. See also "Your Hudson Valley Neighbor," *Kingston (N.Y.) Week*, July 20, 1967, Manuscript Division, LC.

14. McBride, *Out of the Air*, 376, 374.

15. Ruth Gaffney to Stella Karn, March 30, 1956, Manuscript Division, LC. The papers also contain pictures, directions, and descriptions of the house. See especially the clipping from the *Times Union* (Albany, N.Y.), November 3, 1961.

16. Alice Hughes, "A Woman's New York," November 8, 1957, clipping in Manuscript Division, LC. See also the introduction to Mary Margaret McBride, *Mary Margaret McBride's Harvest of American Cooking* (New York: Putnam, 1957), xvii–xix; and Mary Margaret McBride, "Why I Wrote a Cookbook," *McClurg Book News*, clipping in Manuscript Division, LC.

17. Stella Karn to Melville Minturn, November 25, 1953; Theodore Purdy to Stella Karn, December 7, 1953; Elliott Schryver to Stella Karn, August 31, 1956, all in Recorded Sound, LC.

18. McBride, *Out of the Air*, 40; McBride, *Harvest of American Cooking*, xvii.

19. The series ran prominently in the *Woman's Home Companion* from May to September 1956. There was also another project, a twelve-volume *Mary Margaret McBride's Encyclopedia of Cooking*, published in 1958 by Homemakers Research Institute, Evanston, Ill., which was just recipes and had no text (indeed, no discernible contribution) by McBride. Perhaps this was leftover material that did not fit into *Harvest of American Cooking*, but its twelve volumes suggests that it was an independent project.

20. McBride, *Harvest of American Cooking*, 115–22.

21. Ibid., 79.

22. M. E. Davis, "Escape to the Range," clipping from Dallas, Texas; *Wall Street Journal*, February 13, 1958, Manuscript Division, LC.

23. For an excellent introduction to the field, see Barbara Wheaton, "Finding Real Life in Cookbooks: The Adventures of a Culinary Historian," and Barbara Haber, "Food, Sex, and Gender," both in *Food, Cookery and Culture*, edited by Leslie Howsam (Windsor, Ont.: Humanities Research Group, University of Windsor, 1998); and Sherrie A. Inness, ed., *Kitchen Culture in America: Popular Representations of Food, Gender, and Race* (Philadelphia: University of Pennsylvania Press, 2001). For the history of cookbooks, see Mary Anna DuSablon, *America's Collectible Cookbooks: The History, the Politics, the Recipes* (Athens: Ohio University Press, 1994). For general overview of American women and cooking, see Barbara Haber, *From Hardtack to Home Fries: An Uncommon History of American Cooks and Meals* (New York: Free Press, 2002); Laura Shapiro, *Perfection Salad: Women and Cooking at the Turn of the Century* (New York: Farrar, Straus & Giroux, 1986); Sherrie A. Inness, *Dinner Roles: American Women and Culinary Culture* (Iowa City: University of Iowa Press, 2001); and Mary Drake McFeely, *Can She Bake a Cherry Pie? American Women and the Kitchen in the Twentieth Century* (Amherst: University of Massachusetts Press, 2000).

24. "Only Human by Sidney Fields," *Sunday Mirror*, October 4, 1953, clipping in Manuscript Division, LC.

25. Promotional flier, AP Newsfeatures (no date), Manuscript Division, LC.

26. Promotional flier, AP Newsfeatures (1953), Recorded Sound, LC.

27. AP Newsfeatures memorandum to McBride column subscribers (no date), Recorded Sound, LC.

28. A fairly complete set of the columns, typed and ready to be sent off to the Associated Press for distribution, can be found in Recorded Sound, LC. They include the date completed and the intended date of publication. Sometimes the year is given, but often it is not, which is why not all footnote citations include a year. The title of these typed drafts was always "Mary Margaret McBride Says," but in some markets (like New York's *Daily Mirror*) the column ran as "As Mary Margaret McBride Sees It." See the clipping dated August 24, 1954, found in Recorded Sound, LC.

29. A rare case is "Mary Margaret McBride Says—Emotions Need Outlets," AP column, June 29 (1953–56), Recorded Sound, LC. McBride confesses that when she is down, "I repair to the kitchen where I substitute cooking for wound-licking." She then gives examples of how other friends have their own outlets, identifying them simply as "Jane," "Frank," "Stella," and "Cynthia."

30. "Some Sentimental Tears—A Columnist Bids a Fond Farewell," February 3, 1956, clipping in Manuscript Division., LC. For reactions from fans, see Joe to Mary Margaret McBride, January 18, 1956, and January 27, 1956, Recorded Sound, LC.

31. Mary Bard Jensen to Mary Margaret McBride, April 27, 1955, Recorded Sound, LC.

32. McBride, *Out of the Air*, 367. It is not clear what kind of cancer Stella had. There are references to a herniated esophagus, which may have been another way of referring to esophageal cancer, a strong possibility for a lifetime smoker like Stella. Lung cancer is also a possibility.

33. McBride, *Out of the Air*, 369.

34. Mary Margaret McBride, *A Long Way from Missouri* (New York: Putnam, 1959), 83.

35. Title page, McBride, *Harvest of American Cooking*.

36. Obituaries appeared in the *New York World-Telegram and Sun* on March 13, 1957, and the *New York Times* on March 14, 1957.

37. McBride, *Out of the Air*, 371. See also Mary Margaret McBride, "My Most Unforgettable Character," *Reader's Digest*, January 1962, 98–102.

38. Note on the bottom of a letter from Mary B. Hunt to Mary Margaret McBride, April 17, 1957, Recorded Sound, LC.

39. McBride, *Out of the Air*, 98–102.

40. M. E. Davis, "Escape to the Range," February 13, 1958, clipping in Manuscript Division, LC.

41. "Mary Margaret Sets a Bountiful Table," *New York Herald-Tribune Book Review*, November 17, 1957, clipping in Manuscript Division, LC, which also contains other reviews. Showing a certain laxity of professional standards, her close friend Cynthia Lowry reviewed the book for the AP wire services, calling it "a dandy gift book for ladies and gents who have everything."

42. Tie-ins, such as to a line of aluminum pots produced by Kaiser Aluminum (clipping found in Recorded Sound, LC), also enhanced the book's visibility, as did Mary Margaret's numerous radio and television promotions to boost sales. See the material in Manuscript Division, LC.

43. McBride, *Out of the Air*, 41.

44. Alice Hughes, "A Woman's New York," November 10, 1957, and Eleanor Roosevelt, "My Day," November 3, 1957, both in Manuscript Division, LC. See also Harry Hansen, "Two Women Authors Feted by Celebrities," *Chicago Tribune Magazine of Books*, November 10, 1957.

45. Ogden Nash, quoted in a *New York Post* syndicated column, November 3, 1957, clipping in Manuscript Division, LC. This widely repeated quotation also appeared on the dust jacket of *Out of the Air*.

46. Typed tribute, dated for release November 28, 1957, Manuscript Division, LC.

NOTES TO CHAPTER 20

1. The original news story seems to have been a column blurb by Hy Gardner dated May 2, 1957: "Mary Margaret McBride, saddened at the passing of her closest friend, confidante and longtime right arm, Stella Karns [*sic*], is wavering and may marry her childhood sweetheart, Dr. Richard Dorris of Jefferson City, Mo." This led to her disavowals, picked up by the wire services: "No Plans to Marry, Says Miss M'Bride" (AP) and "Don't Plan to Wed—Mary Margaret," all clippings found in the Mary Margaret McBride papers, Manuscript Division, Library of Congress (hereafter cited as Manuscript Division, LC).

2. "Marie Torre Reports," May 27, 1958, clipping found in McBride papers, Manuscript Division, LC. See also Jack Gould's media column in the *New York Times*, June 1, 1958.

3. Ellen Derges, "Warmth, Sincerity Are McBride Trademarks," *Peoria (Ill.) Journal Star*, May 14, 1958, clipping in Manuscript Division, LC.

4. See Ted Cott to Matthew Keating, January 22, 1958 [1959], and Sid Sirulnick to Mary Margaret, January 5, 1959, Manuscript Division, LC. Cott noted in his letter to a listener upset at the demise of the program: "As I am sure you realize, the cost of presenting a personality of Miss McBride's quality is tremendous and while we can present the program for a good long period of time (which we have done since May 7, 1958), we must eventually secure sponsor support for such an endeavour or we must wind up in a very poor economic position."

5. Mary Margaret McBride, *Out of the Air* (Garden City, N.Y.: Doubleday, 1960), 139. She told television host Tom Snyder in 1975, "I left broadcasting when Stella died; I couldn't front for myself." Quoted in Jacquelyn D. St. John, "Sex Role Stereotyping in Early Broadcast History: The Career of Mary Margaret McBride," *Frontiers* 3 (1978): 37.

6. For discussion of these general trends, see Susan J. Douglas, *Listening In: Radio and the American Imagination* (New York: Times Books, 1999); Michele Hilmes, *Only Connect: A*

Cultural History of Broadcasting in the United States (Belmont, Calif.: Wadsworth, 2002); and Donna Halper, *Invisible Stars: A Social History of Women in American Broadcasting* (Armonk, N.Y.: Sharpe, 2001).

7. Mcbride, *Out of the Air*, 266. Her papers at the Library of Congress contain many reviews of the books. See, for example, Helen Bates, "No Echo Answers Ad Libs," *Times-Union* (Jacksonville, Fla.), December 18, 1960: "That apologetic cliché, 'It loses something in translation,' could be applied in another way to this summing up of the McBride era on the air. Put down in black and white, things that may have been thrilling to the ear, flop dismally." Priscilla T. Campbell, in the *Worcester Sunday Telegram*, December 18, 1960, pointed to another problem: "Reviewing a book by MMM [*sic*] offers continual temptation to make it a review of her partner and business manager, the late Stella Karn, because Stella was a character and McBride isn't."

8. The contracts and itineraries with W. Colston Leigh are in the Mary Margaret McBride papers, Motion Picture, Broadcasting, and Recorded Sound Division, Library of Congress (hereafter cited as Recorded Sound, LC). McBride received between $500 and $750 for each lecture and almost always traveled by air.

9. Ellen Scott, "Mary McBride Found More Like Favorite Aunt Than a Celebrity," *Albany (N.Y.) Times Union*, September 13, 1966. See also Emma Bugbee, "Mary Margaret McBride Is Back on Air Tomorrow," *New York Herald-Tribune*, July 10, 1960, both in Manuscript Division, LC.

10. Mary Margaret McBride to Eleanor Roosevelt, undated letters from 1960 and 1962, found in the Eleanor Roosevelt papers, Franklin D. Roosevelt Library, Hyde Park, New York. In 1958 Roosevelt and McBride had talked about doing an interview show together, but nothing came of it. See McBride, *Out of the Air*, 326.

11. "Marie Torre Reports," June 30, 1960, clipping in Manuscript Division, LC. Material about WGHQ and Harry Thayer is in Recorded Sound, LC. Surviving tapes of *Your Hudson Valley Neighbor* include the programs of September 24, 1964, and August 9, 1971 (LWO 12747 R5, Recorded Sound, LC). The 1971 tape describes visiting an air show. McBride initially sounds old and tired as she broadcasts in the hot sun but becomes more animated as the show goes on.

12. McBride, *Out of the Air*, 329. The Eleanor Roosevelt papers at the Roosevelt Library contains warm and active correspondence between the two women right up until Roosevelt's death. For a description of appearing on McBride's show, see Eleanor Roosevelt, "My Day," August 9, 1960, where she pronounces Mary Margaret "one of the most expert interviewers I have ever known."

13. Mary Margaret McBride to Fannie Hurst, 1962, Fannie Hurst papers, Harry Ransom Humanities Research Center, University of Texas at Austin. See also a letter from Nannine Joseph to McBride, December 26, 1962, Manuscript Division, LC, saying that she had heard the tape ("You have done a wonderful thing—too good to be lost") and wondering whether it could be distributed commercially. No copy of the tape seems to survive.

14. Norman Jackson, "Nostalgia: Mary Margaret McBride," clipping, October 1975, in Manuscript Division, LC.

15. "People," *Time*, May 15, 1964, 50. The telegrams and the clipping can be found in the Manuscript Division, LC.

16. Harry Thayer to Mary Margaret McBride, August 12, 1968, Manuscript Division, LC. The quotation comes from Kay Bartlett, "At 75, Mary Margaret McBride Is Still on the Air," AP feature, *New Brunswick, N.J. News*, May 13, 1975.

17. Thayer to Mary Margaret McBride, January 28, 1966, Manuscript Division, LC.

18. Thayer to Mary Margaret McBride July 3, 1968, Manuscript Division, LC.

19. McBride to Josephine Thayer, no date, Manuscript Division, LC.

20. Her accident was carried by the news services and the *New York Times*, August 13, 1970), which brought her letters and get-well wishes from her old fans.

21. David Richards, "Mary Margaret's Still in Love with the Mike," *Washington Star News*, October 31, 1973, clipping in Manuscript Division, LC. Mary Margaret admitted the same thing in 1974: "Radio is the breath of life to me. I might be in a dismal swamp by the end of the day, but I always wake up feeling I could lick my weight in wildcats." "Radio Is Still 'The Breath of Life to Me,' Says 74-year-old Mary Margaret McBride," *National Tattler*, January 6, 1974, clipping in Manuscript Division, LC.

22. Bert Greene, *Bert Greene's Kitchen Bouquets: A Cookbook of Favored Aromas and Flavors* (Chicago: Contemporary Books, 1979), 70.

23. "She Swaps Fame for Rural Life," AP feature, ca. 1960, clipping in Manuscript Division, LC.

24. Mary Margaret McBride to Abel Green, 1961 typescript, Manuscript Division, LC. The article ran in *Variety* in January 1962.

25. This ran variously as "Highlights of the Airwaves" or "Confessions of a TV Fan," July 8, 1964, as a substitute for Cynthia Lowry's AP column. Clipping found in Manuscript Division, LC.

26. Mary Margaret McBride, "Wonderful World of Soap Opera," July 13, 1967, written as a substitute for Cynthia Lowry's AP column. Clipping found in Manuscript Division, LC.

27. Background information on Cynthia Coleman Lowry (1912–94) has been gleaned from mentions by Mary Margaret McBride in various articles and books, as well as a brief entry in *Foremost Women in Communications* (New York: Foremost Americans Publishing Company, 1970). In a phone conversation with me on August 10, 1999, Heywood Hale Broun characterized Lowry as a female version of the hard-driving newspaperman and thought she was probably a lesbian. It was Lowry who donated all of McBride's papers and recordings to the Library of Congress in 1977.

28. Typescript of Norman Jackson article, "Nostalgia: Mary Margaret McBride" (1974), Manuscript Division, LC.

29. The fullest discussion of McBride's last years and the role of Lowry in them can be found in Beverly Merrick, "Mary Margaret McBride: At Home in the Hudson Valley," *Journalism History*, August 1996, 110–18. Another close friend in her final years was Sister Mary Charles McCarthy, president and chief administrator of Kingston's Benedictine Hospital, where McBride was hospitalized for her broken hip.

30. Barbara Bedell article, March 24, 1971, *Cheyenne Sunday Magazine*, clipping in Manuscript Division, LC.

31. Bartlett, "At 75, Mary Margaret McBride Is Still on the Air."

32. Ibid. Similar stories include Marcia Hayes, "Quavering in the Catskills," *Pittsburgh Press*, December 28, 1969; Chris Farlekas, "Superstar of Yesteryear's Radio Lives in Ulster," *Sunday Record*, April 23, 1972; and Richard Lamparski, "What Ever Became of . . . Mary Margaret McBride: The First Lady of Radio," no date (ca. 1960–62), clippings all found in Manuscript Division, LC.

33. Donna Knight, "At 75, Still '1st Lady of Radio,'" *Indianapolis Star*, September 18, 1975, clipping found in Manuscript Division, LC. St. John, "Sex Role Stereotyping in Early Broadcast History," mentions her appearance on the show, but all attempts to find a surviving copy through NBC or Tom Snyder himself (Snyder to Susan Ware, May 14, 2001) were unsuccessful. Even as late as 1975, tapes of television shows were not always kept systematically.

34. "Paris Farm Girl Comes Full Circle," *Barrytown, New York Explorer*, November 1962, clipping in Manuscript Division, LC.

35. Steve Tinney, "Mary Margaret Mcbride Is Still Broadcasting at 74," April 1974 clipping, Manuscript Division, LC.

36. Obituaries appeared in the *New York Times, Washington Post, Poughkeepsie Journal*, and *The Freeman* (Kingston, N.Y.), all on April 8, 1976.

NOTES TO EPILOGUE

1. For general background on the history of public radio, see James Ledbetter, *Made Possible By . . . : The Death of Public Broadcasting in the United States* (New York: Verso, 1997); Michele Hilmes, *Only Connect: A Cultural History of Broadcasting in the United States* (Belmont, Calif.: Wadsworth, 2002); and Jack Mitchell, "Lead Us Not into Temptation: American Public Radio in a World of Infinite Possibilities," in *Radio Reader: Essays in the Cultural History of Radio*, edited by Michele Hilmes and Jason Loviglio (New York: Routledge, 2002), 405–22. To revisit the early days of National Public Radio, see *Every Night at Five: Susan Stamberg's All Things Considered Book* (New York: Pantheon Books, 1982).

2. Diane Rehm, *Finding My Voice* (New York: Knopf, 1999), 167.

3. Probably the closest radio personality to Mary Margaret Mcbride on commercial radio today is Joan Hamburg, who hosts a daily two-hour talk show each morning on WOR in New York. See Valerie Gladstone, "New York Radio's Folksy Powerhouse," *New York Times*, July 9, 2000. For the continuing problems women face as talk show hosts, see Mark Jurkowitz, "Examining Women's Radio Silence," *Boston Globe*, June 4, 2003.

4. In her *Listening In: Radio and the American Imagination* (New York: Times Books, 1999), Susan Douglas sees NPR and talk radio as mirror images, emphasizing that they both grew from a sense of public exclusion from the mainstream news. She especially stresses them both as "electronic surrogates for the town common" (pp. 284–85). For overviews of the talk show phenomenon, see Wayne Munson, *All Talk: The Talkshow in Media Culture* (Philadelphia: Temple University Press, 1993); and Howard Kurtz, *Hot Air: All Talk All the Time* (New York: Times Books, 1996).

5. Quoted in Kurtz, *Hot Air*, 287.

6. Ibid., 3.

7. Ibid., 270–72.

8. Munson, *All Talk*, 98. See also Susan Douglas, "Letting the Boys Be Boys: Talk Radio, Male Hysteria, and Political Discourse in the 1980s," in Hilmes and Loviglio, eds., *Radio Reader*, 485–504.

9. In her *Only Connect*, Michele Hilmes traces the links as far back as the nineteenth century: "But the greatest influence from magazines may have been the women's daytime talk show, based on the kind of familiar and intimate domestic address pioneered in women's magazines since the days of *Godey's Ladies' Book*" (p. 96). For further background in addition to Munson and Kurtz, see Jane Shattuc, *The Talking Cure: TV Talk Shows and Women* (New York: Routledge, 1997; Jane Shattuc, "The Oprahification of America: Talk Shows and the Public Sphere," in *Television, History, and American Culture: Feminist Critical Essays*, edited by Mary Beth Haralovich and Lauren Rabinovitz (Durham, N.C.: Duke University Press, 1999), 168–80; Gloria-Jean Masaciarotte, "C'mon, Girl: Oprah Winfrey and the Discourse of Feminine Talk," *Genders* 11 (fall 1991): 81–110; and Jennifer Hyland Wang, "'Everything's Coming Up Rosie': Empower America, Rosie O'Donnell, and the Construction of Daytime Reality," *The Velvet Light Trap* 45 (spring 2000): 20–35.

10. Kurtz, *Hot Air*, 149–57.

11. Ibid., 58.

12. Material on the Oprah Winfrey phenomenon includes Katherine Krohn, *Oprah Winfrey* (Minneapolis: Lerner Publications, 2002); Janet Lowe, *Oprah Winfrey Speaks: Insight from the World's Most Influential Voice* (New York: Wiley, 1998); and Bill Adler, ed., *The Uncommon Wisdom of Oprah Winfrey: A Portrait in Her Own Words* (Secaucus, N.J.: Birch Lane Press, 1998). In some ways, the contemporary television figure to whom McBride may be closest is not Oprah Winfrey but Barbara Walters, with her soft but sometimes probing interviews of celebrities and newsmakers. The main difference is that when you watch a Barbara Walters interview, you always are as much aware of the interviewer as of the interviewee, which rarely happened with Mary Margaret McBride.

13. Kurtz, *Hot Air*, 70.

14. Overviews of these trends can be found in Hilmes, *Only Connect*, and Christopher H. Sterling and John M. Kittross, *Stay Tuned: A Concise History of American Broadcasting*, 2nd ed. (Belmont, Calif.: Wadsworth, 1990). See also Bruce J. Schulman, *The Seventies: The Great Shift in American Culture, Society, and Politics* (New York: Free Press, 2001).

15. Shattuc's *The Talking Cure* explores the implications of identity politics for the talk show genre.

16. An excellent example is all the men who went off to war during the 1940s and never discussed their experiences or feelings when they came back. Similarly, Holocaust survivors often hid their experiences from their children and grandchildren. These silences were not generally broken until the 1980s and 1990s.

17. Masciarotte, "C'mon Girl," makes an interesting point about the differences between Sally Jesse Raphael's radio and television programs: "While her radio call in show does share the television talk show's territory of the painful experience, it is still not a group experience and exchange. It is more in line with Ann Landers's and the print advice columnists' advice to the lovelorn and the lifeworn. It is an individual problem-solving show without the element of a coalition of the painful mass subject. Her mixing of the media genres probably accounts for the fact that she has both a radio call in show and a television talk show" (p. 104).

18. Ed Kintzer, Des Moines, Iowa, to Susan Ware, June 7, 1999.

Index